'Think on my words'

'You speak a language that I understand not.' Hermione's words to Leontes in *The Winter's Tale* are likely to ring true with many people reading or watching Shakespeare's plays today. For decades, people have been studying Shakespeare's life and times, and in recent years there has been a renewed surge of interest into aspects of his language. So how can we better understand Shakespeare? How did he manipulate language to produce such an unrivalled body of work, which has enthralled generations both as theatre and as literature? David Crystal addresses these and many other questions in this lively and original introduction to Shakespeare's language. Covering in turn the five main dimensions of language structure – writing style, pronunciation, grammar, vocabulary, and conversational style – the book shows how examining these linguistic 'nuts and bolts' can help us achieve a greater appreciation of Shakespeare's linguistic creativity.

DAVID CRYSTAL is one of the world's foremost authorities on language. He is author of the hugely successful *Cambridge Encyclopedia of Language* (1987; second edition 1997), *Cambridge Encyclopedia of the English Language* (1995; second edition 2003), and *English as a Global Language* (1997; second edition 2003). An internationally renowned writer, journal editor, lecturer and broadcaster, he received an OBE in 1995 for his services to the study and teaching of the English language. His previous work on Shakespeare includes two books written with his actor son, Ben, *Shakespeare's Words* (2002) and *The Shakespeare Miscellany* (2005), essay contributions to *Shakespeare: An Oxford Guide* and *The Oxford Shakespeare, Pronouncing Shakespeare* (2005), and regular essays for *The Times Educational Supplement* and the theatre magazine, *Around the Globe*.

'Think on my words'
Exploring Shakespeare's Language

David Crystal

CAMBRIDGE
UNIVERSITY PRESS

CAMBRIDGE UNIVERSITY PRESS

Cambridge, New York, Melbourne, Madrid, Cape Town, Singapore, São Paulo, Delhi

Cambridge University Press
The Edinburgh Building, Cambridge CB2 8RU, UK

Published in the United States of America by Cambridge University Press, New York

www.cambridge.org
Information on this title: www.cambridge.org/9780521700351

First published 2008
Reprinted 2008

Printed in the USA at Edwards Brothers, Inc.

A catalogue record for this publication is available from the British Library

ISBN 978-0-521-87694-0 hardback
ISBN 978-0-521-70035-1 paperback

Contents

List of figures and tables

Preface

The title of this book means what it says: it is an exploration of Shakespeare's language, not a comprehensive survey. It is an introduction from a particular point of view. Books and anthologies with the words *Shakespeare* and *Language* in the title are numerous, and they represent a coming together of several traditions in theatre, literary criticism, philology, and linguistics. Mine is basically a nuts-and-bolts approach, governed by one basic principle – that one should never examine a linguistic nut or bolt without asking 'what does it do?' And 'what does it do?' means two things: how does it help us understand the meaning of what is said (a semantic explanation), and how does it help us appreciate the dramatic or poetic effect of what is said (a pragmatic explanation)? I have found my own understanding immensely enhanced by the kind of approach I employ. I just hope I have managed to convey something of that insight in these pages.

I have used three First Folio sources: the edition of the plays held at the Electronic Text Center, University of Virginia Library, my copy of the 1910 Methuen facsimile, and the Norton facsimile. For my statistical data, I have used the concordance which was compiled to accompany the *Shakespeare's Words* website (www.shakespeareswords.com). The spelling of quotations is modern in Chapters 1 and 2, but after the description of Elizabethan orthography in Chapter 3, most quotations come from the First Folio or contemporary texts.

Hilda Hulme, my Shakespeare teacher at university, said in her insightful book *Explorations in Shakespeare's Language*: 'it is not easy to argue about Shakespeare's meaning without being excited by it'. Or explore it, even, now that we have such powerful electronic search capabilities. Every time I do even the most menial search of my Shakespeare database, I discover something I have never noticed before. It is an excitement open to anyone who wishes to increase their understanding of Shakespeare and his works.

DAVID CRYSTAL
Holyhead, March 2007

Play and poem abbreviations

Ado	*Much Ado About Nothing*
Ant	*Antony and Cleopatra*
AWW	*All's Well That Ends Well*
AYLI	*As You Like It*
Cor	*Coriolanus*
Cym	*Cymbeline*
Err	*The Comedy of Errors*
Ham	*Hamlet*
1H4	*Henry IV Part 1*
2H4	*Henry IV Part 2*
H5	*Henry V*
1H6	*Henry VI Part 1*
2H6	*Henry VI Part 2*
3H6	*Henry VI Part 3*
H8	*Henry VIII*
JC	*Julius Caesar*
John	*King John*
KE3	*King Edward III*
Lear	*King Lear*
LLL	*Love's Labour's Lost*
Lover	*A Lover's Complaint*
Luc	*The Rape of Lucrece*
Mac	*Macbeth*
MM	*Measure for Measure*
MND	*A Midsummer Night's Dream*
MV	*The Merchant of Venice*
Oth	*Othello*
Per	*Pericles*
R2	*Richard II*

R3	*Richard III*
Rom	*Romeo and Juliet*
Shr	*The Taming of the Shrew*
Sonn	*Sonnets*
STM	*Sir Thomas More*
Temp	*The Tempest*
TGV	*The Two Gentlemen of Verona*
Tim	*Timon of Athens*
Tit	*Titus Andronicus*
TN	*Twelfth Night*
TNK	*The Two Noble Kinsmen*
Tro	*Troilus and Cressida*
Ven	*Venus and Adonis*
Wiv	*The Merry Wives of Windsor*
WT	*The Winter's Tale*

OTHER ABBREVIATIONS

a	adjective
adv	adverb
int	interjection
n	noun
OED	*Oxford English Dictionary*
pr	preposition
v	verb

I 'You speak a language that I understand not': myths and realities

There is a story that, if you travel into the most isolated valleys of the Appalachian Mountains in eastern USA, you will find people who still speak the language of Shakespeare. They are said to be the descendants of those early settlers who left England for Virginia in 1606, when Shakespeare was age 42. Several settlers, it seems, moved inland and away from the larger centres of population. And there, the story goes, cut off from the changes in society and language which would take place in the seaboard cities, and rurally conservative by temperament, generation after generation carried on speaking the tongue that the pioneers brought with them.

The story varies a bit, depending on who is telling it. In some accounts, it is Roanoke Island, off the east coast of Virginia, where you will hear pure Shakespearean English – or 'Elizabethan English', as it is often put. In others, you do not have to leave the British Isles. Just turn off the main road in Northern Ireland, or in County Kerry, or in deepest Warwickshire, and there it will be, unchanged, unchanging.

Anyone who believes this has, as Thersites says of Agamemnon, 'not so much brain as ear-wax' (*Tro.* 5.1.49). It is a myth. Speech never stands still – not even between two generations, let alone the sixteen or so that separate the reigns of the first and second Queen Elizabeth. Listen to the speech of young and old people from the same part of a country, and you will hear all kinds of differences in pronunciation, grammar, and vocabulary. Wicked! It was the same in Shakespeare's day. He even refers at one point to language change taking place within a generation. Mercutio sneeringly describes the way Tybalt speaks: he calls him one of the 'new tuners of accent' (*Rom.* 2.4.29).

It is true that the language used in some parts of a country will change less rapidly than others. There is always a grain of truth inside a myth. Isolated communities will indeed be more conservative in the way they speak. But no community is so isolated that it is immune from contact with those who speak differently from themselves. And the evidence? All you need do is listen to the modern communities. In the BBC television series *The Story of English* (1988), the programme makers visited Roanoke. What we heard was regional, rural, but definitely modern American English. Not a *forsooth* in earshot. No *thou*s or *goeth*s. And the accent – as we will see in Chapter 6 – was some distance away from that used in the early 1600s.

The idea that the English of Shakespeare's time is rurally alive and well in modern times is a remarkably persistent myth. I hear someone come out with it, on the radio or in the press, every few months. It's a myth born of ignorance of the basic facts about the way language changes. And the chief problem in approaching the language of Shakespeare, to my mind, is that a whole spider's web of myths has grown up around it, which has to be brushed away to enable our eventual linguistic encounter to be with something real.

THE QUANTITY MYTH

'Shakespeare had the largest vocabulary of any English writer.' If I had a pound for every time I've heard someone say that, I'd have enough to buy a First Folio. He certainly had a wide-ranging vocabulary for his time, as we shall see, but – 'the largest of any English writer'? That certainly isn't the case. Any modern writer uses far more words than Shakespeare. Indeed, you, reader, if you are understanding all the words I use in this book, command more words than Shakespeare. The reason is the way English vocabulary has grown over the past 400 years.

It's never going to be possible to do precise calculations about how much vocabulary was in use during a particular historical period. The best we can do is count the words in whatever texts remain – and even that is not yet practicable (though it will become more so, one day, as texts increasingly achieve an electronic presence on the Internet). So we have to rely on 'best guesses'. And on that basis it is thought that there were about 150,000 different words in English by the end of the sixteenth century. Today, the unabridged *Oxford English Dictionary* contains over 600,000 different words. There are simply far more words available to be used now, compared with Shakespeare's time.

So how many of these words do you and I use? You can work out the totals, approximately, by using a dictionary. Choose one with about 1,500 pages, such as the *Concise Oxford*: dictionaries of this size contain about 100,000 different headwords. (Headwords are the units in bold type, such as **cat**, **good**, **ask**, and **quick**, which appear at the beginning of a dictionary entry, or sometimes – as with **goodness** and **quickly** – within the entry.) If you go through a small sample of the pages, noting which words you can imagine yourself using, then work out the average number per page, and then multiply by the number of pages in the book, you will get a rough idea of your active vocabulary. Having done this with a few dozen people, over the years, I can say that most of us use at least 50,000 words. That is, we know at least half the words in the dictionary. Think about such clusters as *nation, national, nationally, nationhood, nationalize, nationalization...* It doesn't take long to build up an appreciable total.

The usual figure given for the size of Shakespeare's vocabulary is about 20,000 different words. Today we have over twice as many words at our command – and yet none of us are Shakespeares. The moral is plain. Quantity is not enough. It is not so much the number of words we have as what we *do* with those words that makes the difference between an ordinary and a brilliant use of language. Also critical is our ability to choose the most effective words from the language's wordstock to express our intentions. And, if the wordstock does not have the words we need, we have to be prepared to invent new ones to make good the deficiency, and to use old ones in unprecedented ways. Shakespeare, as we shall see in Chapter 7, is excellent at all this. More than anything else, he shows us how to be daring with language.

Many commentators on Shakespeare's language nonetheless seem to be obsessed with quantity rather than creativity – probably because it is far easier to count than to analyse. But even the task of counting has some hidden complexities, so that we should never take someone's vocabulary estimate at its face value. We have to ask: 'What has the counter counted?' Take the estimate of '20,000 different words' above, and compare it with another widely cited Shakespearean estimate of '30,000 words'. Notice the phrasing. 'Different' words are those which differ in their dictionary meaning. *Cat*, *dog*, and *ask* have different dictionary meanings, as do *bear* ('animal') and *bear* ('carry'). But *cat* and *cats*, although they look different, do not have different dictionary meanings, nor do *ask*, *asks*, *asking*, and *asked*. These are simply different forms of the 'same' word, expressing different grammatical meanings, such as singular and plural or present and past tenses. If you count all of these forms separately, obviously you will get a much higher total than if you do not.

When someone talks about the number of words in Shakespeare, then, it is always important to know what kind of word they have been counting. People who say Shakespeare has 'about 20,000' words are grouping all the variants together. Those who say he has 'over 30,000' words are counting all the variant forms separately. The contrast is very noticeable in Shakespeare because the language of his time had more grammatical variants than exist today. We shall look at this in Chapter 8, but for the moment just consider *bear, bears, bearest, beareth, bearing, boar'st, bore,* and *born,* which are the variant forms of *bear* (ignoring spelling variants) in the First Folio. They count as 'one' under the first procedure, but as 'eight' under the second.

'About 20,000'. That 'about' is an important qualification, for there is quite a large variation surrounding this estimate. The figure is sometimes as low as around 18,000. A lot depends on which works you include as part of the canon. If you include, say, disputed or partially authored texts such as *King Edward III* and *Sir Thomas More*, your total is going to be appreciably greater than if you do not. But even within the 'core' texts, there are problems in deciding what to count. There are five types of difficulty.

- We have to decide whether a word is a compound or not. When Edgar calls Oswald a 'base, proud, shallow, beggarly, three suited, hundred pound, filthy worsted stocking knave' (*Lear.* 2.3.14), do we count this as twelve words (if all hyphens are omitted) or as eleven (if just *worsted-stocking* is hyphenated, as the Arden edition does) or as ten (if it is *filthy-worsted-stocking*, as the Penguin edition has it) or as nine (if *three-suited* and *hundred-pound* are separately hyphenated, as in Penguin) or as eight (if it is *three-suited-hundred-pound*, as in Arden)? (for the First Folio version, see p. 99).

- Do we include all editorial emendations, modernizations, and variants between Folio and Quarto texts (p. 23)? What exactly is being 'sledded' (*Ham.* 1.1.63) – *poleaxe* or *Polacks* or something else? Is it *auncient* or *ancient*? The total will grow if we include every variant.

- Do we include proper names? These are usually excluded in word-counting exercises, as they relate more to encyclopedic knowledge than to linguistic intuition. Just because I know the words *Hamburg* and *Frankfurt* does not mean that I can speak German! On the other hand, some proper names do have more general significance – as in modern English *Whitehall* (in the sense of 'the civil service'). This means that perhaps we should include such words as *Ethiop* ('person with a dark complexion') in our total.

- Do we include foreign words? Shakespeare uses 288 Latin word-forms, 310 French word-forms, and 36 Spanish or Italian word-forms (it is sometimes difficult to decide which language it is). When characters are definitely speaking a foreign language, the words might reasonably be excluded, but it is not always clear when something is foreign, as when the gravedigger says *argal*

(= Latin *ergo*, 'therefore', *Ham.* 5.1.19) or Polonius says *videlicet* (= 'that is to say', *Ham.* 2.1.61). Are these better treated as loan words into English – much as we talk about 'a tour de force' or 'a je ne sais quoi' today?

- Do we include onomatopoeic 'words', as when Edgar shouts *sesey* (a hunting cry, *Lear.* 3.4.97) or Doll Tearsheet says (or should it be burps?) *hem* (*2H4.* 2.4.29).
- Do we include humorous forms, such as malapropisms? When Mistress Quickly says *allicholy* as a variant of *melancholy* (*Wiv.* 1.4.148), is this the 'same' word or a different one?

Depending on how we answer these questions, our Shakespearean total will vary by a thousand or so.

But 20,000 cannot be very far from the truth. And it will certainly do to focus our attention on the linguistic reality that it represents. For 20,000 *was* a large vocabulary, in its day. If we compare a work of a similar size to the Shakespearean canon, the contrast is striking. There are 884,647 words in the Riverside edition, according to Martin Spevack's *Concordance*; and there are around 880,000 words in the 1611 King James Bible. But if we exclude all the proper names in the latter, we find that the Bible uses only some 6,000 different words. It is of course a very different genre, and the translators deliberately cultivated a conservative style; but the contrast is nonetheless noteworthy. Shakespeare uses over three times as many words.

Why is Shakespeare's vocabulary so large? Partly because he wrote so much, but mainly because of what he wrote about. It is the difference between people, situations, and subject-matter which generates different kinds of vocabulary, and Shakespeare is acknowledged to be unmatched in the range of his characters, settings, and themes. Here is Montjoy the herald addressing King Harry (*H5.* 3.6.122).

Now we speak upon our cue and our voice is imperial. England shall repent his folly, see his weakness, and admire our sufferance. Bid him therefore consider of his ransom, which must proportion

the losses we have borne, the subjects we have lost, the disgrace
we have digested – which in weight to re-answer, his pettiness
would bow under.

If you write only historical plays, your vocabulary is going to be
focused on the kind of things that kings and princes talk about.
Conversely, if you write only street-comedy, a very different kind of
vocabulary is going to appear. Here is Doll Tearsheet haranguing
Pistol (*1H4*. 2.4.119):

> Away, you cutpurse rascal, you filthy bung, away! By this wine,
> I'll thrust my knife in your mouldy chaps an you play the saucy
> cuttle with me! Away, you bottle-ale rascal, you basket-hilt stale
> juggler, you!

If you write love stories, that will motivate a further lexical domain.
Here is Mercutio satirizing Romeo the lover (*Rom*. 2.1.9):

> Cry but 'Ay me!' Pronounce but 'love' and 'dove'.
> Speak to my gossip Venus one fair word,
> One nickname for her purblind son and heir,
> Young Adam Cupid, he that shot so trim
> When King Cophetua loved the beggar maid.

And if you write about the most profound kinds of mental conflict,
you will employ words that go well beyond the everyday. Here is one
of Hamlet's reflections (*Ham*. 3.1.85):

> Thus conscience does make cowards of us all,
> And thus the native hue of resolution
> Is sicklied o'er with the pale cast of thought,
> And enterprises of great pith and moment
> With this regard their currents turn awry
> And lose the name of action.

If you do all of these, and more, inevitably you will end up with a
lexical total that makes you stand out from your contemporaries.

THE INVENTION MYTH

Part of this 'more' is the creation of new words, and this introduces another linguistic myth about Shakespeare – that he invented (the fraction varies enormously among accounts) a quarter, a third, a half ... of all the words in the English language. Even if we restrict the notion to 'the English language as spoken in Jacobethan times', such fractions are far from the truth – insofar as the truth can be established at all. For working out the linguistic facts in relation to word-creation is an even more difficult procedure than in the case of word-counting. Even today, with all the media and computer resources available to us, it is rare to find a word where we can say unequivocally that a particular person invented it. An exception is *blurb*, which we know was devised by the American author Gelett Burgess at a dinner party in New York in 1907. Very few words are like that.

In earlier periods, the only evidence we have to go on are the surviving texts, which allow us to establish the 'first recorded user' of a word. There is no greater collection of historical lexical usage than the unabridged *Oxford English Dictionary* (*OED*), and that is the usual source of information when someone tries to establish how many words a particular author introduced into the language. Thus no one has yet found an earlier use of *trippingly* than when Oberon uses it (*MND.* 5.2.26). But to say that the first recorded user actually invented the word is to take a leap into the dark. In some cases, it would be absurd to suggest that the first recorded user was the inventor: the earliest *OED* citation for the common oath '*sblood* ('God's blood') is when Falstaff uses it (*1H4.* 1.2.83). This is hardly an invention! Shakespeare is simply the first person we know to have written it down.

The first person *we know*. It is perfectly possible that someone else wrote '*sblood* before 1596 and the lexicographers have not yet come across it. Lexicography has its limitations: nobody can read everything or even have ready access to everything. And when compiling a historical dictionary, decisions have to be made about which texts to include. Shakespeare, of course, was a special target of the first

OED editors: they went through his work with a toothcomb. As a result, there are rather more usages attributed to him than might have been the case if some of his contemporaries had been given the same treatment. Every now and then someone notices an earlier usage in a previously ignored text, and tells the *OED* editors about it. *Lonely* is a case in point. In the *OED* it is first recorded as 1607 (in *Cor.* 4.1.31); but there are numerous instances of this word appearing earlier, in both poetry and prose. To take just one example, Mary Sidney, the Countess of Pembroke, talks about the 'lonely ghosts' in her *Tragedie of Antonie*, and that is 1592. As more texts come to be on the Internet, this kind of discovery will take place more often.

Of the 2,200 words in the *OED* whose first recorded use is in Shakespeare, about 1,700 are plausible Shakespearean inventions – words like *anthropophaginian, assassination, disproperty, incardinate, insultment, irregulous, outswear,* and *uncurse* – and about half of them stayed in the language. That is a remarkable total. No other writer of the time – or indeed since – comes anywhere near it. Even more remarkable is the fact that 1,700 is approaching 10 per cent of his known vocabulary.

When we talk of Shakespeare's influence on the English language, we should not be thinking solely of his invented words. There is a distinction to be made between 'inventing a word' and 'introducing a word into the language'. Many invented words have a very short life and never achieve a permanent place in English: there are several examples in the previous paragraph. Equally, many words and phrases which were not invented by a particular author entered the language because he or she used them: Shakespearean examples include dozens of idioms such as *to the manner born* and proverbial expressions such as *brevity is the soul of wit,* both of which owe their present-day status to their use in *Hamlet.*

At the same time, it is important not to over-rate what Shakespeare was doing. The age in which he wrote (in linguistics, technically called Early Modern English) was one of the most lexically inventive periods in the history of the language. The sixteenth century saw a huge expansion of vocabulary as scholarly writers tried to make good the deficiencies they perceived to exist in English. Thousands of words were taken from Latin and Greek, and new words created on the basis of the patterns found there. And as there was no dictionary in which these new words could be recorded – the first attempt at an English dictionary was not until Robert Cawdrey's short (2,521 head-words) *Table Alphabeticall* in 1604 – writers invented anew, in most cases unaware that someone else might have attempted the word before them. Modern English *discontented*, for example, is first recorded in 1548, but before it became the standard usage others had invented *discontentive* (1605), *discontenting* (1605), and *discontentful* (1615).

The interesting question, of course, is a more particular one – not 'why did Shakespeare invent words?' (for everyone did) but 'why did he invent one particular word rather than another?' When, in the Prologue to *Henry V*, the Chorus asks 'Can this cockpit hold the vasty fields of France', we are presented with a coinage, *vasty*. Why did he invent this word when a perfectly satisfactory word, *vast*, already existed in the language – a word, moreover, which he used himself? We shall explore this and related questions in Chapter 5.

THE TRANSLATION MYTH

Claims about the supposed difficulty of Shakespeare's language are frequently made these days, especially in relation to the teaching of Shakespeare in schools. 'We need to translate him into modern English if he is to be understood' runs one assertion, and several texts are in print which try to do just that. In most cases, more is involved than translation: a better term would be 'simplification'. When long speeches are reduced to one or two basic points, or long words replaced by contemporary slang, it is not just the poetry of the lines which disappears; the nuances of thought go also. I am not the first to suggest that Romeo's lines, such as

With love's light wings did I o'erperch these walls,
For stony limits cannot hold love out

(*Rom.* 2.1.108)

are a mite denuded by the crude directness of 'I want a snog'. Not surprisingly, rewriting of this kind has generated harsh criticism from those who feel that Shakespeare is being 'dumbed down'.

How difficult is Shakespeare's language? To what extent does he need 'translating'? A distinction has to be drawn, first of all, between difficulty of language and difficulty of thought. Simple language can express a complex thought: 'to be or not to be, that is the question'. Conversely, complex language can express a simple thought: Edgar's harangue of Oswald, which I quoted earlier ('base, proud, shallow, beggarly, three-suited, hundred-pound, filthy worsted-stocking knave') means essentially 'I don't like you', and we get the pragmatic point from the insulting way the actor says the lines, whether we know what the individual words mean or not. It is true that some of Shakespeare's thought is difficult to grasp. But this is not always because of the language he uses.

Linguistic difficulty chiefly arises from unfamiliar grammar and unfamiliar vocabulary. It may also arise from unfamiliar spelling and punctuation, such as we encounter in the First Folio, but most editions of the plays remove orthographic problems in advance, and of course on stage they do not exist. There may also be some unfamiliar ways of carrying on a conversation, as we shall see in Chapter 9. But difficulty with grammar and vocabulary are the two factors that are most commonly cited when talking about texts needing translation. And the chief reason for this difficulty? It is asserted that the English language has changed so much in these respects, in the 400 years since Shakespeare was writing, that it is no longer comprehensible.

What is the evidence? There are indeed some tricky passages in Shakespeare, such as the Edgar harangue, which continues:

> ... a lily-livered, action-taking, whoreson, glass-gazing,
> super-serviceable, finical rogue ...

Virtually every word here needs a modern English gloss. But against this we have to place such passages as this one, from King Harry's speech before Agincourt (H5. 4.3.40):

This day is called the Feast of Crispian.
He that outlives this day and comes safe home
Will stand a-tiptoe when this day is named
And rouse him at the name of Crispian.
He that shall see this day and live t'old age
Will yearly on the vigil feast his neighbours
And say, 'tomorrow is Saint Crispian.'
Then will he strip his sleeves and show his scars
And say 'These wounds I had on Crispin's day.'

Here, no words need a Modern English gloss. So the question is: how much of Shakespeare's language is like the first example and how much like the second?

How much has grammar changed, in the past 400 years? We shall look at the main differences in Chapter 8. But we can get a rough idea of the scale of the problem if we compare two grammars. G. L. Brook's *The Language of Shakespeare* (1976) conveniently sets out points of grammatical difference between Early Modern and Modern English in numbered paragraphs – and there are about 250 of them. Norman Blake's *A Grammar of Shakespeare's Language* (2002) is organized similarly, but with many more sub-divisions, making some 350 points in all. This sounds like a lot, until we reflect on just how many grammatical points there are in English – about 3,500 described in the large grammar compiled by Randolph Quirk and his associates, *A Comprehensive Grammar of the English Language* (1985). So only some 10 per cent of Shakespeare's grammar is likely to cause a comprehension problem. The vast majority of the grammatical rules are the same then as now.

What about vocabulary? How many words have changed their meaning between Early Modern English and today? Notice that the question here is one of difference, not difficulty. Shakespeare uses plenty of words which haven't changed their meaning but might still be difficult. Classical allusions are a good example. There is no linguistic problem in the sentence which Paris uses to explain why he has not mentioned his feelings to the grieving Juliet: 'Venus smiles not in a house of tears' (*Rom.* 4.1.8), but it makes no sense until you know who Venus is. She turns out to be the same goddess of love today as she was 400 years ago. This is not a matter of language change. Nor is it a matter of language change if someone does not know what a 'vigil' is, in the *Henry V* quotation. That word has not changed its meaning either.

Shakespeare's Words (see Preface) is a book which collates examples of all the words in Shakespeare's texts which have changed their meaning between Early Modern and Modern English. The associated website database presents 47,365 instances altogether – which at first seems like a lot, but as a proportion of the 884,647 words in Shakespeare it is quite a small total, just over 5 per cent. Hardly a case for translation.

But certainly a case for a glossary. *Shakespeare's Words* groups those 47,365 instances into 13,626 headwords, listing them alphabetically from *'a* (a contracted form of 'have') to *zwagger* (a dialect form of 'swagger', used in *King Lear*). That also sounds like a lot, but now we have to take into account a second factor: *degree* of difficulty. The list includes everything from really difficult words, such as *incarnadine* and *finical*, to words which would hardly give you a second thought, because they are so close to modern words, and in some cases continue to be used in special contexts (e.g. poetry or religion), such as *morn* ('morning'), *plumpy* ('plump'), and *thou*. So the really interesting question is: how many of these different words pose a *serious* difficulty of interpretation.

I shall explore this issue in detail in Chapter 7. For now, it is only necessary to point out that there are two types of candidate. First, there are words which are totally opaque – like *fraughting* (when Miranda describes the people in the sinking ship as 'fraughting souls', *Temp.* 1.2.13), where neither the form of the word nor the context is of any help, and no amount of guessing will produce a correct interpretation. (The word means 'making up the cargo' – *fraught* is related to *freight*.) Second, there are words which *look* easy but which are very deceptive – the 'false friends' – such as *merely* meaning 'totally' or *ecstasy* meaning 'madness'. There are about a thousand words which fall into one or other of these categories, and these are the items we see routinely glossed in the notes to an edition. But that's only one in twenty of Shakespeare's vocabulary.

A number of other 'different words' are of what we might call 'moderate difficulty'. These are cases where the context is sufficiently clear to enable us to make a guess at the meaning. We are able to extract enough information from the accompanying language to make rough sense of what is being said. For example, when Demetrius says to Helena (*MND*. 2.1.227)

> I'll run from thee, and hide me in the brakes,
> And leave thee to the mercy of wild beasts

we may not know what *brakes* are, but we can easily understand that they must mean 'somewhere to hide'. And because we know they are in a forest, the likelihood is that a *brake* must be some sort of bush-cluster or thicket. Which is exactly what it is. (The word *bracken* is related.)

With a really unusual word, Shakespeare himself often helps us out, providing us with context in the form of his own gloss. What does Macbeth mean when he talks about making 'the multitudinous seas *incarnadine*' (*Mac*. 2.2.62)? The line continues: 'making the green one red'. What does the Duke mean when he says he is going to make a judgement 'as a *grise*...' to help Othello and Desdemona receive Brabantio's favour (*Oth*. 1.3.198)? The line continues: 'as a grise or step'.

There are about 2,000 words which fall into this intermediate category. They include many cases where the form of the word provides a clear indication of the meaning – such as *dismasked*, *bethumped*, *languageless* and *steepy*. We use our present-day knowledge about prefixes and suffixes (whose meaning usually hasn't changed since Early Modern English) to work out what these words must mean. They also include cases where the effect of the word on the listener is more important than its actual meaning. Indeed, often the actual meaning may not be known.

Here's a Modern English example. If I call you a 'blithering idiot', you know the strength of my feeling – but if I were to ask you what 'blithering' meant, you probably wouldn't be able to answer. (It literally means 'senselessly talkative'. *Blither* comes from the same source as *blether* and *blather*.) In fact, the literal meaning is not important, in such cases. What is important is to appreciate the force of the word – that a 'blithering idiot' is a much more idiotic idiot than a non-blithering one. The same point applies to many Shakespearean exclamations, such as Mistress Quickly's *tilly-fally* (2H4. 2.4.81), King Richard's *hoyday* (R3. 4.4.390), and the ubiquitous *whoreson*. In such cases, it is the pragmatic force of the expression that matters, not its semantic content. And pragmatic force is what actors effectively convey. (I shall discuss pragmatic effects further in Chapter 9.)

None of this adds up to a strong argument for translation or modernization. At worst we are talking about somewhere between 5 and 10 per cent of Shakespeare's grammar and vocabulary posing a problem. Rather than modernize Shakespeare, therefore, our effort should be devoted to making ourselves more fluent in 'Shakespearean'. If we are to take the linguistic fear out of Shakespeare studies, we need to devise appropriately graded Early Modern English syllabuses and to write carefully graded introductions, phrase books, and other materials – just as we would in the foreign-language teaching world. All fluent modern English speakers, native or non-native, have an immensely powerful start, in that they already know over 90 per cent of the language that Shakespeare uses. That remaining 10 per cent or so is admittedly an impediment, and I shall explore it further in Chapters 7 and 8, but it should be seen as an opportunity and a challenge to be overcome, not as a barrier to be evaded. The sense of achievement, once the energy has been devoted to the task, is tremendous, and yields a reward which is repeated every time we go to see one of the plays.

THE STYLE MYTH

It is the easiest phrase in the world: 'Shakespeare's style'. And insofar as there is something in the way he writes which we feel is distinctive, and which differentiates him from other writers, then we will continue to use it. But as soon as we try to identify this style with reference to particular linguistic features, the notion starts to disintegrate. Very few authors, in fact, can be identified with reference to a linguistic feature (or set of features) which can be found throughout their whole body of work. Nor would we expect this to be so. Style always varies on two dimensions: dia-chronically, over time, as people grow older; and synchronically, at any one point in time, as people adapt their writing to suit different types of subject matter. With a writing career extending over some twenty-five years and a range of content extending from high tragedy to low comedy, we must expect stylistic variation rather than homogeneity. And that is what we get. If it were otherwise, questions about the authorship of Shakespeare's plays would have been settled years ago.

By style I mean the set of linguistic features that, taken together, uniquely identify a language user. The notion presupposes that there has been a choice – that someone has opted for Feature P rather than Feature Q (or R, S, . . .). In this view, if we have no choice in the use of a feature, that feature cannot be a part of our style. For example, I have the option in English of putting an adverb earlier or later in a sentence: *Quickly we ran down the road* vs *We ran down the road quickly*. If I have a preference for one position rather than the other, that would be a feature of my style. By contrast, I do not have an option over where I place the definite article *the* in English. It has to appear before the noun: I can only say *the cat* and never *cat the*. This is an obligatory feature of the language, and it can therefore play no part in my style. All English speakers and writers have to use it in the same way.

There are thousands of options available to us, when we use a language, and it is possible to group these into types.

- Vocabulary offers the largest number of options: there is almost always room for choice, when we select a word – *I'm buying a new car / auto / automobile / banger / jalopy . . .* – and often these choices convey distinctive effects. An example is the choice which can often be made between an Anglo-Saxon, French, or Latin word: different stylistic resonances result when we select *fire* vs *flame* vs *conflagration* or *kingly* vs *royal* vs *regal*. In linguistics, vocabulary is part of the subject of *semantics*. I shall explore some of Shakespeare's semantic choices in Chapter 7.

- English offers us many options in the way we vary sentence length, sentence structure, word-order, and word structure – all part of the study of *grammar*. Adverbs, for example, are very useful in this respect, because they are so mobile: in addition to the two variants above, we can also have *We quickly ran down the road* and *We ran quickly down the road*. I shall explore some of Shakespeare's grammatical choices in Chapter 8.

- Sounds (as reflected in the orthography) are a third dimension, allowing us options in the way we can build patterns of vowels, consonants, syllables, rhythms, and melodies, and generating effects which are traditionally described using such notions as alliteration, rhyme, and metre. In linguistics, the orthographic side is handled under the heading of *graphology*, and the pronunciation side under the heading of *phonology*. I shall explore some of Shakespeare's orthographic choices in Chapters 3 and 4 (or at least, the choices we find in Shakespearean texts), and some of his phonological choices in Chapters 5 and 6.

- And there are options in the way we interact, too, when we engage in verse or prose dialogue with each other. The choices here are more flexible, including a wide range of notions such as the way we question and answer each other, interrupt, repeat, change topic, or express things politely or rudely. The choice between *thou* and *you* is an especially interesting variable under this heading, which is often referred to as *pragmatics*. I shall explore some of Shakespeare's pragmatic choices in Chapters 8 and 9.

Because all four of these types of variation enter into any characterization of a style, with hundreds of variables implicated, it is easy to see that a succinct statement of stylistic individuality is unlikely, for any author. It is not difficult to select a small group of features and exaggerate their use, so that they bring to mind their author. That is how comedians and parodists achieve their effects. But this is a long way from the comprehensive and balanced stylistic account which we need if we want to claim we have captured an author's linguistic identity. With writers who are orthographically or lexically idiosyncratic, such as e e cummings or James Joyce, the task of producing a representative stylistic statement is relatively straightforward. For Shakespeare, it is mind-bogglingly difficult.

None of this is to deny the possibilities offered by 'forensic' linguistic studies of author identification. Individual linguistic 'fingerprints' can be established, and it only takes a single plausible negative point to throw doubt on an authorship hypothesis. For example, I know – and it could be demonstrated by analysing every word I have ever published – that I do not use the conjunction *whilst* in such constructions as *Do not remove the cable whilst your computer is on*. I use *while*. So, if someone were to present a piece of anonymous writing which contained the word *whilst*, it could not possibly have been written by me – even if there were a hundred positive characteristics in it which suggested it could have been mine.

To be so certain, two things have to be present. We need to be sure that there is a choice available in Modern English grammar between *whilst* and *while*. And we need to have an intuition to interrogate. If I didn't have a clear intuition about my usage (and how many of us would?), I could be tested. You could ask me to fill in the blank in sentences using one of the two alternatives: *Do not remove the cable – your computer is on*. That is the sort of thing which linguists often do. Unfortunately, neither of these options is available in relation to Shakespeare. We are often not sure what choices were present in Early Modern English grammar. And, unless seance science takes a huge leap forward, we have no direct access to Shakespeare's intuition. All we have are the surviving texts, and a body of linguistic research which is patchy, to say the least. So firm statements about style are going to be elusive.

But careful analysis can certainly identify stylistic preferences, and sometimes even a quite small observation can be intriguing. Take the phrase *in the midst of*. Uses both with and without the definite article are recorded during the sixteenth century. Spenser, for example, uses both, depending on whether he needs the extra syllable to make up a metrical line. In Book 2 of *The Fairy Queen*, we find:

A flaming fire in midst of bloody field

as well as

And in the midst of all, a fountain stood.

There are several other examples of both usages in his writing. Shakespeare, by contrast, uses only *in the midst of* (the word is spelled *midst*, *mid'st*, *midds't* and *middest* in the First Folio). Here are all six instances:

Whom leprosy o'ertake! – i'th'midst o'th'fight

(*Ant.* 3.10.11)

I'th'midst o'th'body, idle and unactive

(*Cor.* 1.1.97)

But, in the midst of this bright-shining day

(*3H6.* 5.3.3)

But in the midst of his unfruitful prayer

(*Luc.* 344)

Make periods in the midst of sentences

(*MND.* 5.1.96)

What, in the midst of the street?

(*Shr.* 5.1.133)

Seven, if you allow:

The birds sang sweetly in the midst of the day

(*STM.* scene 9.185)

It is important to note that, even in the first two examples, where he wants to drop a syllable to maintain a strict metrical rhythm, he opts to reduce the words to *i'th'*, rather than drop the article altogether. Both the following would have worked:

> Whom leprosy o'ertake! – in midst o'th'fight
> In midst o'th'body, idle and unactive.

We can thus conclude that, if we encountered a line which contained the phrase *in midst of*, it is less rather than more likely to be by Shakespeare.

Such a case appears in the 'Denbigh' or 'Danielle' poems. These are two poems found in a collection of verses in Welsh, English and Latin mainly praising Sir John Salusbury and his family; they are in the library of Christ Church, Oxford (Christ Church Mss 183 and 184). Poems XXI and XXII in Ms 184 are written in the same hand, which is different from any other hand in the collection. At the end of each poem is a signature in a different hand: *finis quoth Danielle* – 'finish said Danielle' – hence the name 'Danielle poems'. There are seventeen six-line verses in the two poems, in the manner of *Venus and Adonis*. Internal references to various personalities suggest that the poems were written between late 1593 and early 1594. Here is the closing stanza of the first poem (with original spelling retained):

> And I'le intreat dianas trayne to stand
> to lend ye help with all their siluer stringes
> The nimphes shall dance with Salusbury hand in hand
> treadinge the measures on the pleasant plaines
> And thus in myddest of all his mirth & glee
> I'le take my leaue of courteus Salusbury.

John Salusbury inherited estates at Lleweni, near Denbigh, in North Wales, and married Ursula Stanley (a daughter of Lord Derby). He developed an interest in poetry while at Oxford, and at Lleweni built up a literary circle. Nobody knows where Shakespeare was, in the early 1590s, but several people have argued that he visited Lleweni, and that these poems were written as a kind of 'thank you for having me'. There are certainly Shakespearean echoes and parallels in several stanzas, but my feeling is that, if Shakespeare *had* written these lines we would have found:

> And thus i'th'midst of all his mirth & glee.

A single piece of linguistic evidence based on so few examples can never be conclusive about authorial identity, but it can be strongly suggestive.

Given the extraordinary range of character and content in Shakespeare, and the period of time (over twenty years) over which he wrote, valid stylistic generalizations are likely to be impossible – or, at least, to be of such generality as to be uninformative. However, these very limitations can themselves act as pointers to areas of linguistic analysis which are likely to prove stylistically insightful. The language of characters can be compared, either in groups (e.g. male vs female, upper vs lower class) or as individuals (e.g. Romeo vs Juliet, Henry IV vs Henry V). So can the language associated with particular genres or themes (e.g. comedy vs tragedy, romance vs revenge). So can the language of different chronological periods, adding a stylistic sharpness to such notions as 'early' and 'late' Shakespeare. And – probably most insightful of all – so can the stylistic effects which result from the choices made between alternative possibilities of expression in individual lines and speeches. 'That which we call a rose / By any other word would smell as sweet' (*Rom.* 2.2.43), but stylistically there is always going to be a difference of meaning or effect. The task facing the stylistician is to determine exactly what that difference is.

2 'Now, sir, what is your text?' Knowing the sources

It is often said that we know so little about Shakespeare – there are so few biographical facts. But the one incontrovertible fact is the language, as seen in the texts which have survived – the First Folio of 1623, the Quarto editions of the plays, and the editions of the poems. Whether you believe that a man called Shakespeare wrote or co-wrote all or some or none of the works ascribed to him in, say, the Cambridge collected works, the fact remains that we have a body of work in (a period of) the English language which has enthralled generations, both as theatre and as literature. And the bottom line, for any linguist, must be: how on earth did he do it? How can anyone manipulate language to produce work like that? As we have seen, it cannot be reduced to such simple notions as 'having a large vocabulary' (the quantity myth), or 'coining a lot of words' (the invention myth). Nor can we avoid the language question by saying such things as 'it is the themes he wrote about', or 'it is the vividness of his characters', for others can present the same themes and characters without achieving the same impact (the translation myth). In any case, the only way we know about those themes and characters in the first place is through the language he has chosen to express them.

The focus for this study of Shakespeare, then, is not so much on 'what he says' as on 'the way that he says it'. And the only way we can find out about the way Shakespeare 'says' things is by hearing, reading, and analysing the written texts which have come down to us. Texts are the primary data, and it is here that any linguistic investigation has to start. But which texts? There are over fifty to choose from, and many printed variants (see p. 31).[1]

TEXTS

All texts of the period, regardless of their literary status, must reflect some sort of contemporary linguistic practice, so everything is of value. Practices do however vary greatly, depending on whether a text is an author's manuscript (a holograph), a copied version (a transcript), or a printed text. If the latter, literary history indicates the importance of distinguishing between the various published types of text which have come down to us, as reflected in the following terminology.

Folio vs quarto vs octavo

These terms refer to the three main book sizes produced by Elizabethan printers. A *folio* is a book made from sheets of paper that have been folded once, making two leaves (four pages), each up to about 15 inches (38 cm) tall (depending on how the pages were trimmed). A *quarto* is a much smaller book, because the sheets of paper have been folded twice, making four leaves (eight pages). An *octavo* has the sheets of paper folded three times, making eight very small leaves (sixteen pages). Nineteen of Shakespeare's plays were issued as quartos before the First Folio edition of 1623. *The Passionate Pilgrim* was published in octavo, as were several later editions of *The Rape of Lucrece* and *Venus and Adonis*. The *Sonnets* appeared in a quarto edition of 1609.

Partly due to the expense of paper, the folio format was used only for books of importance. Plays were not viewed as serious literature, and were printed only as quartos. Then in 1616, Ben Jonson published a folio collection of his own plays, the first Elizabethan dramatist to attempt a collected edition. It was a precedent for Heminge and Condell, the compilers of the Shakespeare First Folio in 1623 (see below).

Good and bad quartos

Two types of quarto have been distinguished, in relation to Shakespeare's plays. 'Good quartos' are those thought to have been produced using a reliable original source. Shakespeare's original manuscripts (or 'foul papers') obviously qualify, as would a 'fair copy' prepared from these papers for publication. So would a transcript made from the manuscript for acting purposes (a prompt-book). 'Bad quartos' are pirated editions, perhaps compiled from memory by actors who had performed in them, or by members of rival companies in the audience, scribbling dialogue down or using shorthand. It was a common practice, according to Heminge and Condell, who refer to the way readers have been 'abus'd with diuerse stolne, and surreptitious copies, maimed, and deformed by the frauds and stealthes of iniurious impostors, that expos'd them'.

The good quartos are listed here with dates of publication:

Titus Andronicus (1594)	*The Merchant of Venice* (1600)
Richard II (1597)	*A Midsummer Night's Dream* (1600)
Richard III (1597)	*Much Ado About Nothing* (1600)
Henry IV Part 1 (1598)	*Hamlet* (1604)
Love's Labour's Lost (1598)	*King Lear* (1608)
Romeo and Juliet (1599)	*Troilus and Cressida* (1609)
Henry IV Part 2 (1600)	*Othello* (1622)

Some of these quartos (such as *Much Ado* and *Hamlet*) are thought to be closer to what Shakespeare originally wrote than any other text.

The most famous bad quartos are the those of *Romeo and Juliet* (1597), *Henry V* (1600), *The Merry Wives of Windsor* (1602), and *Hamlet* (1603). In two instances, *Romeo and Juliet* and *Hamlet*, a bad quarto was published before the good one appeared. Some speeches in bad quartos are quite accurately reproduced; others are seriously distorted, heavily paraphrased, assigned to the wrong character, or omitted altogether. They do however provide interesting suggestions about theatrical practice and they can sometimes shed light on textual problems. The opening lines of a famous speech (*Ham.* 3.1.56) illustrates a rather poorly memorized passage:

> *First Folio version*
> To be, or not to be, that is the Question:
> Whether 'tis Nobler in the minde to suffer
> The Slings and Arrowes of outragious Fortune,
> Or to take Armes against a Sea of troubles,
> And by opposing end them: to dye, to sleepe
> No more; and by a sleepe, to say we end

The Heart-ake, and the thousand Naturall shockes
That Flesh is heyre too? 'Tis a consummation

Good quarto version (1604)
To be, or not to be, that is the question,
Whether tis nobler in the minde to suffer
The slings and arrowes of outragious fortune,
Or to take Armes against a sea of troubles,
And by opposing, end them, to die to sleepe
No more, and by a sleepe, to say we end
The hart-ake, and the thousand naturall shocks
That flesh is heire to; tis a consumation

Bad quarto version (1603)
To be, or not to be, I there's the point,   [*I* = 'ay']
To Die, to sleepe, is that all? I all:
No, to sleepe, to dreame, I mary there it goes,
For in that dreame of death, when wee awake,
And borne before an euerlasting Iudge,
From whence no passenger euer retur'nd,
The vndiscouered country, at whose sight
The happy smile, and the accursed damn'd.

The bad quarto version echoes some later lines of the Folio speech, but they are only echoes.

Not everyone views everything in the 'bad' quartos as bad, because they do at least maintain a connection with contemporary performance – for example, they contain helpful stage directions which are not found in other texts. Hamlet's father's ghost appearing 'in his nightgown' (3.4.93) is a case in point. These 'short quartos' (to use the more neutral expression) do at least, as Laurie Maguire puts it, 'represent what Shakespeare wrote, in a text he didn't write'.

Folios

The 'First Folio' is so named in contrast with later editions. The Second Folio of 1632 was a reprint with some modernized spellings and corrections of stage directions and proper names. The Third Folio of 1663 made some more corrections but included fresh errors. In the second impression of this book, in 1664, seven plays were added 'never before Printed in Folio', including *Pericles, Prince of Tyre*. This was reprinted as the Fourth Folio in 1685, with more corrections and errors. As most of my examples in this book are from the First Folio (other sources are mentioned as they occur), a brief summary of its contents follows.

- A ten-line address to the reader by B. I. (= Ben Jonson)
- A title-page containing a copper-engraved image of Shakespeare made by Martin Droeshout
- A dedication by John Heminge and Henrie Condell to the Earls of Pembroke and Montgomery
- An address to the reader by Heminge and Condell
- An eighty-line memorial poem by Ben Jonson
- A fourteen-line poem from the scholar and poet Hugh Holland
- A 'Catalogve' of thirty five of the plays grouped into Comedies (pp. 1 to 303), Histories (pp. 1 to 232, but the numbers from 69 to 100 are repeated), and Tragedies (pp. 1 to 399 [this last page actually misprinted as 993], with page 156 followed by 257, and no correction made thereafter); *Troilus and Cressida* is missing from the list, and has no page-numbering at all (see below)
- A twenty-two-line poem from the poet Leonard Digges
- An eight-line poem from Digges' friend James Mabbe (signed only as I. M.)
- The names of 'the Principall Actors in all these Playes'
- The plays themselves, beginning with *The Tempest*; in seven cases, there is a list of 'The Names of all the Actors' (*Temp, TGV, MM, WT, 2H4, Oth, Tim*) – really the dramatis personae – usually crammed into a small space at the very end of a play, but in two instances (*2H4, Tim*) displayed in large type, taking up the whole of a page
- Eleven of the plays are shown divided into Acts, and eighteen are divided into Acts and Scenes, using Latin titles (*Actus primus,*

Scena or *Scoena prima/secunda*, etc); however, six plays (*2H6, 3H6, Tro, Rom, Tim, Ant*), though they open promisingly with 'Actus Primus. Scoena Prima', contain no further divisions, and in *Hamlet* the divisions stop after Act 2 Scene 2.

A page from the First Folio is reproduced as Figure 1 and some of its linguistic features will be referred to in later chapters.

Troilus and Cressida is included in the First Folio but not mentioned in the Catalogue at the front of the book. It was inserted between the Histories and Tragedies. The first page is the Prologue, set in a larger type than the other play texts, and this is followed by the opening of Act 1 Scene 1. The next two pages are numbered 79 and 80, and the remaining twenty-six pages carry no numbers at all. What accounts for this curious pagination?

The bibliographic evidence suggests that *Troilus* was originally placed at p. 80 in the Tragedies section, and that four pages had already been printed before it was decided to withdraw it – perhaps because it was felt to be in the wrong place, or perhaps there were problems over permission to use the text. It was then replaced by *Timon of Athens*. At a later stage, when the problems were resolved, a place had to be found for *Troilus*. Evidently the most convenient solution was to put the play between two of the major sections, but without revising the page numbers. By then, however, the Catalogue at the front had been printed.

PRINTING

The *Troilus* issue illustrates an important point about the way books were printed in Shakespeare's time. Modern typesetting practice makes it inconceivable that a book today should be printed in any way other than as a single work, with all the typeset pages kept until the work is finished (and often stored for future editions). If, upon reaching the final page of the present book, I decide to make a correction on the opening page, I can do so, because everything is available in my computer. That kind of storage was not possible in Elizabethan

Mer. Tut, duns the Mouse, the Constables owne word,
If thou art dun, weele draw thee from the mire.
Or saue your reuerence loue, wherein thou stickest
Vp to the eares, come we burne day. light ho.
  Rom. Nay that's not so.
  Mer. I meane sir I delay,
We wast our lights in vaine, lights, lights, by day;
Take our good meaning, for our Iudgement sits
Fiue times in that, ere once in our fine wits.
  Rom. And we meane well in going to this Maske,
But 'tis no wit to go.
  Mer. Why may one aske?
  Rom. I dreampt a dreame to night.
  Mer. And so did I.
  Rom. Well what was yours?
  Mer. That dreamers often lye.
  Ro. In bed asleepe while they do dreame things true.
  Mer. O then I see Queene Mab hath beene with you:
She is the Fairies Midwife, & she comes in shape no bigger then Agat-stone, on the fore-finger of an Alderman, drawne with a teeme of little Atomies, ouer mens noses as they lie asleepe: her Waggon Spokes made of long Spinners legs: the Couer of the wings of Grashoppers, her Traces of the smallest Spiders web, her coullers of the Moonshines watry Beames her Whip of Crickets bone, the Lash of Philome, her Waggoner, a small gray-coated Gnat, not halfe so bigge as a round little Worme, prickt from the Lazie-finger of a man. Her Chariot is an emptie Haselnut, made by the Ioyner Squirrel or old Grub, time out a mind, the Faries Coach-makers: & in this state she gallops night by night, through Louers braines: and then they dreame of Loue On Courtiers knees, that dreame on Curfies strait: ore Lawyers fingers, who straits dreamt on Fees, ore Ladies lips, who strait on kisses dreame, which oft the angry Mab with blisters plagues, because their breath with Sweet meats tainted are. Sometime she gallops ore a Courtiers nose, & then dreames he of smelling out a sure:& somtime comes she with Tith pigs tale, tickling a Parsons nose as a lies asleepe, then he dreames of another Benefice. Sometime she driueth ore a Souldiers necke, & then dreames he of cutting Forraine throats, of Breaches, Ambuscados, Spanish Blades: Of Healths fiue Fadome deepe, and then anon drums in his eares, at which he startes and wakes; and being thus frighted, sweares a prayer or two & sleepes againe: this is that very Mab that plats the manes of Horses in the night: & bakes the Elflocks in foule sluttish haires, which once vntangled, much misfortune bodes,
This is the hag, when Maides lie on their backs,
That presses them, and learnes them first to beare,
Making them women of good carriage:
This is she.
  Rom. Peace, peace, *Mercutio* peace,
Thou talk'st of nothing.
  Mer. True, I talke of dreames:
Which are the children of an idle braine,
Begot of nothing, but vaine phantasie,
Which is as thin of substance as the ayre,
And more inconstant then the wind, who wooes
Euen now the frozen bosome of the North:
And being anger'd, puffes away from thence,
Turning his side to the dew dropping South.
  Ben. This wind you talke of blowes vs from our selues,
Supper is done, and we shall come too late.
  Rom. I feare too early, for my mind misgiues,
Some consequence yet hanging in the starres,

Shall bitterly begin his fearefull date
With this nights reuels, and expire the tearme
Of a despised life clos'd in my brest,
By some vile forfeit of vntimely death.
But he that hath the stirrage of my course,
Direct my sute: on lustie Gentlemen.
  Ben. Strike Drum.
  They march about the Stage, and Seruingmen come forth with their napkins.
    Enter Seruant.
  Ser. Where's *Potpan*, that he helpes not to take away? He shift a Trencher? he scrape a Trencher?
  1. When good manners, shall lie in one or two mens hands, and they vnwasht too, 'tis a foule thing.
  Ser. Away with the Ioynstooles, remoue the Court-cubbord, looke to the Plate: good thou, saue mee a piece of Marchpane, and as thou louest me, let the Porter let in *Susan Grindstone*, and *Nell*, *Anthonie* and *Potpan*.
  2. I Boy readie.
  Ser. You are lookt for, and cal'd for, askt for, & sought for, in the great Chamber.
  1 We cannot be here and there too, chearly Boyes, Be brisk awhile, and the longer liuer take all.
    Exeunt.
  Enter all the Guests and Gentlewomen to the Maskers.
  1. *Capu.* Welcome Gentlemen,
Ladies that haue their toes
Vnplagu'd with Cornes, will walke about with you:
Ah my Mistresses, which of you all
Will now deny to dance? She that makes dainty,
She Ile sweare hath Cornes: am I come neare ye now?
Welcome Gentlemen, I haue seene the day
That I haue worne a Visor, and could tell
A whispering tale in a faire Ladies eare:
Such as would please: 'tis gone, 'tis gone, 'tis gone,
You are welcome Gentlemen, come Musitians play:
    Musicke plaies: and the dance.
A Hall, Hall, giue roome, and foote it Girles,
More light you knaues, and turne the Tables vp:
And quench the fire, the Roome is growne too hot.
Ah sirrah, this vnlookt for sport comes well:
Nay sit, nay sit, good Cozin *Capulet*,
For you and I are past our dauncing daies:
How long ist now since last your selfe and I
Were in a Maske?
  2. *Capu.* Berlady thirty yeares.
  1. *Capu.* What man: 'tis not so much, 'tis not so much,
'Tis since the Nuptiall of *Lucentio*,
Come Pentycost as quickely as it will,
Some fiue and twenty yeares, and then we Maskt.
  2. *Cap.* 'Tis more, 'tis more, his Sonne is elder sir: His Sonne is thirty.
  3. *Cap.* Will you tell me that?
His Sonne was but a Ward two yeares agoe.
  Rom. What Ladie is that which doth inrich the hand Of yonder Knight?
  Ser. I know not sir.
  Rom. O she doth teach the Torches to burne bright:
It seemes she hangs vpon the cheeke of night,
As a rich Iewel in an Æthiops eare:
Beauty too rich for vse, for earth too deare:
So shewes a Snowy Doue trooping with Crowes,
As yonder Lady ore her fellowes showes:
The measure done, Ile watch her place of stand,
And touching hers, make blessed my rude hand.
    Did/

Figure 1: A page from the First Folio (p. 57 of *Romeo and Juliet*)

times, for the simple reason that there was not enough type available to print a whole book.

Printing took place using the letterpress method. Letters, certain letter combinations (*ligatures*, such as *ff*), punctuation marks, and other characters were manufactured to produce individual pieces of lead type. These were placed into the specially designed individual compartments of a type-holding case (the *distribution box*). Compositors selected their pieces of type from the box with one hand and placed them backwards and in reverse order on a composing stick that they held in the other, making sure that all the characters were at the same height. Blank pieces of type were used as space separators. The page was then built up, line by line.

When the compositor had finished setting the number of pages he needed to fill one side of a sheet of paper, he would lock them into a framework, or *forme*, which was then inked and placed onto the press. The whole of that side of paper would be printed – as many copies as was needed. After the paper dried, a different forme would print the second side. Once printed on both sides, the paper would be folded (as mentioned above: once for a folio, twice for a quarto, three times for an octavo) to make up a single section (or *quire*) of a book. The whole book then consisted of a sequence of quires, each assigned a letter or number (*signature*), to ensure that everything came out in the right order. In modern book-production, the typesetting is done electronically, but the basic procedure (and much of the terminology) remains the same.

Elizabethan printers usually had only a small quantity of type available – enough to print a quire, but not much more. Consequently, as soon as one forme had been printed, its type would be broken up and reused to make the next one. The identifying material at the top of each page (the *running head*) would be kept on one side (in *standing type*), ready for use on the next forme, but all other text would go, the pieces of type being returned to the different compartments of the distribution box. How do we know that type was reused in this way? The evidence comes from detailed work by analytical bibliographers, who can establish the minute characteristics of pieces of type (especially if a piece has been damaged) to show how they were repeatedly used throughout a book. In just a few cases, such as title pages with especially complex setting, a page might be kept for repeated use.

Editions of an Elizabethan book rarely went beyond a thousand copies. This was partly because the Stationer's Company limited the size of issues (to keep typesetters in work), but – given the expense of paper – it also ensured that no more copies would be printed than would be likely to be sold. Elizabethan printers were just as concerned as their modern counterparts not to have too many unsold books occupying warehouse shelves. If a book sold well, a reprint would be needed quite quickly, and had to be reset all over again.

This typographical excursus has several important linguistic implications. The printing procedure was prone to error. For example, it is easy to imagine someone (especially an apprentice – and one of the compositors of the First Folio was thought to be such) setting a letter the wrong way round in his composing-stick or confusing two similar-looking letters in the distribution box. Then again, the compositor would expect that all the pieces of type in, say, bin *f*, would contain instances only of *f*; but his colleague who had refilled the bins using type from the previous forme might have put some other, similar-looking letters in there by mistake. Anyone typesetting on autopilot would insert the wrong letter without a second glance. It would then be up to the proofreader to spot the error – and the proofreaders of those days, by all accounts, lacked the professional training they are expected to have today. Contemporary comments remark on the lax standards of the printing houses. In the case of the First Folio, several pages were proof-read and corrected while the printing was going on – which is why different copies of the Folio are not always identical (and why any statistics about Folio usage may vary slightly depending on which copy is used).

Reprinting a book was done by copying the text of the previous edition. Any errors in that text would very likely be transmitted into the new edition – which would have its own fresh errors. Some of the earlier errors (and some of the new ones) would be spotted and corrected, but never all. As a result, the printing history of a particular text can quickly become very complex, especially when numerous editions were published. There were no less than six consecutive quartos of *Henry IV Part 1* – designated Q0, Q1, Q2, Q3, Q4, and Q5 – each one printed from its predecessor, with the First Folio and another quarto, Q6, adapted from Q5. Tracking the changes across editions, in such cases, is the stuff of bibliographic nightmares.

MANUSCRIPTS?

At the beginning of the 1998 film *Shakespeare in Love*, we see the author bent over a table, writing studiously with a quill. At intervals he crushes a piece of paper and throws it onto a shelf, which – apart from the crumpled paper – contains a skull and a mug which says 'A present from Stratford-upon-Avon'. As the camera moves in, we see that he is practising his signature.

Signatures we have, but nothing else. There are six of them thought to be authentic, all in legal documents – a deposition, a conveyance, a mortgage deed, and three in Shakespeare's will. They are reproduced in Figure 2. There are several similarities between them (notably the strongly written capital *W* and *S*), but there is a degree of uncertainty about the identity of some of the letters, and the signatures vary significantly – though that is hardly surprising, considering the circumstances in which they were written. The conveyance signature is crammed into one of the labels that carry the seal, at the bottom of the document. And the three will signatures are written by someone who, judging by the shaky look of the writing, was not at all well. It is possible to see differences in the way the 'long *s*' and the *a* are formed, and there are different kinds of abbreviation. The spellings, evidently, vary. That is the joke in Marc Norman and Tom Stoppard's screenplay. The writer needs practice!

But the joke is spurious. Shakespeare would never have felt the need to get his signature 'right'. As we shall see in Chapter 3, there was no system of standardized spelling at the time he was writing; the

Figure 2: Shakespeare signatures (a) Shakp (b) Shakspe(r) (c) Shaksper (d, e) Shakspere (f) Shakspeare

concept of 'correct spelling', with its associated social sanctions, did not clearly emerge until the eighteenth century. Before that, people unselfconsciously spelled their names in different ways. David Kathman collected as many variants as he could find for the Shakespeare surname between 1564 and 1616 and found 25 variants in 342 instances, such as *Shackspeare, Shagspere, Shaxberd,* and *Shekspere.*[2] 60 per cent of the cases are *Shakespeare* or *Shake-speare,* however, and it is this form which triumphs, presumably because it

[a] *Shakp*, 1612, Belott-Mountjoy Deposition

[b] *Shakspe(r)*, 1613, Gatehouse Conveyance

[c] *Shaksper*, 1613, Gatehouse Mortgage

[d, e] *Shakspere*, 1616, first and second sheet of will

[f] *Shakspeare*, 1616, third sheet of will

Figure 2: (cont.)

was the one chosen by his publishers. The name first appears in print in the letter of dedication which precedes his first publication, *Venus and Adonis*, in 1593, and printers thereafter generally retained it. The standardization would have been greatly reinforced by its use in the First Folio.

But why the middle *e*? There is no sign of it in the six signatures. And why the hyphen? The two points are probably related. Ever since the Middle Ages, printers had manipulated the spelling of words in order to avoid typesetting problems. They would add an *e* to the end of a word to help fill out a line of type, or remove a letter they felt to be unnecessary if a line was too long (p. 62). Adding extra symbols, such as a hyphen, was also a means of separating pieces of type which would

To the memorie of M. *W. Shake-fpeare.*

Figure 3: Type-setting instance of Shakespeare's name in the First Folio

otherwise be awkwardly juxtaposed. A noticeable feature of printed works from the Elizabethan period was the way some letters had long curling upward and downward strokes – ascenders (as in k and h) and descenders (as in p and y). Two of these, side by side, could clash, in certain typefaces, and this would have been the case when a k with a long curling right-hand leg came up against the left-curling foot of the 'long s'. We can see the possible problem in the italic font used for the name in Figure 3, which is the version printed above the memorial by I. M. at the beginning of the First Folio. Evidently the typesetter felt he needed both an e and a hyphen to maintain an elegant appearance.

Every text Shakespeare wrote must have been originally hand-written, and it is one of the great literary puzzles of our age why none of his manuscript work – with one possible exception – has survived. By all accounts, he was a fluent writer. The editors of the First Folio, John Heminge and Henrie Condell, say in their prefatory address to the reader:

> His mind and hand went together: And what he thought, he vttered with that easinesse, that wee haue scarce receiued from him a blot in his papers.

The point was evidently accepted by Ben Jonson, who in his miscellany, *Timber or Discoveries*, reflects that there were lines in Shakespeare which would have been improved by some rewriting:

> *I remember*, the Players have often mentioned it as an honour to *Shakespeare*, that in his writing, (whatsoever he penn'd) hee never blotted out line. My answer hath beene, Would he had blotted a thousand.

Blot in these quotations does not mean 'ink-stain'; it means any erasure or correction. 'Blot, blot, good Lod'wick', King Edward instructs his secretary (*KE3*. 2.1.173), who has written a line of unpleasing poetry. He is telling him to strike it out. Shakespeare made few corrections, it seems.

The 'possible exception' referred to above appeared in the later decades of the nineteenth century. Scholars examined the poorly preserved manuscript of *Sir Thomas More* (Ms Harley 7368, British Library), which displays several different kinds of handwriting, and suggested that one of these hands – the so-called 'Hand D' – was produced by Shakespeare himself. Hand D is used in over three pages, a total of 147 lines (see Figure 4, which shows folio 9 of the manuscript).[3] The play is a collaboration which fell foul of the censor, who demanded revisions to be made, and Shakespeare, it is suggested, was one of the revisers.

The original arguments were based on perceived similarities of style and subject-matter. The scene dramatizes an event in 1517, when Londoners rioted in protest against foreign immigrants, and More acted as a peace-maker. His long speech, affirming the values of tolerance, has images and phrasing which echo passages in *Coriolanus* and the English history plays, notably the Jack Cade scenes in *Henry VI Part 2*. Later, scholars pointed to similarities between some of the *More* spellings and those in early printed editions of Shakespeare's works, such as *scilens* (p. 62). And there seemed to be similarities between certain letter shapes and those in the known signatures. For example, Hand D has an initial letter *w* which typically begins with an opening upstroke – the feature can clearly be seen in Figure 4 at the beginning of lines 13, 31, 35, 39, and (very noticeably) 47 – and a similar flourish is found in most of the signatures too. The capital *S* at the beginning of line 49 bears a striking resemblance to the *S* in the signatures, especially in the conveyance (*b*, in Figure 2). (A virtually identical capital *S* and upstroke *W* is also visible at the beginning of some lines of the Danielle manuscript, as it happens: see p. 20.)

But the arguments against are strong. The most obvious point to make is that the sample of undisputed handwriting in the signatures is

why certainly you ar
for to the king god hath his office lent
of dread of Justice, power and commaund
hath bid him rule, and willd you to obay
and to add ampler matie to this
he hath not only lent the king his figure
his throne his sword, but gyven him his owne name
calls him a god on earth, what do you then
rysing gainst him that god himsealse installes
but ryse gainst god, what do you to your sowles
in doing this o desperat as you are
wash your foule mynds wt teares and those same hands
that you lyke rebells lyft against the peace
lift vp for peace, and your vnreuerent knees
make them your feet to kneele to be forgyven
tell me but this what rebell captaine
as mutines are incident, by his name
can still the rout who will obay a traytor
or howe can well that proclamation sounde
when ther is no adicion but a rebell
to quallyfy a rebell, youle put downe straingers
kill them cutt their throtes possesse their howses
and leade the matie of lawe in liom
to slipp him lyke a hound, saying saie now the king
as he is clement, yf thoffendor moorne
shoold so much com to short of your great trespasse
as but to banish you, whether woold you go
what country by the nature of your error
shoold gyve you harber go you to ffraunce or flanders
to any Iarman prouince, to spane or portigall
nay any where that not adheres to england
why you must needs be straingers, woold you be pleasd
to find a nation of such barbarous temper
that breaking out in hiddious violence
wold not affoord you an abode on earth
whet their detested knyves against your throtes
spurne you lyke dogges, and like as yf that god
owed not nor made not you, nor that the elaments
wer not all appropriat to your comforts
but charterd vnto them, what would you thinck
to be thus vsd, this is the straingers case
and this your mountanish inhumanyty
fayth a saies trewe lett vs do as we may be doon by
woold be ruld by you master moor yf youle stand our
freend to procure our pardon

Submit you to theise noble gentlemen
entreate their mediation to the kinge
geve vp yorself to forme obay the magistrate

too small to provide much of a comparison. The names *William* and *Shakspeare* are sometimes abbreviated, and the only other words which appear are *by me*. That means only half the alphabet is represented (*a, b, e, h, i, k, l. m, p, r, s, w, y*) and there are only about eighty readable letters in all. Letters vary in their handwritten shape depending on whether they occur at the beginning, in the middle, or at the end of a word; and these options are not available in the signatures. Moreover, as already suggested, there are noticeable differences between the six signatures.

Caption for Figure 4: Transcript of part of the Shakespearean section of *Sir Thomas More*

marry god forbid that   1

---

nay certainly yo^{u} ar
for to the king god hath his offyc lent
of dread of Iustyce, power and Comaund
hath bid him rule, and willd yo^{u} to obay   5
and to add ampler ma(ies)tie to this
he [god] hath not [le] only lent the king his figure
his throne [z] (&) sword, but gyven him his owne name
calls him a god on earth, what do you then
rysing gainst him that god himsealf enstalls   10
but ryse gainst god, what do yo^{u} to yor sowles
in doing this o desperat [ar] as you are.
wash your foule mynds w^{t} teares and those same hand(e)s
that you lyke rebells lyft against the peace
lift vp for peace, and [yor] your vnreuerent knees   15
[that] make them your feet to kneele to be forgyven
[is safer warrs, then euen yo^{u} can make]
                    [in in to yor obedienc.]
[whose discipline is ryot; why euen yo^{ur} warrs hurly]
tell me but this
[cannot p(ro)ceed but by obedienc] what rebell captaine
as muty(n)es ar incident, by his name   20
can still the rout who will obay [th] a traytor
or howe can well that p(ro)clamation sounde
when ther is no adicion but a rebell
to quallyfy a rebell, youle put downe straingers
kill them cutt their throts possesse their howses   25
and leade the matie of lawe in liom
                    [alas alas]
to slipp him lyke a hound; [sayeng] say nowe the king

And in any case, how far dare we extrapolate from a signature to a person's handwriting generally? Signatures are automatic, formulaic things, meant to be recognized but hardly 'read'. They tend to look nothing like a person's other handwriting.

The *More* text displays all the lower-case letters, except for *x*, but it has very few capitals – they are not even used at the beginning of the poetic lines (unlike the usual printing practice of the time), which makes a systematic comparison with the striking *W* and *S* of the signatures difficult (apart from the case noted above). Punctuation is

---

Caption for Figure 4 (cont.)

as he is clement, yf thoffendor moorne
shoold so much com to short of yor great trespas
as but to banysh yo^u, whether woold yo^u go.   30
what Country by the nature of yor error
shoold gyve you harber go yo^u to Fraunc or flanders
to any Iarman p(ro)vince, [to] spane or portigall
nay any where [where yo^u] that not adheres to Ingland
why yo^u must need(e)s be straingers. woold yo^u be pleasd   35
to find a nation of such barbarous temper
that breaking out in hiddious violence
woold not afoord yo^u, an abode on earth
whett their detested knyves against yor throtes
spurne yo^u lyke dogg(e)s, and lyke as yf that god   40
owed not nor made not yo^u, nor that the element(e)s
wer not all appropriat to [tho] yor Comfort(e)s.
but Charterd vnto them, what woold yo^u thinck
to be thus vsd, this is the straingers case
and this your momtanish inhumanyty   45

---

fayth a saies trewe letts [] do as we may be doon by

---

weele be ruld by yo^u master moor yf youle stand our
freind to p(ro)cure our p(ar)don

Submyt yo^u to theise noble gentlemen
entreate their mediation to the kinge   50
gyve vp yor sealf to forme obay the maiestrate
and thers no doubt, but mercy may be found yf you so seek it

Notes: [] deleted text, () unclear transcription, Speaker designations (all, moo) are no⸱
shown; they are written on the left of the page (*moo* stands for 'Moor').

of no relevance, in relation to signatures, but there is so little of it in Hand D that even a comparison with the punctuation of printed plays is of dubious value. The character of the writing varies somewhat between the three pages, with words less clearly formed towards the beginning, suggesting a varied speed. There are several signs of rushed or casual writing. Several letters appear in varying forms, especially *a*, *b*, *g*, *h*, *p*, *s*, and *t*. The *n* of *and* in line 6 looks like an *m*, and there are only three downward strokes (*minims*) in the *un* of *sounde* in line 22, when there should be four. And, most obviously of all, there are many crossings out (though whether these are all made by the same hand is unclear). This does not look like a page from someone who 'never blotted out line'.

There are two critical difficulties with any argument based on spelling. The first has already been mentioned: there was no standardized spelling at the time, and writers would vary. The word *sheriff* is used five times on the opening page of Hand D, and it is spelled in five different ways, as *shreiff*, *shreef*, *shreeve*, *shreiue*, and *shreue*; other variants, seen in the First Folio, are *sheriffe* and *sherife*. Only a very large corpus of examples would indicate a personal preference, under such circumstances, and this we do not have. Secondly, an uncertain number of people stand between Shakespeare's original manuscript and the printed versions that have come down to us. When we encounter an unusual spelling, we need to establish whether the idiosyncrasy was due to the author, or to someone who copied the author's manuscript, or to the compositor who turned it into print. This means making a detailed comparative study of the spelling choices made in different versions, and it is difficult to be conclusive. The effects of time also need to be considered: what might have been an unusual spelling in the 1590s might no longer have been a decade or so later. And it is always possible that an apparently idiosyncratic spelling turns out to be less so, once more texts from the period have been taken into account, as we shall see in the case of *scilens* (p. 62).

Having said all that, the accumulation of interesting-looking spellings which are found in Hand D and in Shakespeare texts is at least suggestive. Those who have made a detailed study of the text have on the whole concluded that there are enough similarities of handwriting to make a case. Three points are made. The similarities between the signatures and the *More* text outweigh the differences. The similarities between the signatures and the *More* text are greater than those between the *More* text and any other known dramatic manuscript of the period. And no other Elizabethan playwright whose handwriting is known closely resembles Hand D. The rewriting of a politically sensitive scene would need a playwright of some experience, and one whom the company of players would trust.

It is possible, of course, that even if Shakespeare were the author of the scene, it would not follow that he actually wrote this manuscript himself. What we have here may be a scribe's copy, or some of the changes might have been introduced by someone else. On the other hand, the manuscript does not give the general impression of someone copying out text in a calm and restrained manner, but of someone creatively writing and changing his mind as he goes along.

Whoever wrote it, the *More* text does give us a good indication of the kind of manuscript copy that was around in Shakespeare's time, and the sort of thing that would have been given to a printing house – unless of course a scribe had intervened to produce a 'fair copy'. Even allowing for scribal differences between then and now, they are not the easiest things to read. Compositors have usually been given a bad press by Shakespearean editors; but one has to commiserate with them at times.

SHAKESPEARE'S LANGUAGE?
Students of Shakespeare's language need to be aware of the layers of uncertainty surrounding the texts we have available, and understand the bibliographic variables involved, but they should never be overawed by them. Despite the limited size of the Shakespearean corpus – less than a million words – and the incomplete state of Early Modern English textual resources, considerable progress has been made in understanding both what he said and the way that he said it (p. 22).

The next chapters of this book, accordingly, review aspects of the language encountered in Shakespearean texts, examining in turn features of their graphology (writing system), phonology (sound system), grammar, vocabulary, and discourse organization. An epilogue reflects on the linguistic character of the work as a whole, and its contribution to the historical development of the English language.

We must expect that some linguistic features of the texts will refer to properties of Early Modern English in general; some will relate to particular varieties or styles of the period; some will define the linguistic creativity of the individual author – or authors (for it has long been known that some of the plays are the result of collaboration); and some, as we have seen, will be the result of interference by someone other than the author, such as a compositor, proofreader, transcriber, actor, or editor. It can often be a problem distinguishing these variables, so that the phrase 'Shakespeare's language' is perhaps better rephrased as 'the language used in Shakespearean texts'. But the primary aim of this book is not to identify sources. Its aim is less ambitious: to explore the meaning and effect of the plays and poems by analysing the way the language – whoever originated it – has been used, and to compare the impact of alternative readings where these exist. Linguists professionally do not comment on the literary or dramatic merit of the texts they study; but linguists are also human beings, and if from time to time an evaluative remark of mine slips in, I make no apology for that.

What we have are the plays and poems as dramatic and literary wholes, expressed in a language which is sometimes different from what we know today, and sometimes difficult. The job of any linguist must be to find ways of explaining the differences and reducing the difficulty, but without interring the author beneath a mound of technical linguistic apparatus. I come, after all, to praise Shakespeare, not to bury him.

3 'In print I found it': Shakespearean graphology

Graphology is the study of the writing system of a language – the orthographic conventions that have been devised to turn speech into writing, using any available technology (e.g. pen and ink, typewriter, printing press, electronic screen). For Modern English, the core of the system is the alphabet of twenty-six letters, in its lower-case (*a, b, c...*) and upper-case (*A, B, C...*) forms, along with the rules of spelling and capitalization which govern the way these letters are combined to make words. The system also includes the set of punctuation marks and the conventions of text positioning (such as headings and indents), which are used to organize text by identifying sentences, paragraphs, and other written units. Additionally, a huge array of visual features is available to express contrasts and nuances of meaning, such as underlining, colours, and typefaces, and these contribute to the overall visual appearance of a text – a property which, today, falls within the professional remit of graphic designers.

When used with reference to individuals, graphology refers to the way that we personally exploit the properties of the writing system. Having been taught to write, we each have a distinctive style of handwriting. And when the system displays variation in punctuation and spelling, we have to choose what to do. In punctuation: do I insert a comma before *and* in such phrases as *tall, dark, and handsome*? do I insert a full stop after abbreviations such as *Mr*? do I write *King's Cross* or *Kings Cross*? In spelling: do I write *judgment* or *judgement*? *encyclopaedia* or *encyclopedia*? *flowerpot, flower-pot,* or *flower pot*? Thanks largely to differences between British and American English, about a quarter of the words in a college dictionary offer spelling alternatives, so there is plenty of opportunity for each of us to develop an idiosyncratic spelling profile. Different contexts also promote idiosyncratic usages, such as multiple exclamation marks in informal letter-writing (*Hey*!!!!) or the use of a lower-case *i* for *I* in emails. And, because the English spelling system is notorious for its irregularity, different levels of proficiency can contribute to our graphological distinctiveness.

These examples are all in relation to Modern English. In the Early Modern English of Shakespeare's time, the writing system displayed several differences compared with today, but the same basic properties are present, and the same opportunities for individual expression offered themselves. In this chapter, I examine the properties of the basic 'segments' of graphology – letters and their combinations. The organizational aspect of graphology I examine in Chapter 4.

THE ALPHABET

By the end of the Middle English period, the alphabet had already evolved its modern tally of twenty-six letters, so that in most respects the printed version of Shakespearean texts (as in Figure 1, p. 28) looks exactly the same as the one we use today. The most noticeable difference is the use of two forms of *s*. The first few lines in column 2 of Figure 1 show the familiar 'sigma' form, which is used at the ends of words (*nights reuels*) and when *s* is capitalized initially (*Shall*). They also show the 'long *s*', which has the shape of an *f* without the crossbar, which is used initially and medially (*deſpiſed, ſome*). In the typeface chosen for the First Folio, the two characters *f* and *ſ* are remarkably similar. Not surprisingly, then, there are a number of cases where alternative readings depend on whether the author/transcriber/compositor used the one or the other. A famous instance is the line in *The Tempest* (4.1.123) where Ferdinand declares:

> Let me liue here euer,
> So rare a wondred Father and a wise
> Makes this place Paradise.

The *s* of *wiſe* is a 'long *s*', but a tradition beginning in the eighteenth century has suggested that the line makes better sense if it ends in *wife*, the error having been caused by broken type or a compositor mistake. The arguments are well reviewed in the Introduction to the Arden edition (3rd series) of the play, which stays with *wise*, as do most modern editions. The linguist has little to add here, other than to affirm that the unusual adjective construction (*and a wise*) has many parallels in Shakespeare (see p. 188), as has the rhyming couplet (*wise . . . Paradise*). (Indeed, we can hardly blame Ferdinand for slipping into rhyme, given that Iris, Juno, and Ceres have done nothing else but exchange rhyming couplets over the previous fifty lines.)

There was thus a strong likelihood of confusion, with a compositor using an *s* instead of *f*, or vice versa, and this was exacerbated by another characteristic of the printed alphabet – the use of ligatures ('joined letters'). It was a standard typesetting practice, which saved a great deal of time, to use single pieces of type for very common sequences of letters, such as *ct*, *ff*, *ffi*, *ʃi*, *ʃt*, and *ʃh* (the *s* forms are always 'long'). In Figure 1 (p. 28), line 6 of column 2 shows two of them, in *Direct* and *lustie*. But similarities between the appearance of some of the ligatures meant that there was a reasonable chance of compositors mixing them up. Awareness of these possible sources of confusion has sometimes led editors to propose alternative readings when they have had trouble accepting a usage, such as suggesting *lazy-passing clouds* instead of *lazy-puffing clouds* (*Rom.* 2.2.31) or *gentle fine* instead of *gentle sin* (*Rom.* 1.5.93).

Another notable alphabetical feature of the time involved the pairs of letters *i* and *j*, and *u* and *v*. We find *u* and *i* in Old English manuscripts. French scribes introduced the letter *v* into English in the early Middle Ages. *J* was originally an elongated form of *i*, introduced to make *i* more clearly distinguishable from other letters consisting of single downward strokes (*minims*), such as *n*, *m*, and *u* – a particular problem in cursive ('joined-up') writing. *J* was slower to achieve recognnition than *v*: all the letters of the alphabet are listed at the top of Elizabethan hornbooks, from which children learned to read, and while *v* is invariably included, *j* is usually missing.

The big difference with Modern English is that the modern contrast between *u* (the vowel) and *v* (the consonant) and between *i* (the vowel) and *j* (the consonant) had not emerged. The pairs of letters were interchangeable, each of them being used for either a vowel or a consonant. We can see this practice in the heading of the Contents page of the First Folio:

> A CATALOGVE of the seuerall Comedies, Histories, and Tragedies contained in this Volume.

Here we have *v* both as a vowel (*catalogve*) and a consonant (*volume*) and *u* also both as a vowel (*volume*) and a consonant (*seuerall*).

The Folio title is not entirely typical of Elizabethan usage. By the end of the sixteenth century there had already emerged a strong tendency for *v* to be used when it was the first letter in a word and for *u* to be used within words, regardless of the sound being represented, and this distinction is strongly present in the Folio. We see it in *veluet*, *Venus*, and *vniuersity*. There are no words beginning with a *u-* in the Folio: it is always *vnborne*, *vnckle*, *vnder*, *vs*, and so on. *V* as a vowel within a word, as in *CATALOGVE*, is unusual, and restricted to words in capital letters (there are just two other examples in the Folio, also both used in titles: *IVLIET* and *IVLIVS*).

Gradually the graphic distinction came to be associated with a phonetic one. The *v* at the beginning and end of a syllable increasingly began to represent the consonant sound, and the *u* in the middle of a syllable the vowel sound. This was reinforced by a tendency to use the *v* symbol to avoid an inelegant or confusing sequence of vowel letters). We can see a hint of this trend in the Folio, in fact, in such occasional spellings as *avoid*, *avow*, *ev'n*, *have*, and *lov'd* (words which would normally be spelled with a *u*), but it is only a hint, as the totals show:

auoid 46	avoid 1
auow 1	avow 1
eu'n 23	ev'n 3
haue 5779	have 1
lou'd 148	lov'd 1

Interesting, though, are the Folio's five instances of *divulge* and its variant forms (*divulged, divulg'd, divulging*), which are always spelled with a *v*. Two adjacent *us* were evidently unpalatable, at least to the Folio typesetters if not to Shakespeare, unless they were words in a foreign language (Latin *fatuus, suum, carduus;* French *louure* ('Louvre') and *pouure* ('pauvre'). There is just one English exception: *slauuer* ('slaver').

The phonetic use of *v* was reinforced by its use in foreign words, as in *mauvais, maves* (= *m'avez*), and *novum*, and also in the pseudo-foreign language used to fool Parolles – *mavousus, vauvado* (*AWW*. 4.1.63, 72). And on the one occasion when Shakespeare uses a regional dialect of England, *v* is clearly being used to show a regionally voiced form of *f*:

> Chill not let go Zir, Without vurther 'casion
>
> (*Lear*. 4.6.235)

and likewise *volke* (folk), *vortnight*, and *vor* in the following lines. During the middle decades of the seventeenth century, the association between letter and sound became standard. From around 1640, in most publications, *v* represented only a consonant, wherever it appeared within a word, and *u* only a vowel. (An exception was in dictionaries, which tended to conflate words beginning with *u/v* and *i/ j* into a single list – a practice which can be found as late as 1755, with Johnson's *Dictionary*, and even later, in its early-nineteenth-century editions.)

A similar trend affected *i* and *j*. The *i* symbols, whether short or elongated, were used both for a vowel (with the sound of modern *y* in *yes*) and for a consonant (as in modern *j* in *judge*). In the Folio we find such spellings as *iustifie, Iuliet, inioy*, and *iniustice*, which show the two values in the same word. The *j* form in fact was rare in English – we see it most often in Latin words (*filij*) and in numerals (*ij, iij, viij*), where it would appear in final position. This use occurs just once in the Folio (*LLL*. 1.2.35), where 'Brag.' (Don Armado) says:

> I haue promis'd to study iij. yeres with the Duke

(Normally, *iii* has three *i*s.) With just one other exception, no use is made of *j* in the Folio. That is in the phrase *Scotch jigge* (*Ado*. 2.1.65–6), used twice – an unusual spelling, for elsewhere the writer/ typesetter uses *i* (*iigge, iigging, iigge-maker*, and the curious *iygge*). In all other cases, *j*- words are spelled with *i*-, as in *ioy, iourney, iack* and *iudge*, and also in such French words as *iour* (= *jour*).

As with *u/v*, the association between letter and sound took some time to emerge. A few printers, copying continental practice, tried to introduce a systematic distinction between *i* and *j* in the late sixteenth century, but it did not really come to be common until the early 1600s. According to the *OED*, the distinction was generally recognized by 1630, and began to appear routinely in print soon after – which makes it somewhat surprising that the First Folio, a 1623 publication, did not use it, and suggests that the editors were rather scrupulously following earlier orthographic practice.

As a result, when reading a text in original Shakespearean spelling, there can be patches of easy reading and of difficult reading, depending on how the *u/v* and *i/j* combinations come out. Some words are exactly as they are today, and present no problems: *vouchsafe, value, volubility*. Others can cause momentary difficulty: *Vrsula, vsurpe, iuly, iutty* ('projecting wall'), *iohn, ioane* ('Joan'), *iuorie*. When an older *i* and *u* usage coincide within a single word, our pause can be longer, but there are not many examples of this kind. Who was *ioue*? The god Jove. And *Vtruuio*? The widow Utruvio, invited to Capulet's feast (*Rom*. 1.2.65). And *iuuenall*? The 'tender juvenal', Don Armado's description of Moth (*LLL*. 1.2.8,ff.).

The *u/v* overlap regularly causes problems of interpretation when reading original manuscripts and printed texts. Sonnet 129, for example, is a commentary on the effects of 'lust in action', in which several lines express a contrast between anticipated pleasure and anti-climactic despondency, such as line 5 ('long *s*' has been replaced by a modern *s* in this transcript):

Inioyd no sooner but despised straight . . .

In this context, line 11 in the 1609 printing made no sense:

A blisse in proofe and proud and very wo.

The problem arose, evidently, because *proud* could represent both the adjective *proud* and the verb *provd* (= *proved*). The text we read today is thus:

A bliss in proof, and proved, a very woe.

CAPITALIZATION

There are several well-recognized rules governing the use of capital letters in present-day English. Capitals mark the opening of a sentence, proper names (of people, places, weekdays, etc), the chief words in titles (of books, films, etc), and the beginning of a line of verse (unless the poet chooses to depart from the convention). The first-person pronoun is conventionally capitalized as *I* (though not always in electronic communication). We also have the option of capitalizing in special contexts, when making a special point (as in *She Who Must Be Obeyed*). However, there is also a great deal of variation in practice, such as with brand names, headings, titles (is it *Prime Minister* or *prime minister*?), and nouns perceived to be of special significance (is it *the Moon* or *the moon*?). British and American practices also differ, especially over whether to use a capital letter after a colon (American English doing so much more often than British English).

Capitalization in the Early Modern English of Shakespeare's time was even less predictable, for the conventions were still evolving. The practice of beginning a sentence with a capital letter had long been established, both in manuscripts and in print, as had the use of a capital for the pronoun *I*. Then as now, we would expect all sentences, other than the first in a document, to have their initial capital letter preceded by a mark of final punctuation, typically a period. But in Shakespearean texts we occasionally find an unusual usage, such as line 7 in the 1609 Quarto text of Sonnet 113, where a capital on a word other than a proper name follows a semi-colon:

For compound sweet; For going simple fauor.

Or this one, where the semi-colon is doing the job of an exclamation mark (*2H4*. 2.3.67):

What ho; Is Gilliams with the Packet gone?

A capital also sometimes follows a colon (as in much modern American, but not British usage), especially when the colon is being used to express the kind of major break normally conveyed by a period, as in these examples from *The Tempest*:

And Ile besworne 'tis true: Trauellers nere did lye,

(3.3.27)

And take his bottle from him: When that's gone,

(3.2.65)

The practice of using a capital to show the beginning of a line of verse had developed in the printing-houses during the sixteenth century, motivated especially by the need to clearly demarcate the lines in blank (that is, unrhymed) verse. If a line took up a whole column measure (as in the first line of column 1 in Figure 1, p. 28), the only way of knowing that the next line was verse and not prose was through the presence or absence of an initial capital. The problem is not so great with handwriting, where words can be compressed or spaced in ways that print cannot; and initial capitals were rarely and irregularly used in Elizabethan poetic manuscripts. But in print, by Shakespeare's time, initial capitalization was standard. (There are some intriguing exceptions, such as in the Q1 text of *The Merchant of Venice*.)

There was a huge amount of variation in the way individual words were capitalized – something that the writers and printers of the time were well aware of. Here is Simon Daines, writing in his *Orthoepia Anglicana* (1640), where there is evidently still enough uncertainty in the popular mind for him to feel the need to spell out which words should be capitalized:

> The pronoun, or word (I) must alwayes be written with a great letter;
> so must every proper name, or peculiar denomination of every
> individuall: as all the Attributes of God Almighty, the names of
> Angels, Saints, and evill spirits; the titles given by the Heathens to
> their faigned Gods and Goddesses; the names of men and women of
> all sorts whatsoever; the names of moneths, winds, rivers, Cities,
> townes, Islands and Kingdoms: the particular name of any peculiar
> dog, horse, or beast of any kind soever: The first word of every verse,
> at least Heroique: any letter set for a number, as you had in the
> beginning of our Orthoepie: any letter standing for any such, or the
> abbreviation as we there mentioned. Lastly, all names or Titles of
> Magistrates, Arts, Offices, and Dignities, in what respect soever
> taken. In these, I say, altogether consists the use of Capitall Letters,
> in all other we use onely the smaller.

The problem is clear, even in this extract. Why *Titles* but not *names*?
Cities but not *townes*? *Islands* but not *rivers*? The printers struggled
to bring consistency, but they were faced with a grass-roots trend
among authors to capitalize on the basis of such subjective notions
as the 'importance' of a word in a particular context or whether a
concept had been personified to some degree (*Justice, Truth*). The
further into the seventeenth century we go, the worse the problem
becomes.

Daines' list is by no means complete, when we look at actual
printer practice. The top of column 1 in Figure 1 shows such forms as
Mouse, Judgement and *Maske*, which do not fit into his categories.
Nor do most of the capitalized words in the Queen Mab speech further
down (the speech is set as prose in the Folio, an issue discussed in
Chapter 9). The pattern suggests that someone has decided to use
capitals to show semantically related words, or perhaps words which
should be given special emphasis by an actor:

Waggon Spokes ... Spinners legs
Couer ... Grashoppers
Chariot ... Haselnut

Some modern directors and actors do set great store by this practice. Philip Voss, for example, talking about his Prospero, comments:[1]

> the punctuation of the First Folio, and particularly the capitalization of nouns, has been very influential on the way I stress some of the sentences.

He cites such lines as:

> The Cloud-capped Towers, the gorgeous Palaces
> The solemn Temples, the great Globe itself . . .

and adds:

> Look at the way Shakespeare writes, and he'll tell you what he wants.

But of course we have no way of knowing whether the Folio capitalization reflects the preferences of Shakespeare, or an intermediary transcriber, or a compositor.

The problem is that for every case where it is possible to suggest a meaningful use of capitals there is another where all the signs suggest a mechanical process. Lady Hotspur starts promisingly when she says (*1H4.* 2.3.549):

> I by thee haue watcht,
> And heard thee murmure tales of Iron Warres

where the capitalization does indeed suggest a dramatic emphasis; but two lines later we are flooded with a conventional list:

> Cry courage to the field. And thou hast talk'd
> Of Sallies, and Retires; Trenches, Tents,
> Of Palizadoes, Frontiers, Parapets,
> Of Basiliskes, of Canon, Culuerin,
> Of Prisoners ransome, and of Souldiers slaine,

When everything is capitalized, it is as if nothing is capitalized.

It would be unwise to place too much reliance on a system where there is so much obvious inconsistency. In many cases, words have been capitalized where there is no real possibility of semantic emphasis, and where the use of a capital must be purely a printer's convention – as in *Gentlemen* and *Drum* (lines 6–7 in column 2, Figure 1). Conversely, many words are uncapitalized yet require emphasis. The semantic link between *Lawyers* and *Fees* is clear enough in this line:

ore Lawyers fingers, who strait dreamt on Fees,

but so is the link between *Ladies* and *kisses* in the next:

ore Ladies lips, who strait on kisses dreame . . .

(There is a further example on p. 72, where the word *entertainment* is printed with and without a capital within a few lines of each other.) Evidently, we need to exercise a great deal of caution when considering the role of capitalization in relation to textual interpretation and dramatic performance.

Just occasionally, it is possible to suspect an intention behind a use of capitals. If we ignore the capitals that begin lines, spelling variants, and repeated forms, there are 130 capitalized words in the 1609 Quarto edition of the *Sonnets*. That is a very small number, out of a total of around 18,000 words. The vast majority are nouns, with just the occasional adjective (e.g. *Antique* in *Sonn.* 17) or other form (e.g. *Amen* in *Sonn.* 85). There is no obvious system behind the usage, other than the possibility that individual words have been capitalized to suggest extra prominence, and this is a matter of individual interpretation, line by line. Two scribes with different preferences may have been involved. Occasionally, we can see a clear contrast, such as *Nature* vs *Art* (*Sonn.* 68), or a focused word, as in *You are my All* (*Sonn.* 112), or a deliberate pun (*Will* in *Sonn.* 135–6) and some sonnets draw attention to themselves by containing a group of capitalized words, such as the 6 items in Sonnets 66 and 154. But these are the exceptions. A.C. Partridge is slightly overstating when he concludes his summary of Elizabethan practice with the very definite statement:[2]

There is no ground whatever, except accident, for supposing that the capitalization of substantives before 1600, and even as late as 1610, indicated dramatic or elocutionary emphasis.

But only slightly.

SPACE-SAVERS

Several conventions can be found in printed Shakespearean texts whose role seems to be no more than to ensure that the lines of text do not exceed the width of the column measure.

Logograms

These are symbols which stand for a word or a meaningful unit within a word (a *morpheme*); in bibliography they are called *brevigraphs*; in linguistics, *logographs* or *logograms*. The ampersand (&) is a well-known example:

> Of Guns, & Drums, and Wounds: God saue the marke;
>
> *(1H4.* 1.3.55)

Seen on the Folio page, it is clear that to have printed *and* in full would have exceeded the column measure. The problem is especially notice-able in the opening line of a speech, where there is both a character name and an indention, taking up valuable space:

> *Nor.* What? drunke with choller? stay & pause awhile,
>   Heere comes your Vnckle.
>
> *(1H4.* 1.3.127)

There are 587 instances of & in the Folio, and 237 of them (40 per cent) are in an opening line. Of the remainder, 265 occur later in a speech, 63 occur in stage directions or the list of actors, and 22 are italicized in pieces of Latin or French (where it is sometimes used in error, a compositor having misread *est* 'is' for *et* 'and'). When the & occurs in a medial line, the presence of several space-consuming capital letters can prompt its use, even twice:

> Me thinkes the Realmes of England, France, & Ireland,
>
> > (*2H6*. 1.1.230)
>
> Sir *Iohn Norberie*, & Sir *Robert Waterton*, & *Francis Quoint*,
>
> > (*R2*. 2.1.284)

but often it is there simply because a line is very long:

> Then vp he rose, & don'd his clothes, & dupt the chamber dore
>
> > (*Ham*. 4.5.53).

When space is tight, as in Mercutio's Queen Mab speech illustrated in Figure 1 (p. 28), we would expect to see & being used as a useful space-saver, and so it is (it occurs there in seven of the eleven instances of 'and'). What is puzzling is when we see it used in a line where there is no space constraint:

> And mouncht, & mouncht, and mouncht:
>
> > (*Mac*. 1.3.5)

Linguistic factors can sometimes motivate a usage. In a fixed phrase, a writer/compositor might habitually use an & instead of *and*. We can see this happening, from time to time, in such phrases as *vp & downe* or *Lords & Ladies*, as well as in song choruses:

> With a hey, and a ho, & a hey nonino;
>
> > (*AYLI*. 5.3.16)

but there is no such explanation for the *Macbeth* typesetting. Probably once again we are dealing with a compositorial idiosyncrasy.

Another useful logogram was &c., used sporadically in the Folio (forty times) more as a text-saver than a space-saver. As in modern English, it saves having to spell out unnecessary detail – such as all the names in a group of characters:

> *Iohn*, &c.   We hope no other from your Maiesty.
>
> > (*2H4*. 5.2.62)
> >
> > *Exit Duke, &c.*

or all the items in a group:

> Enter Ariell, *loaden with glistering apparell, &c.*
>
> (*Temp.* 4.1.194)

It is especially used to avoid restating something that everyone is assumed to know, such as the bulk of a proclamation or the chorus of a song.

> *Crier. Henry* King of England, &c.
>
> (*H8.* 2.4.8)

> In spring time, &c.
>
> (*AYLI.* 5.3.24)

And it saves having to read a letter out all over again:

> And looke you, heeres your letter: this it sayes,
> When from my finger you can get this Ring,
> And is by me with childe, &c.
>
> (*AWW.* 5.3.310)

However, the &c. sometimes needs to be made clear. When Brutus reads 'Shall Rome, &c.' in a letter, he has to work out what it means:

> *Shall Rome &c.* Thus must I piece it out:
> Shall Rome stand vnder one mans awe?
>
> (*JC.* 2.1.51)

Abbreviations

Abbreviations in Shakespearean texts are primarily space-savers, as is clear from cases where a full form and an abbreviated form occur near each other. Thus at one point Talbot shouts:

> God, and S. *George, Talbot* and Englands right,
>
> (*1H6.* 4.2.55)

and at another:

> Saint *George,* and Victory, fight Souldiers, fight:
>
> (*1H6.* 4.6.1)

And in the same sentence we find:

> None my Lord, but old Mistris *Quickly*, and M. [*M.* = *Mistris*]
> *Doll Teare-sheet.*

(2H4. 2.2.145)

Titles such as *Saint*, *Master*, *Lord*, and *King* are abbreviated in this way, usually to the initial letter, but sometimes the first few letters (as with *Doct*[or]). Most character names at the beginning of a speech are abbreviated, of course, as is still common modern practice. And occasionally we see abbreviations for amounts of money, as in the list which Peto finds in Falstaff's pocket (*1H4*. 2.4.520), using roman numerals alongside *s* (= shillings), *d* (= pence), and *ob* (= obolus, halfpenny).

> Item, a Capon. ii.s.ii.d.
> Item, Sawce iiii.d.
> Item, Sacke, two Gallons. v.s.viii.d.
> Item, Anchoues and Sacke after Supper. ii.s.vi.d.
> Item, Bread. ob.

In the *More* extract on p. 36, there is also an instance of a *pro*-abbreviation, which was a common Elizabethan orthographic practice: a *p* with a concave curve through the stem has replaced the *pro* of *proclamation* (l. 22).

Omitted letters

An ancient scribal practice was to place a tilde (~) over a letter to show that a following letter – or letters – was being omitted. Most commonly the missing letter is an *m* or *n*, especially when the word contains a double *mm* or *nn*.

> *Fal.* He that buckles him in my belt, cãnot liue in lesse

(2H4. 1.2.139)

> *Hot.* Hath *Butler* brought those horses frõ the Sheriffe?

(1H4. 2.3.69)

Aga. His blowes are wel dispos'd there *Aiax*.   *trũpets cease*

(*Tro.* 4.5.116)

The practice is usually employed in print to save space, as can be seen in the *Sonnets* or *Venus and Adonis*, where the final two lines of each stanza are indented and the printer sometimes had difficulty making a long line of text fit into the reduced space. We find the problem twice in the last lines of sonnets: *whē* for *when* (*Sonn.* 33.14) and *Sõmers* for *Sommers* (56.14).

Occasionally we see a word with the letter omitted but the tilde absent:

A back friend, a shoulder-clapper, one that countermads

(*Err.* 4.2.37).

It is impossible to say whether this is due to compositorial error or broken type.

Superscript letters

Another scribal practice was to shorten common words by placing a tiny raised letter (a *superscript*) above the word's initial letter. In the Folio there are many instances of *y* with a superscript *u* standing for *thou*, *t* for *that*, and *e* for *the*.

Mort. Thou do'st then wrong me, as $\overset{t}{y}$ slaughterer doth,

(*1H6*.2.5.109)

Char. So we be rid of them, do with him what $\overset{u}{y}$ wilt.

(*1H6*. 4.7.94)

Rather less often, we find a *w* with a small *c*, standing for *which*. We find both *which* and *the* superscripts used in this example (*AYLI*. 3.2.401):

of madnes, $\overset{c}{w}$ was to forsweare the ful stream of $\overset{e}{y}$ world,

In the handwritten extract from *Sir Thomas More* (p. 36), we find two other superscripts: $y\overset{o}{}$ for *your* (line 11) and $\overset{t}{w}$ for *with* (line 13).

SPELLING

I have left spelling to last, in this chapter, because although in many ways the most important aspect of Shakespearean graphology – it is, after all, the means whereby we recognize words, and thus sentences – there is least that can be said about it by way of generalization. The reason is that the Elizabethan spelling system was in – what we linguists technically call – a mess. Or, to put it more circumspectly, in the words of the orthoepist John Hart, in his influential *An Orthographie* (1569, folio 2): there is 'such confusion and disorder, as it may be accounted rather a kind of ciphring' than English spelling.

The causes of the disorder lay in the diversity of factors which had influenced the evolution of the spelling system to that date. French scribes had superimposed new spellings on the Old English model (e.g. *qu* for *cw*, as in *queen*). Continental printers working in England had brought some of their spellings with them (hence an originally Dutch *gh* in *ghost*). The Renaissance had introduced many new foreign words into English, often with novel and not always consistent spellings (e.g. *bazaar, guitar*). There had been a major shift in pronunciation of English vowels during the fifteenth century, without a corresponding shift in spelling, so that the gap between the spoken and written word had widened. And, during the sixteenth century, the well-meaning efforts of the first spelling reformers had actually increased the complexity of the system. Several had recommended adding letters to words in order to show their etymology: for example, a silent *b* was introduced into *debt* to show its Latin source in *debitum*. To some scholars, of course, such new letters were excellent features, but they had to be spoken aloud to achieve their best effect. People who did not do so, such as Don Armado, were considered by such pedants as Holofernes to be (glossing the Folio's opening lines) 'intolerable, affectedly precise, extravagantly behaved individuals, torturers of correct spelling' (*LLL.* 5.1.17):

> I abhor such phanaticall phantasims, such insociable and poynt
> deuise companions, such rackers of ortagriphie, as to speake dout

fine, when he should say doubt; det, when he shold pronounce debt;
debt, not det: he clepeth a Calf, Caufe: halfe, haufe: neighbour
vocatur nebour; neigh abreuiated ne: this is abhominable, which he
would call abhominable it insinuateth me of infamie: *ne inteligis
domine*, to make franticke, lunaticke?

It drives me mad, says Holofernes. (*Fine*, incidentally, here means 'in
an affectedly elegant way'. There are no grounds for emending the
word to *sine b* (i.e. 'without *b*'), as if it arose out of an orthographic
confusion between *f* and *s* (see p. 44).)

There is a definite error in the spelling of one word in this
extract: *abhominable* is spelled the same way both times, which
makes no sense, as the whole point (as with the other words) is to
illustrate the contrast between two spellings. The Quarto text of the
play has *abbominable*: evidently a *b* has been mistaken for an *h* by a
compositor unable to follow (and who could blame him?) the sense of
the text at this point. Holofernes, of course, wants the *h* pronounced,
for he believes that *abhominable* come from Latin *ab homine* – that is,
'away from man', and therefore 'inhuman, beastly'. This isn't the
actual etymology, in fact (the word is *abominabilis* in Latin), but the
h spelling was nonetheless widely viewed to be correct at the time,
and that is how it is spelled in Shakespeare's other sixteen uses in the
First Folio.

By the time Shakespeare had begun to write, scholars had tried
to sort out English spelling. Richard Mulcaster, the headmaster of
Merchant Taylors' School, had written a work on the principles of
early education, called the *Elementarie* (1582). It is, he says, 'a very
necessarie labor to set the writing certaine, that the reading may be
sure', and to that end he set about compiling a word list of 8,500
recommended spellings, which proved to be extremely influential.
Over half the words in it give spellings that are still in use today. He
died in 1611 aged about eighty. Shakespeare would certainly have
known him, as the boy actors of Merchant Taylors were a well-
known theatre company, and both of their companies played at

Hampton Court. The boys may even have been the ones chiefly in mind when Hamlet and Rosencrantz pour scorn on the 'eyrie of children' who were so fashionable that they were putting real actors out of work (*Ham.* 2.2.338). And Mulcaster may (or, of course, may not) have been the model for Holofernes.

The wheels of spelling change turn slowly, but by 1623 a remarkable amount of standardization had already taken place, as we can see if we look at one of the most distinctive features of English spelling (and the source of some of the strongest complaints) in the mid-sixteenth century: the use of 'superfluous letters'. The usual way of marking a short vowel was to double the following consonant (as in modern English: the *a* of *matting* sounds short, whereas in *mating* it is long). But a tendency had also emerged to add a final *e* as well – thus producing such forms as *fitte*, *hadde*, *sette*, and *gette*. In the Folio, however, these forms hardly appear. Of the 300 instances of 'get', only one is *gette*; the rest are *get*. Similarly, *fitte* turns up just once, compared with 160 instances of *fit*; and *hadde*, even more curiously, just once out of 1,399 instances of *had*.

It is possible to quantify the degree of difference between Shakespearean and Modern English spelling by comparing older spellings to modern ones. For example, here are the spellings of all the words in the opening fifty lines of Hamlet, apart from common grammatical words (e.g. *the, of, wilt*), proper names (e.g. *Francisco*), and singular/plural variants (e.g. *night/nights*).

Old spellings

againe, appear'd, appeare, assaile, beleefe, burnes, centinels, downe, eares, fantasie, farewel, hast, heare, houre, intreated, leige-men, peece, reliev'd, saies, seene, selfe, sicke, speake, starre, strook, thinke

Modern spellings

against, all, along, answer, apparition, approve, beating, bed, bell, bid, carefully, come, course, Dane, dreaded, enter, exit, eyes, fortified, friends, get, give, good, goodnight, ground, guard, have, heart, heaven, hold, holla, honest, illume, king, last, let, live, long, made, make, meet, minutes, mouse, night, nothing, one, part, place, pole, quiet, rivals, same, say, sight, sit, soldier, stand, stirring, story, take, there, therefore, thing, touching, tush, twelve, twice, two, unfold, watch, welcome, westward, yond

This is a typical result: the spellings in the First Folio are roughly 70 per cent identical with modern English.

Why then do we have the impression that Folio spellings are so different? It is partly because a very small number of old spellings turn up with great frequency. The addition of a final -e alone accounts for over half of all instances. In fact, just five processes account for over 80 per cent of the difference between spellings then and now:

- the presence or absence of a final -e (*againe*)
- the use of an apostrophe to replace a letter *e* (*arm'd*)
- the use of *ie* instead of *y* at the end of a word (*busie*)
- the use of double instead of single consonants, especially double -*ll* (*royall*)
- the use of *ie* or *ee* for vowels with an 'ee' phonetic character (*neere*)

What small samples do not show is the unpredictability of spellings, and this contributes to the impression of difference – *do* as well as *doe*, *hearts* and *harts*, *too* and *to*, *being* and *beeing*, *demand* and *demaund*, *truely* and *truly*, and so on. In some cases, the vacillation is even in the same line or adjacent lines:

If you are arm'd to doe, as sworne to do,

(*LLL*. 1.1.22)

thou hast forgotten to demand that truely, which thou wouldest truly know.

(*1H4*. 1.2.5)

A wide range of factors lie behind such variations. In most cases we cannot talk of an 'error', as there was no standard spelling in use at the time. Nor was there any climate of demand for 'correct' spelling (apart from in the minds of a few orthoepists). Printers did their best to produce consistent copy, but with a wordstock of around 150,000 words to deal with, produced by writers that could be as arcane and scholarly as Mulcaster, on the one hand, and as innovative and playful as Shakespeare, on the other, it is hardly surprising that an intuition about norms would be difficult to achieve. Also, printing factors interfered. If a word did not fit into a line, it might be abbreviated. We see a clear case of this during this speech of Vincentio (*Shr.* 5.1.80, a prose passage, shown here in Folio lineation):

> *Vin.* Lucentio: oh he hath murdred his Master: laie
> hold on him I charge you in the Dukes name: oh my
> sonne, my sonne: tell me thou villaine, where is my son
> Lucentio.

The Folio norm is *sonne* – there are 555 instances of it and only 68 instances of *son*.

It is therefore most unwise to place any great weight on arguments based on spelling, when examining Shakespearean texts. As we saw in Chapter 2, one such argument has been used in the search for evidence to support the claim that an extract from *Sir Thomas More* is in Shakespeare's handwriting. The first scholars who made this claim suggested that there were idiosyncratic spellings in the extract, and that these could also be found in the text of plays known to be by Shakespeare. The spelling of *silence* as *scilens* was one, found also as the name of a character in the Quarto edition of *2H4* (not in the Folio, where it is *Silence*). F. W. Bateson's comment in a 1975 essay was typical: this is a spelling 'to be found nowhere else in the whole of English literature'.[3] But such claims are premature. The *OED* has examples from 1225, and although that dictionary gives no illustrations of *sc* in *silence* after 1513, they are there, awaiting discovery. A. C. Partridge, for example, 'without any search for parallel spellings', came across two from the Elizabethan period.[4] *Scilens* has since been spotted in the writing of the playwright John Mason, in *The Puritan*

(1607) and *The Turke* (1610). And it has to be said that spellings with an *sc* representing the sound /s/ are not at all uncommon in Early Modern English, as every Folio play illustrates (with the word *scene*). Followed by an *i*, we see the spelling in *science, sciatica, conscience* (pronounced with an [s] at the time: see Chapter 6), *discipled, discipline, lasciuious,* and many more. Conversely, words with modern *sc* sometimes had *s*, as in *sent* (= *scent, Ham.* 1.5.58) and *symitare* (= *scimitar, MV.* 2.1.24). *Scythe* appears as *sythe* (three times in the Folio), *sieth* (in *Sonn.* 12, 60, 100), *syeth* (*Sonn.* 123), and in *sithed* (*Lover.* 12). Sometimes *sc* appears as *c*, as in *Cizers* (*Err.* 5.1.75) and a further guess at *scimitar: Cemitar* (*Tro.* 5.1.2). With a sound/spelling relationship plainly in evolution, it would be unwise to make any claims about individual preferences. If we want to argue that *Sir Thomas More* is Shakespearean, we must look to other kinds of evidence than spelling.

4 'Know my stops': Shakespearean punctuation

Also falling under the heading of graphology is the set of orthographic practices that we call English punctuation. The conventions have taken a millennium to develop, and (as Internet innovations show) the process is not over yet. From a time (in Old English) when manuscripts were almost totally unpunctuated, apart from a few indications of voice inflection, we have moved to a stage where a full use of punctuation is a mark of education. Grammars and publishing houses formulate rules governing usage, and we struggle to follow them – struggle, because the recommendations of different grammarians and publishers do not always agree, even within British (as opposed to American) English. Punctuation is not so much a system, more a set of practices of varying rigour.

Why is punctuation such a problem? Because a huge amount of linguistic responsibility has been placed on a very small number of marks:

the *period* (.), also called a *point* or *full stop*
the *semi-colon* (;)
the *colon* (:)
the *comma* (,)
single (' ') or double (" ") *inverted commas* (especially in UK usage), also called *quotation marks* or *quote marks*
the *hyphen* (-)
the *dash* (–)
parentheses ( ), also called *round brackets*
the *question mark* (?)
the *exclamation mark* or (especially US usage) *exclamation point* (!)
the *apostrophe* (')

Leaving aside more specialized features, such as square brackets ([ ]) and obelisks (§), this amounts to not even a dozen marks, and these have to perform a range of overlapping functions.

- Conveying a pause, of varying duration, e.g. two dashes longer than one; periods longer than commas.
- Suggesting a tone of voice, e.g. question marks with a rising pitch; exclamations with a falling pitch; parentheses with a lower, faster, and quieter mode of speech.
- Marking a grammatical construction: a period ending a sentence (as does a question mark and exclamation mark); inverted commas demarcating direct speech.
- Adding a meaning: inverted commas identifying the title of a work or giving 'special' emphasis; repeated exclamation marks raising the emotional tone.
- Marking types of word, e.g. a period showing an abbreviation (*Mr.*); a hyphen identifying a compound word (*washing-machine*).
- Organizing the text, e.g. a hyphen at the end of a line signalling a word-break; a colon relating numerals (as in times, *6:15*).

In particular, faced with a punctuation mark, it can be unclear whether the writer has used it as a guide to pronunciation (a 'phonetic' or 'elocutional' function) or to make the text easy to read (a 'grammatical' or 'semantic function'). Even in Modern English, despite two centuries of familiarity with standard English marks and practices, the punctuation of many sentences can be read aloud in several different ways. The problem is very much greater in reading original Shakespearean texts because during his lifetime not just the conventions of using punctuation, but the marks themselves, were still in the process of being established.

The modern set of marks slowly emerged during the sixteenth century, with English writers influenced by continental practices. Earlier marks, such as the *virgule* (/) used by William Caxton, gradually fell out of use in print, though it was still often used in manuscripts to mark major pauses. It was a time of erratic growth, as can be seen in the sporadic arrival in English of punctuation nomenclature. The word *punctuation* is first recorded in the *OED* in 1539. *Comma* in its sense as a punctuation mark is known from 1530. (In its senses of 'pause' or 'detail', it turns up twice in Shakespeare.) And during the second half of the century we encounter the first recorded uses (again, in their sense of marks) of *apostrophe* (1588), *colon* (1589), *full stop* (1596), and *point of interrogation* (1598 – the term *question mark* arrives surprisingly late, in 1905). The next two decades provide instances of *hyphen* (1603), *period* (1609), and *stop* (1616). *Semi-colon* – sometimes also called a *comma colon* – is much later (1644), as is the *note of exclamation* (1657) and *quotation quadrats* (1683 – what would in the nineteenth century be called *quotation marks*; a *quadrat* was a small metal block used for spacing). *Dash* and *bracket* are eighteenth century.

Interestingly, Shakespeare is the first recorded user of two of these words. 'You find not the apostrophus, and so miss the accent', says Holofernes, criticizing the way Nathaniel has read Don Armado's letter to Jaquenetta (*LLL.* 4.2.119), which the *OED* dates – somewhat prematurely – as 1588. He means: 'you are ignoring the marks of elision'. And Salerio shuts up the burbling Solanio with an abrupt: 'Come, the full stop!' (*MV.* 3.1.15). The *OED* assigns 1596 to that one.

We should never read too much into 'first recorded uses', of course: they tell us only the first time lexicographers have (so far) discovered that someone has written a word down (see p. 8). Punctuation terms would have been in spoken usage, especially among printers, for some time before they first appeared in writing. Semi-colons, for instance, began to be used in English books with some frequency in the 1580s, and isolated uses can be traced back to 1538. They were probably described in several ways before the term *semi-colon* became the norm. But the dates nonetheless do reinforce the main point, which is that the basis of English punctuation practices was being established at precisely the time that Shakespeare was writing. New usages are inevitably prone to inconsistency and error.

We must expect, then, to find a great deal of variation in the way writers, copyists, and compositors employed them.

Some scholars were already trying to impose order on what was happening. George Puttenham, in his *Art of English Poesie* (1589, quoted here with modern spelling and punctuation), reminded his readers that English could do no better than follow Classical models:

> The ancient reformers of language invented three manner of pauses, one of less leisure than another, and such several intermissions of sound to serve (besides easement to the breath) for a treble distinction of sentences or parts of speech, as they happened to be more or less perfect in sense. The shortest pause or intermission they called 'comma', as who would say a piece of a speech cut off. The second they called 'colon', not a piece but as it were a member for his larger length, because it occupied twice as much time as the 'comma'. The third they called 'periodus', for a complement or full pause, and as a resting place and perfection of so much former speech as had been uttered, and from whence they needed not to pass any further unless it were to renew more matter to enlarge the tale.

What he is recommending is a three-grade system, using the formula 'one period = two colons = four commas'. Some writers, such as the author of the influential *An Orthographie* (1569), John Hart, used a musical analogy: if a comma is a crotchet, then a colon is a minim.

The approach was frequently advocated until the nineteenth century, and may still be encountered today in recommendations for public speaking. If you try it, you will quickly see that it is far too mechanical a system to cope with the complexities of English syntax. When followed pedantically it produces the most bizarre rhythms and a kind of oratory which is miles away from Hamlet's recommendation to have speech come 'trippingly upon the tongue' (*Ham.* 3.2.2). But in Elizabethan England, many felt it was an ideal to be aimed at, and certainly the way commas and colons are distributed in Shakespearean texts, often being used in places where periods would be grammatically expected, suggests that at least some people were following it. When the semi-colon arrived, making a four-grade system, its length was usually considered to be between that of the comma and the colon.

The big question was whether punctuation marks were there to help speaking or reading. If the former, then they had to be given clear phonetic values. If the latter, then it did not matter what length the marks represented as long as they made the sense clear. It is easy to see that the former approach would appeal to actors, wanting their scripts to give them as many clues as possible about how a speech should be read; and the latter would appeal to publishers, wanting their books to be as readable as possible. Between 1590 and 1630 it is possible to sense a sea-change in the way people thought of punctuation: early on, the phonetic/elocutional approach was the dominant one; later, the grammatical/semantic approach ruled.

How we interpret the periods, colons, semi-colons, and commas of a Shakespearean text thus involves our judgement about whether their use is motivated by phonetic or grammatical considerations. When we see a mark interfering with a grammatical construction, we might well infer that the only reason it is there (transmission errors of copying or printing aside) is to give the actors a clue about how to say it. A good example is the coordination of two nouns with *and* (as in *boys and girls*). Today we do not allow a comma before the *and*, and the same practice was normal in Elizabethan texts:

> hee is pure Ayre and Fire, and the full elements of Earth and
> Water neuer appeare in him

> (*H5*. 3.7.20).

It is grammatically unnecessary, therefore, in King Henry's description of Hotspur:

> Who is sweet Fortunes Minion, and her Pride

> (*1H4*. 1.1.82).

But we can easily imagine a rendition in which an actor gives that comma some dramatic value.

The principle is easy to state, more difficult to interpret: when a punctuation mark is used that is not required by Early Modern English grammar, then it has to be explained, and – once an error in transmission is ruled out – the most likely explanation is that it is there for phonetic purposes. We can rule out transmissional error if we find repeated examples of the same pattern over a wide range of texts – which is what we do find if we go looking for examples of coordinated noun phrases with *and*. But often we do not have to look so far for a norm, as the immediate context illustrates it. When Antony shakes hands with Caesar's murderers (*JC*. 3.1.186), there are no commas between the names and the pronouns – apart from Casca:

> Next Caius Cassius do I take your hand;
> Now Decius Brutus yours; now yours Metellus;
> Yours Cinna; and my valiant Caska, yours;
> Though last, not least in loue, yours good Trebonius.

Casca was the first to stab Caesar ('Speake hands for me'). Might we therefore imagine the actor playing Antony to take that comma seriously, delaying the onset of *yours*, and perhaps doing some business with Casca's hands at that point? This is somebody else's problem, not mine. But having been present at the rehearsals of the Globe's 2005 production of *Troilus and Cressida*, where director Giles Block used the Folio text, I can affirm that there were many discussions between director and actors over precisely how much value to attach to a comma.

The same principle applies to the other marks. Here is a common version of the last two lines of *A Midsummer Night's Dream* (before the fairies arrive to clear up):

> A fortnight hold we this solemnity
> In nightly revels and new jollity.

That, indeed, is the simplest present-day punctuation, and it is what I find in all the modern editions I have. But the Folio has this:

> A fortnight hold we this solemnity.
> In nightly reuels; and new jollitie.

It looks erratic, on first glance. But if we allow *In nightly reuels* a separate status, a fresh nuance emerges, and perhaps an actor might want to make something of it.

Not everyone likes to pay close attention to punctuation. Some directors think that the plays have too much. Peter Hall, for example, has this to say (in his *Diaries*, 21 August 1975, edited by John Goodwin):

> Shakespeare's text is always absurdly over punctuated: generations of scholars have tried to turn him into a good grammarian. Even the original printed texts are not much help – the first printers popped in some extra punctuation. When punctuation is just relaxed to the flow of the spoken word, the actor is liberated.

Well, up to a point. It is certainly true that some compositors added a great deal of fresh punctuation. We know, for example, that compositor B of the First Folio was a heavy punctuator, adding many marks (especially commas) to the text. We also know that the scrivener Ralph Crane, who prepared some of the transcripts for the Folio compositors, had some idiosyncratic punctuation habits. But there are many cases where, either through accident or design, a text appears which can suggest an interesting reading or performance, and these have to be given every consideration. The following extract is, from a grammatical point of view, over-punctuated; but it could be argued that the commas well reflect Morton's nervously excited report on the battle of Shrewsbury (*2H4*. 1.1.131):

> The summe of all,
> Is, that the King hath wonne: and hath sent out
> A speedy power, to encounter you my Lord,
> Vnder the Conduct of yong Lancaster

Writers on the whole avoided the problem by putting the bare minimum of punctuation into their manuscripts. The extract from

Sir Thomas More shown in Figure 4 (p. 36) is a good example. It has hardly any periods, few commas, two semi-colons (if that is what they are), no question marks, no colons. Some lines cry out for punctuation:

> marry god forbid that [1]
> 　　　　what rebell captaine …
> can still the rout who will obay [th] a traytor [21]
> kill them cutt their throts possesse their howses [25]

When marks are used, they are often idiosyncratic. The *More* writer seems to give the semi-colon the value of a period, and in line 28 we see a comma and a period used together.

Before the 1580s, the period, comma, colon, question mark, and round brackets are regularly found in printed texts. Sometimes an inverted semi-colon is used where we would expect a question mark. Why? There are lots of questions asked in plays, and with a limited supply of pieces of type available at any one time, we can easily imagine a compositor using up all the 'marks of interrogation' in his distribution box and finding it necessary to adapt another piece of type for the purpose. When the semi-colon started to be used routinely, during the 1580s, we often find it being used interchangeably with the colon, perhaps for the same reason. The primary function of the colon was to mark a pause (it is actually called *pause* in Ben Jonson's *English Grammar*), and as pauses are the sort of thing that actors need to know about, it is not surprising to find colons far more in demand in printed plays than they would be in a piece of scholarly prose.

Whatever the reason, we often encounter a mixture of colons and semi-colons in Shakespearean texts, with compositors (such as those who set the First Folio) varying in their preferences for the one or the other. As a result, it is difficult to know whether a contrast in usage was introduced in order to show different lengths of pause, or whether it was a random choice. For example, there seems to be dramatic purpose behind the several marks in this speech of Leontes (*WT.* 1.2.108), for they break up the text into disjointed units of discourse that well reflect his emotional turmoil as he imagines Hermione's infidelity.

> *Leo.* Too hot, too hot:
> To mingle friendship farre, is mingling bloods,
> I haue *Tremor Cordis* on me: my heart daunces,
> But not for ioy; not ioy. This Entertainment
> May a free face put on: deriue a Libertie   5
> From Heartinesse, from Bountie, fertile Bosome,
> And well become the Agent: 't may; I graunt:
> But to be padling Palmes, and pinching Fingers,
> As now they are, and making practis'd Smiles
> As in a Looking-Glasse; and then to sigh, as 'twere   10
> The Mort o'th'Deere: oh that is entertainment
> My Bosome likes not, nor my Browes.

The sequence in line 7 certainly seems to have contrastive value, with the semi-colon expressing a shorter pause than the colon; but in other lines, the contrast is not so clear. I can imagine one actor giving a longer pause for the colon after *Deere* than he would use for the semi-colon after *Glasse*, and another hardly pausing after *Deere* at all. Both would work in performance.

EXCLAMATION MARKS

Exclamation marks can be one of the most noticeable features of a modern edition, but few of them are original. They began to be used in English texts during the 1590s, and were immediately often confused with question marks, both physically (by compositors mixing up pieces of type) and editorially, when the grammatical function of a sentence was unclear. Rhetorical questions posed a particular difficulty (a modern example: *How should I know*), as did exclamatory questions (*Hasn't she grown*). Even today, there can be uncertainty over which end-mark to use, and – judging by the confusion – it was a real problem for Elizabethan writers/editors/compositors. Sometimes, the meaning of the sentence is the dominant factor, and the result is an exclamation mark (the 'note of admiration', or 'wonderer', as John Hart called it). At other times we see texts where the user has plainly been influenced by the grammatical 'look' of the sentence and gone for a question mark (Hart's 'note of interrogation', or 'asker'). These are the ones which can cause some confusion when reading an original text, as in these lines (*Ham.* 1.2.132):

> O God, O God!
> How weary, stale, flat, and vnprofitable
> Seemes to me all the vses of this world?
> Fie on't? Oh fie, fie, 'tis an vnweeded Garden …

The first question mark is easy to explain, given that the sentence begins with a question-word, *How*. The second is a puzzle, and has to be put down to uncertainty on the part of the user, who certainly knew about exclamation marks, for there is one just two lines before. A similar vacillation appears later in the play (2.2.303), where a series of parallel rhetorical questions begins with an exclamation mark and then continues with question marks:

> What a piece of worke is a man! how Noble in Reason? how
> infinite in faculty? in forme and mouing how expresse and admir-
> able? in Action, how like an Angel? in apprehension, how like
> a God?

The problem is a recurring one: to give just one more example, here is Portia talking to herself about her situation (*JC.* 2.4.39):

> Aye me! How weake a thing
> The heart of woman is?

She is alone, and plainly the force of the sentence is exclamatory rather than questioning.

We can sometimes see the uncertainty going in the other direction, with an exclamation mark used in place of a question mark. The error is not common in the Folio, as there are only 350 exclamation marks in the whole book, but there are three clear cases.

– A messenger arrives for Caius Martius (*Cor.* 1.1.221):

> *Mess.* Where's *Caius Martius*?
> *Mar.*   Heere: what's the matter!

The exclamation mark is wrong, for this is a genuine question, and taken as such: the Messenger immediately answers it.

– When Demetrius wakes and sees Helena, he expostulates (*MND.* 3.2.137):

> O *Helen*, goddesse, nimph, perfect, diuine,
> To what, my loue, shall I compare thine eyne!
> Christall is muddy,

The second line is rhetorical, but it is undoubtedly a question, for he answers it himself.

– Apemantus and Timon have been rudely interrogating each other in several exchanges, and after each question there is a question mark. But we then find this, from Apemantus (*Tim.* 4.3.312):

> What man didd'st thou euer know vnthrift, that was beloued
> after his meanes!
> *Tim.* Who without those meanes thou talk'st of, didst thou euer
> know belou'd?
> *Ape.* My selfe.

It is the only exclamation mark in the sequence, and is clearly an error.

We might have expected the Folio compositors to have gone in for exclamation marks, following the lead of Ben Jonson, who shows no reluctance to use them in his prefatory memorial:

> I, therefore will begin. Soule of the Age!
> The applause! delight! the wonder of our Stage!

But they are rarely found in the plays, and are missing even in places where the exclamatory function of the language is undeniable, as in the climactic ending of King Henry's speech before Agincourt (*H5.* 3.1.34):

> Cry, God for *Harry*, England, and S. *George*.

or the Ghost's heartbroken cry (*Ham.* 1.5.80):

> Oh horrible Oh horrible, most horrible:

All we get is an unexciting period and a colon, respectively.

There is no correlation between the distribution of exclamation marks in the First Folio and the assumed chronological order of the plays. Seven plays have none at all (*TGV, Shr, 1H6, Wiv, H5, TN, MM, WT*). The exclamation mark was only just beginning to make its appearance when Shakespeare was writing his first plays, so it is perhaps not surprising to see none there. But any thought of a developmental explanation for the distribution of these marks in the First Folio disappears when we see that *The Winter's Tale* has none either. Far more likely is that the presence or absence of exclamation marks reflects different awareness and preferences on the part of the Folio compositors.

The vast majority of the exclamation marks (319 out of 350, 91 per cent) appear in a sentence or line which begins with an interjection – and in 265 cases (83 per cent) this is *Oh* or *O* – either the emotional noise or the vocative form of address (it is often unclear which is which). To illustrate, here are all the Folio examples from *Romeo and Juliet* (with Norton line numbers):

700:    O deare account! My life is my foes debt.
1574:   O! I am Fortunes foole.
1721:   O God!
1732:   O Nature! what had'st thou to doe in hell,
1827:   O deadly sin, O rude vnthankefulnesse!
1977:   To heare good counsell: oh what learning is!
2087:   O God! I haue an ill Diuining soule,
2251:   O God!
2285:   Auncient damnation, O most wicked fiend!
2608:   O Lamentable day!
2963:   O true Appothecarie!
3075:   O heauen!
3076:   O wife looke how our Daughter bleedes!

There was evidently a strong association of the mark with emotional discourse. But it was not general printing-house practice to set an exclamation-mark after a sentence beginning with *O(h)*, for there are dozens of such sentences in *Henry VI Part 1*, *The Winter's Tale*, and the other plays which have no instances (we can see one in line 11 of the Leontes speech on p. 72). We must be seeing typesetting idiosyncrasy here.

Whoever set *Much Ado About Nothing* and *A Midsummer Night's Dream* (the only two plays in which exclamation marks appear more frequently than one in a hundred lines) had a much more sophisticated (and modern) set of ideas about how these marks should be used. These compositors still made the occasional error, but they knew about the force of exclamatory sentences beginning with *What* or *How* (without any preceding interjection) and they were beginning to experiment with the use of the mark for statements uttered with extra feeling, and seeing how it could be carried through a sequence of sentences to mark a continuing mood. Here are the non-*O(h)* examples from these two plays:

Exclamatory 'what/how' sentences
Ado, 302: How sweetly doe you minister to loue,
              That know loues griefe by his complexion!
MND, 1591: My *Oberon*, what visions haue I seene!

An imperative sentence
MND, 1690: Behold how like a maid she blushes heere!

Emphatic statements
Ado, 609:   the Princes foole!
Ado, 1562:   A maid and stuft!
Ado, 1977:   Princes and Counties!
Ado, 2130:   Some haste my Lord!
Ado, 2484:   Suffer loue! a good epithite, I do suffer loue
               in-deede,

In four of these last five cases, the exclamatory utterance is repeating or taking up an utterance made by a preceding speaker.

The text of *A Midsummer Night's Dream* also illustrates a rare sequence of marks, during one of Pyramus' hyperbolic outpourings (*MND*. 5.1.273):

> 2080: Eyes do you see! How can it be!
> O dainty Ducke: O Deere!
> Thy mantle good; what staind with blood!

The only other case I have found of this happening is in *Julius Caesar*, where the citizens (here numbered 1, 2, 3, and 4) echo each other's horror at the murder of Caesar (*JC*. 3.2.199):

> 1735: 1. O pitteous spectacle!
> 2. O Noble *Caesar*!
> 3. O wofull day!
> 4. O Traitors, Villaines!
> 5. O most bloody sight!

Four hundred years on, the use of the exclamation mark has expanded and settled down. It is now used routinely with interjections (*Oh!*), greetings (*Happy Xmas!*), peremptory commands (*Stop!*), expressions of surprise (*What a mess!*), loud speech in dialogue (*I'm in the garden!*), and ironic or pointed comments (*He paid, for a change!*). Style-guides advocate caution, noting the tendency for them to be over-used. On the whole, modern editions of Shakespeare do not introduce them excessively (a contrast with Victorian times, when they littered the pages). But it is important to know that, when reading such material as the following, all exclamation marks (and indeed the dashes too) have been added by the modern editor (*Rom*. 3.3.75, Penguin edition):

> Friar: Hark, how they knock! – Who's there? – Romeo, arise.
> Thou wilt be taken. – Stay a while! – Stand up.
>
> *Knock*
>
> Run to my study. – By and by! – God's will,
> What simpleness is this! – I come, I come!

Compare this with the Folio lines:

Harke how they knocke:
(Who's there) *Romeo* arise,
Thou wilt be taken, stay a while, stand up

Knocke.

Run to my study: by and by, Gods will
What simplenesse is this: I come, I come.

PARENTHESES

The use of parentheses in this last example illustrates another distinctive feature of original Shakespearean texts. Parentheses today have a limited set of specialized functions, enabling us to show examples, references, and cross-references, as in the citations to plays throughout this book; numbers or letters in a list, as in (*a*), (*b*), (*c*); and alternative forms of a word, as in O(*h*). But their main function is to enclose an observation which makes an extra or subordinate semantic point; if omitted, the rest of the sentence would still stand. And when such text is read aloud, the parenthesis typically receives reduced prominence. This is certainly not the case with the Folio example above, where the enclosed utterance is a separate sentence, by no means semantically optional, and is being shouted out.

The Folio compositors – as with exclamation marks – seem to have had very different practices concerning the use of parentheses. Again, there is no developmental pattern: plays with over a hundred parentheses occur throughout Shakespeare's career (*TGV*, *Wiv*, *2H4*, *Oth*, *WT*, *Cym*, *H8*). Most of the plays have very light usage: in twenty-five plays there are fewer than sixty instances. A third of all instances occurs in just three plays (*2H4*, *Wiv*, *WT*). This extract illustrates heavy usage (*WT*. 5.1.25):

Were I but twentie one,
Your Fathers Image is so hit in you,
(His very ayre) that I should call you Brother,
As I did him, and speake of something wildly

By vs perform'd before. Most dearly welcome,
And your faire Princesse (Goddesse) oh: alas,
I lost a couple, that 'twixt Heauen and Earth
Might thus haue stood, begetting wonder, as
You (gracious Couple) doe: and then I lost
(All mine own Folly) the Societie,
Amitie too of your braue Father, whom
(Though bearing Miserie) I desire my life
Once more to looke on him.

There may even be parentheses inside parentheses:

(And dead almost (my Liege) to thinke you were)

(*2H4*. 4.5.157)

For the most part, these parentheses identify a less important grammatical construction. Here are some examples.
–Terms of address:

Too true (my Lord:)

(*WT*. 5.1.12)

We are not (Sir) nor are we like to be

(*WT*. 5.1.204)

– Short discourse interpolations:

is Princesse (say you) with him?

(*WT*. 5.1.93)

The one, I haue almost forgot (your pardon:)

(*WT*. 5.1.104)

– Interjections:

But (ah) I will not, yet I loue thee well,

(*KJ*. 3.3.54)

I, or else I would I might be hang'd (la.)

(*Wiv*. 1.1.239)

– Subordinate clauses:

> There is none worthy,
> (Respecting her that's gone)
>
> (*WT.* 5.1.34)

> Infirmitie
> (Which waits vpon worne times)
>
> (*WT.* 5.1.141)

– Reinforcing or amplifying phrases:

> I am sorry
> (Most sorry) you haue broken from his liking
>
> (*WT.* 5.1.210)

> Had our Prince
> (Jewell of Children) seene this houre,
>
> (*WT.* 5.1.115)

The practice can also be seen in stage directions – not very often, admittedly, but eight times in *The Tempest*'s stage directions, as here (3.1):

> *Enter Ferdinand*
>
> *(bearing a Log.)*

In none of these cases is there anything universal about the practices. For every one subordinate clause parenthesized, there are hundreds not.

Some usages stand out. When clauses introducing direct speech are parenthesized in a long narrative, the result still has an impact on the modern reader. This is Launce telling the tale of his dog (*TGV.* 4.4.15):

> Hee thrusts me himselfe into the company of three or foure
> gentleman-like-dogs, vnder the Dukes table: hee had not bin there
> (blesse the marke) a pissing while, but all the chamber smelt him:
> out with the dog (saies one) what cur is that (saies another) whip
> him out (saies the third) hang him vp (saies the Duke.) I hauing bin

acquainted with the smell before, knew it was Crab; and goes me to the fellow that whips the dogges: friend (quoth I) you meane to whip the dog: I marry doe I (quoth he) you doe him the more wrong (quoth I) 'twas I did the thing you wot of: he makes me no more adoe, but whips me out of the chamber:

Here too, the practice was not universal; for example, whoever set *The Comedy of Errors* did not follow it (*Err.* 2.1.62):

'Tis dinner time, quoth I: my gold, quoth he:

It is important to appreciate that not all parentheses in Shakespearean texts convey a reduced semantic force, and we have to disregard the pressure from present-day usage if we are not to misinterpret. As Longaville wonders how to send his letter, he sees Dumaine approaching, and says (*LLL.* 4.3.75):

By whom shall I send this? – Company? Stay.

(Penguin edition)

In the Folio it appears as:

By whom shall I send this (company?) Stay.

Here, *Company* is an important explanatory word, despite the parentheses. Another example is when parentheses enclose *if*-clauses; the meaning can be critical to the sense, as here (*John.* 2.1.555):

To our solemnity: I trust we shall,
(If not fill vp the measure of her will)
Yet in some measure satisfie her so,

In such cases, the original punctuation presents a distraction to modern readers.

The amount that can be parenthesized ranges from single words to whole sentences or more.

Your Grace may starue (perhaps) before that time

(*1H6.* 3.2.48)

> you; whom he loues
> (He bad me say so) more than all the Scepters

(*WT.* 5.1.144)

> He doth nothing but frowne (as who should say, and you will not
> haue me, choose: he heares merrie tales and smiles not, I feare hee
> will proue the weeping Phylosopher when he growes old, being so
> full of vn-mannerly sadnesse in his youth.)

(*MV.* 1.2.44)

Just once (*LLL.* 1.1.241), they provide an economical way of portraying
dialogue, when Don Armado reads from a letter (hence the italics):

> *There did I see that low spirited Swaine, that base Minow of thy*
> *myrth,* (Clown. Mee?) *that vnletered small knowing soule,* (Clow
> Me?) *that shallow vassall* (Clow. Still mee?) *which as I remember,*
> hight Costard, (Clow. O me) *sorted and consorted contrary to thy*
> *established proclaymed Edict*

Why some words, phrases, and sentences are singled out in this way,
and not others, seems to depend entirely on the whim of the compositor, or scribe (Ralph Crane especially seems to have had a liking for
them), or both:

> I saw a Smith stand with his hammer (thus)

(*John.* 4.2.193).

There are over 800 instances of *thus* in the canon: why this one was
given special treatment is a mystery.

Perhaps the most interesting cases of parentheses in original
Shakespearean texts are those which suggest an interesting reading
for an actor. The phrases in this next passage are usually printed as
Eagle England and *Weasel Scot* (*H5.* 1.2.169), but two levels of meaning emerge once the noun phrases are divided:

> For once the Eagle (England) being in prey,
> To her vnguarded Nest, the Weazell (Scot)

Also interesting are the cases which reinforce parallelism in meaning in a way that modern commas (because of their wide range of uses) cannot.

> I (a lost-Mutton) gaue your Letter to her (a lac'd-Mutton) and she (a lac'd-Mutton) gaue mee (a lost-Mutton) nothing for my labour.
>
> (*TGV*. 1.1.96)

This is much clearer than the repeated use of commas, as in the Penguin edition:

> I, a lost mutton, gave your letter to her, a laced mutton; and she, a laced mutton, gave me, a lost mutton, nothing for my labour.

The parentheses are kept in some modern editions (e.g. the Arden).

APOSTROPHES

The modern apostrophe has three functions. It signals the omission of one or more letters, in such words as *here's* and *can't*. It indicates a possessive ending on nouns, as in *cat's* and *cats'* (vs plural *cats*). And it avoids an awkward juxtaposition of symbols, especially with plurals, as in *cross the i's and dot the t's, 2's and 3's*, and so on. The rules governing the modern use were finally established only in the eighteenth century, and were soon disputed (in such cases as whether an apostrophe should be used in place names, as in *Harrods* and *St Pauls*). Variation still exists in such forms as *1970's* vs *1970s*.

The use of an apostrophe developed on the European mainland in the early decades of the sixteenth century, arrived in England in the 1550s, and by the time Shakespeare began to write was appearing sporadically in plays. It was used primarily to mark an omission (*elision*) of a letter, whether spoken or silent, as in *th'* for *the* or *hang'd* for *hanged*, and this is one of the most distinctive features of the graphology of the plays. Sometimes more than one letter is omitted. The opening pages of *The Tempest* display many examples:

> o' ('on'), i' ('in'), th' ('the'), t' ('to'), too't, was't, on't, where's, let's, there's, 'Tis, howr's ('hour is'), now's, vpon's, 'bout, cam'st, do'st, attend'st, saw'st, liu'd, hang'd, dash'd, perish'd, swallow'd, touch'd, heau'd, turn'd, call'd, lou'd, chang'd, form'd, pleas'd, di'd ('died')

Sometimes more than one letter is elided:

> 'twixt, 'em, I'le, Hee'l, I'ld ('would')

And sometimes a whole word is, especially in stock phrases:

> 'Sblud, an arrant Traytor (*H5*. 4.8.9) [= *God's blood*]
> 'Faith that was not so well (*Oth*. 4.1.275) [= *In faith*]
> 'Saue his Maiesty. (*Temp*. 2.1.173) [= *God save*]
> No, 'pray thee. (*Temp*. 1.2.371) [= *I pray*]

The reason for the elision varies: in some cases it enables a word to fit the metrical character of a line or focuses the emphasis within a sentence more sharply (see p. 141); in others it helps to capture the colloquial character of conversational speech or identifies a character's idiosyncratic way of talking. In most cases, the identity of the underlying word is obvious from the context, though some of the more unusual forms can make the reader hesitate – such as Lady Capulet's *thou'se heare our counsell* ('thou shalt', *Rom*. 1.3.10).

In the above examples, the grammatical association of an apostrophe with a final *-s*, *-st*, or *-d* is noteworthy, for it seems to have prompted an overuse (*hypercorrection*) in similar contexts where no such grammatical motivation exists. In particular, there are many instances where the *-s* which expresses the third-person singular ending of the present tense (*she walks*) is preceded by an apostrophe. *Has* seemed especially prone to this:

> He ha's braue Vtensils

> (*Temp*. 3.2.97)

> out-*Herod's Herod*.

> (*Ham*. 3.2.13)

why doe's he suffer this rude knaue

(*Ham.* 5.1.99)

Of one I dan'st withall.

(*Rom.* 1.5.143)

The use of an -*s* ending to show possession did not develop at the same rate as the use to mark elision. Most possessives in the original texts have no apostrophe, whether in singular or plural:

keeping safe *Nerrissas* ring.

(*MV.* 5.1.307)

The fields chiefe flower, sweet aboue compare,

(*Ven.* 2.2)

There is thus no way of showing the difference between a singular and a plural noun, as this pair of examples shows:

The smiles of Knaues
Tent in my cheekes, and Schoole-boyes Teares take vp

[= *school-boys'*]

The Glasses of my sight:

(*Cor.* 3.2.116)

Wilt thou, vpon the high and giddie Mast,
Seale vp the Ship-boyes Eyes, and rock his Braines,

[= *ship-boy's*]
(*2H4.* 3.1.19)

It was not until the eighteenth century that the distinction between '*s* and *s*' for singular and plural was finally established. But plainly some people were well aware of the emerging possibilities in usage, for there are many instances in the Folio of the singular possessive apostrophe. Most of the instances are found after a clearly animate noun – usually the name of a person or god:

the Murtherer gets the loue of *Gonzago's* wife.

(*Ham.* 3.2.273)

> To sacred *Delphos*, to *Appollo's* Temple,
>
> (*WT.* 2.1.183)

> Odd's lifelings heere he is
>
> (*TN.* 5.1.181)

A personified noun occasionally has one:

> Chiefe nourisher in Life's Feast.
>
> (*Mac.* 2.2.40)

So do a few place names:

> *Verona's* ancient Citizens
>
> (*Rom.* 1.1.92)

And the logic of possession even extended to a pronoun (something that would be condemned by nineteenth-century grammarians and judged a major error today):

> How sometimes Nature will betray it's folly?
> It's tendernesse?
>
> (*WT.* 1.2.151–2)

What is of great interest to a linguist (but probably not to anyone else) is that the usage is already being extended to what are technically called 'absolute genitives' (where the possessed noun does not follow the *'s*) and 'double genitives' (where both an *of* and an *'s* occur in the same construction):

> For halfe thy wealth, it is *Anthonio's*
>
> (*MV.* 4.1.367)

> the young Gentleman of the Count *Orsino's* is return'd
>
> (*TN.* 3.4.57)

Despite this, there is still a huge amount of variation:

> With Peircing steele at bold *Mercutio's* breast,
>
> (*Rom.* 3.1.159)

Not *Romeo* Prince, he was *Mercutios* Friend,

(Rom. 3.1.184)

Even in the same line:

Did *Romeo's* hand shed *Tybalts* blood

(Rom. 3.2.71).

The overall impression is one of uncertainty. Frequently we see a usage which can only be explained by people feeling that an apostrophe is needed, but they are unsure exactly where, so (much as present-day greengrocers are claimed to do) they put one in and hope for the best! Here are some further examples:

O *Romeo, Romeo,* braue *Mercutio's* is dead,

(Rom. 3.1.116)

when thou hast 'tane thy stand,

(Cym. 3.4.110)

I that would be knowne: too'th warrs my boy, too'th warres:

(AWW. 2.3.276, and throughout the play)

Sometimes, it is not at all clear what was in the mind of the inserter, as in this opening remark of Fluellen's (*H5* 4.1.65):

'So, in the Name of Iesu Christ, speake fewer:

At other times, we can see the inserter experimenting with the mark to help handle special cases, such as the foreign accent of Dr Caius (*Wiv.* 1.4.105; 2.3.83):

giue-'a this Letter to Sir *Hugh*
I shall procure 'a you de good Guest.

One further practice shows how different the use of the apostrophe was in Shakespeare's time. It was quite often used to mark a plural -*s* ending, especially when the noun ends in a vowel (an unusual type of word in English).

these fashion Mongers, these par-don-mee's,

(*Rom.* 2.4.33)

Of thousand's that had struck anoynted Kings,

(*WT.* 1.2.358)

Vertue it selfe) these Shrugs, these Hum's, and Ha's,

(*WT.* 2.1.74)

And teach *Lauolta's* high, and swift *Carranto's*,

(*H5.* 3.5.33)

All of the above practices were erratic and prone to compositor-ial idiosyncrasy. There are many places where there should be an apostrophe, but it is missing – even with clear cases of elision, as with *have* and *he* in the following:

Will you ha the truth on't:

(*Ham* V.1.23)

God be with his soule, a was a merrie man,

(*Rom.* 1.3.41)

Ben Jonson grumbles in Book 2 of his *English Grammar* (Chapter 1, 9–10) about the way the apostrophe 'through the negligence of Writers and Printers, is quite omitted'. He himself became an enthusiast for its sys-tematic use, so he must not have been greatly amused to see the way his encomium was treated by Heminge and Condell in the First Folio, where we find *seem'd* and *mourn'd* alongside *torned* ('turned') and *filed*; *didst* and *hadst* without apostrophes; and several uses of the possessive with-out them, such as *Shakespeares minde* and *Marlowes mighty line*. Probably today he would have joined the Apostrophe Protection Society.

ITALICS

Italics are another notable feature of the graphology of Shakespearean texts, used with a noticeably different set of functions compared with today. Modern uses are extremely varied. They include emphasizing a word in its context, highlighting technical terms or words which are the focus of discussion, showing examples (especially in linguistic books), and drawing attention to an unusual word, such as a foreign word or a word that has not been fully assimilated into the language (*per se*). They perform a clarifying role when they are used to distinguish titles (such as plays) from other text or to set off single letters ('*A* and *B*', '*p*s and *q*s'). And they can have a purely conventional role, such as when used to identify a vehicle (HMS *Kent*), to show the Latin names of plants and animals (*ficus benjamina*), or to show performance directions, as in plays and musical scores. Because of lower resolution on screens, there is less use of italics on the Internet, boldface or colour being used instead.

Some of these uses can be found in Shakespearean texts. Stage directions and scene titles are always in italics, as are the names (often abbreviated) which precede speeches, as here (*Ham.* 1.4.1):

> *Enter Hamlet, Horatio, Marcellus.*
> *Ham.*   The Ayre bites shrewdly: is it very cold?
> *Hor.*   It is a nipping and an eager ayre.

Words which are plainly foreign in origin – which in Shakespeare means largely Latin or French (see p. 17) – are also italicized. These Latin examples are all from *Hamlet*:

> *Hic & vbique?*
>
> (1.5.156)

> *Videlicet*, a Brothell, or so forth.
>
> (2.1.61)

> It must be *Se offendendo*, it cannot bee else:
>
> (5.1.9)

And this French one is from *Henry V* (5.2.214):

> How answer you.   *La plus belle Katherine du monde mon trescher & deuin deesse.*

The whole of the French exchange between Katherine and her maid in Act 3 Scene 4 is printed in italics.

Then as now, an unfamiliar word – especially if it is a noun and suspected to be foreign – can appear in italics, but everything evidently here depended on the intuition of the compositor. If a word had newly arrived in English, we might expect any compositor to go for the italic font, such as in this case, which the *OED* first records in 1591:

> 'twas *Cauiarie* to the Generall:
>
> *(Ham.* 2.2.435)

Likewise, an unusual Shakespearean usage would attract it:

> Marry this is Miching *Malicho,*
>
> *(Ham.* 3.2.146)

But when a word has been in English for a few decades, or even centuries, the use of italics is more puzzling. *Modicum,* for example, had been known since the fifteenth century, but it is italicized here:

> Lo, lo, lo, lo, what *modicums* of wit he vtters
>
> *(Tro.* 2.1.67).

Similarly, *eisel* had been in the language, in various spellings, since the twelfth century, and yet it must have seemed alien to the *Hamlet* compositor:

> Woo't drinke vp *Esile,* eate a Crocodile?
>
> *(Ham.* 5.1.272)

though not, apparently, to the one who set the *Sonnets* Quarto:

> Potions of Eysell gainst my strong infection,
>
> *(Sonn.* 111.10)

On the other hand, the uses of *Quietus* are italicized both in *Hamlet* and the *Sonnets:*

When he himselfe might his *Quietus* make
With a bare Bodkin?

(*Ham.* 3.1.75)

And her *Quietus* is to render thee,

(*Sonn.* 126.12)

The more instances we observe, the more we get the impression that, when it comes to the use of an unfamiliar word, the choice of italics is very much down to the individual compositor, who might change his opinion even within a single play:

Your *quondam* wife

(*Tro.* 4.5.179)

This is the quondam King;

(*3H6.* 3.1.23)

He lends out money gratis, and brings downe

(*MV.* 1.3.41)

This is the foole that lends out money *gratis.*

(*MV.* 3.3.2)

In the case of *interim*, which is used ten times in the Folio, we see it in italics six times (in *H5, Ham, JC, Ado, Mac, TN* – spelled *intrim*, in the last), and in roman four times (in *AYLI, LLL, Oth, Tim*).

The use of italics for proper names was a very different matter. This was an extremely systematic practice, with only occasional inconsistencies, and it provides one of the most noticeable differences between modern and Elizabethan orthography, especially when there is a long sequence of names, as here (*Tro.* 5.5.6):

Renew, renew, the fierce *Polidamus*
Hath beate downe *Menon*: bastard *Margarelon*
Hath *Doreus* prisoner.
And stands Calossus-wise wauing his beame,
Vpon the pashed courses of the Kings:

> *Epistropus* and *Cedus, Polixines* is slaine;
> *Amphimacus,* and *Thous* deadly hurt;
> *Patroclus* tane or slaine, and *Palamedes*
> Sore hurt and bruised; the dreadfull Sagittary
> Appauls our numbers, haste we *Diomed*
> To re-enforcement, or we perish all.

The practice of italicizing included proper names referring to groups:

> Where are my *Switzers*?

> *(Ham.* 4.5.99)

but it rarely extended to the use of proper names when used as other parts of speech, such as adjectives and adverbs, as we see in:

> Oh this is Counter you false Danish Dogges.

> *(Ham.* 4.5.112)

and this is presumably why *Calassus* (= *Colossus*) remains in roman type in the *Troilus* quotation, because it forms part of an adverb. *Sagittary* (a centaur) must have been taken to be a common noun.

In a few instances, italicization extends to names of places, but cases where a name is in italics are far outnumbered by those where it is not. There are twenty instances of roman *Denmark* in *Hamlet,* and just two in italics. That some compositors, at least, were not entirely sure of the convention can be seen in the occasional inconsistency within a few lines of each other, or even within the same line:

> had I a sister were a *Grace,* or a daughter a Goddesse,

> *(Tro.* 1.2.236)

> And what make you from Wittenberg *Horatio*?

> *(Ham.* 1.2.64)

> But what in faith make you from *Wittemberge*?

> *(Ham.* 1.2.68)

Wittenberg is italicized nowhere else.

Italics were also used systematically in Shakespearean texts in a few other contexts:

– Songs:

> *How should I your true loue know from another one?*
> *By his Cockle hat and staffe, and his Sandal shoone.*
>
> (*Ham.* 4.5.25)

– Letters, or extracts from them:

> *To the vnknowne belou'd, this, and my good Wishes:*
> Her very Phrases:
>
> (*TN.* 2.5.90)

– Lines which have to be delivered in a special way:

> *For vs, and for our Tragedie,*
> *Heere stooping to your Clemencie:*
> *We begge your hearing Patientlie.*
>
> (introduction to 'The Murder of Gonzago', *Ham.* 3.2.158)

– Maxims:

> Therefore this maxime out of loue I teach;
> "*Atchieuement, is command; vngain'd, beseech.*
>
> (*Tro.* 1.2.292)

– Prologues and Epilogues (but not Inductions or Choruses):

> *Put forth toward Phrygia, and their vow is made*
> *To ransacke* Troy, *within whose strong emures*
> *The rauish'd* Helen, Menelaus *Queene,*
> *With wanton* Paris *sleepes, and that's the Quarrell.*
>
> (*Tro.* Prologue.8)

Note that in this last example there is reverse setting, with personal names now in roman type.

Italics in Shakespearean texts, then, provide an intriguing mixture of systematic practice and idiosyncrasy. Cases where the italics have been used to highlight a meaning – presumably by the author – are few; but there is a clear instance in the *Sonnets*, where in 135 and 136 a pun on the writer's first name results in eight examples of an italicized *Will*, with a further example in 143 (though an earlier one at 57.13 remains in roman). If this happens once, it could happen elsewhere, but examining the other 23 examples of italicized words in the 1609 Quarto edition brings to light no obvious pattern of use, apart from the normal italiciza-tion of names of mythical figures (*Adonis*, *Mars*, etc), though *Muses*, *Phaenix*, and *God* are left in roman. Again we see inconsistency. *Audit*, for instance, turns up twice in italics and twice not, and a few other words show a similar duality. As we have seen (p. 52), there are 130 capitalized words in the Quarto edition, but only 23 of them are itali-cized. And why, for example, *Autumne* receives italics in one instance whereas *Summer* and *Winter* do not, is a puzzle. This seems to be a further sign of compositor vacillation. Cases where editors think a word might have been deliberately italicized to make a point, such as *Informer* (125.13) or *Heriticke* (124.9), thus have to be discussed on their merits.

INVERTED COMMAS

Inverted commas, as they are traditionally called in the UK (US usage, and increasingly everyone else, prefers 'quotation marks'), identify the words actually spoken by someone, appearing at the beginning and end of the speech. If the speech goes on for several paragraphs, they appear only at the beginning of each paragraph except the last. They can also be used to draw attention to a word or phrase – 'scare quotes' or 'sneer quotes', as they are often called – and as an alternative to italics in identifying individual words, titles, and so on. Some writers do without them, and some dislike them, on account of their cluttered appearance (especially when doubled: " "). James Joyce once called them 'perverted commas'.

The mark started to appear in English during the 1590s, and increased in frequency throughout the following century, but did not come into regular use until the late eighteenth century. There is hardly any sign of it in Shakespearean texts – just a few cases where an opening mark (but no closing mark) is used to identify a maxim or a high-sounding line, as in the quotation from *Troilus* above, and here:

"Past, and to Come, seemes best; things Present, worst

(*2H4*.1.3.108)

"More than our Brother, is our Chastitie

(*MM*. 2.4.185)

or a sequence of lines:

"Cowards father Cowards, & Base things Syre Bace;
"Nature hath Meale, and Bran; Contempt, and Grace.

(*Cym*. 4.2.26)

For all cases of direct speech, the main graphological device in the texts is to place the reporting verb in parentheses or to follow it with a colon:

Thrise fairer then my selfe, (thus she began)
The fields chiefe flower, sweet aboue compare,

(*Ven*. 7)

'Tis dinner time, quoth I: my gold, quoth he:

(*Err*. 2.1.62)

Good morrow foole (quoth I:) no Sir, quoth he,

(*AYLI* 2.7.18)

but, as this last example shows, that does not always happen. Indeed, usually we have to work out who is saying what from the context. This is not a problem, for we are easily able to process a spoken narrative containing lots of 'he said's – and there are no inverted commas in speech – but, because we are used to the modern convention, the lack of punctuation in a line can give us pause.

Sayes, very wisely, it is ten a clocke

(*AYLI*. 2.7.22)

At hand quoth Pick-purse.

(*1H4*. 2.1.49)

HYPHENS

There is no punctuation mark more prone to variation than the hyphen. It turns up unpredictably at the end of a line of print to mark a word-break, and it has an uncertain presence in many compound words and prefixes. Is it *flower-pot* or *flower pot*, *co-ordinate* or *coordinate*? Publishing style-books (style books?) include lists of hyphenated words in an attempt to ensure stylistic consistency. They are used much more often in British English than in American English. Other functions of the hyphen include a linking function, especially in word sequences (*mother-in-law*), and a separating function to avoid a confusing sequence of vowels (*anti-intelligence, re-use*). There is occasionally a contrastive function: *recover* vs *re-cover*. Sometimes there is a consideration of elegance, as when a prefix is followed by a numeral or a capital (*pre-1980, anti-Blair*). Occasionally, we have no idea what to do: I do not know how to write the past tense of *to samba* (*we samba-ed?*).

The kind of uncertainty illustrated by this last example must have been very much the norm in Elizabethan times. Hyphens became increasingly common in print from the 1570s, after John Hart emphasized their linking role (he called them 'joiners'). We see them in Shakespearean texts, as today, in two types of context: at the ends of lines, indicating a word-break, and within lines, identifying compound expressions.

The conventions governing where to break a word at the end of a line are so complex that style-books today give only very general guidelines. If you want to know where you should insert the hyphen, you have to look for help in those dictionaries that mark the places. For example, *Webster's Third New International Dictionary* shows **con.ster.na.tion**. With the advent of computers, line-end hyphenation is rapidly becoming a thing of the past, as the software can automatically space words so that the right-hand margin is even (*justified*). But, especially with narrow-column setting, as in an encyclopedia or newspaper, it still proves necessary to break words to avoid ugly spaces earlier in the line.

If we examine all the line-break hyphens in one of the plays (*Err*), we find that some of the conventions are the same as today. Many words are broken neatly in the middle, sometimes accurately reflecting the word's internal structure:

> aduer-sitie, bee-ing, for-sake, Porpen-tine, Pro-verbe, res-cue, vn-ruly, yon-der

And if there is a double consonant, the hyphen separates them:

> mer-rie, can-not, writ-ten

Other conventions are very different. Many words are split towards the beginning, sometimes with just one letter before the hyphen:

> an-swer'd, Ar-madoes, As-pect, e-nough, ex-ploits, hi-ther, Idi-ot, Ma-ster, o-bey, ra-ther, re-turn'd, ve-rie

And there is a tendency to divide syllables according to the way the word is spoken, so that the word structure is unclear:

> batte-ring, dea-lers, loo-seth

With compound words and phrases, also, some of the practices are the same as today. If the following items were to appear in a modern text, we would not be surprised to see them hyphenated:

> Aqua-vitae, calues-skin, cherrie-stone, Fortune-teller, headie-rash, Loue-springs, no-face, Rope-maker, shoulder-clapper, spoon-meate

We would also expect hyphenation when a compound ends in -*ing* or (in modern spelling) -*ed*:

> life-preseruing, out-facing, sap-consuming, selfe-harming, well-dealing;
>> ill-fac'd, leane-fac'd, ore-wrought, sweet-fac'd, sweet-sauour'd

especially if the compound occurs before a noun:

> deepe-diuorcing vow, sea-faring men, soule-killing Witches,
> wind-obeying deepe; foole-beg'd patience, ship-wrackt guests

But we would not expect to see the following hyphenations today:

> Base-Viole (= bass viol)
> for her wealths-sake (= wealth's sake)

or these examples from *The Tempest*: *fowle-play, peg-thee, red-pla-gue*. They are written as separate words now. Conversely, these next examples would have no hyphen or space at all (with just a few minor variations in usage):

> else-where, foot-ball, Gold-smith, hand-writing, other-where,
> Pea-cocke, Schoole-master, selfe-same, thred-bare, vn-vrg'd

Particularly distinctive, within this latter category, are word-breaks like these, which have no linguistic justification at all:

> Backe slaue, or I will breake thy pate a-crosse.
>
> (*Err.* 2.1.78)

That is the only instance in this play, but the practice is very common elsewhere (*a-boord, a-farre, a-gaine, a-non*...).

Hyphens display the same kind of compositorial variation that we see in other areas of Shakespearean graphology. *Pea-cocke* turns up in *Err*, but elsewhere in the Folio it is *peacock*; it is *other-where* in *Err* but *otherwhere* in *H8*; *else-where* in *Err* but *elsewhere* in *1H4*; and so on. There is vacillation within the same play: *Gold-smith* appears in *Err*, but the other thirteen instances of this word in the play are all *goldsmith*. And there are several inexplicable examples, such as Alonso's *oo-zie bed* (*Temp.* 5.1.151) or Hamlet's *North, North-West* (*Ham.* 2.2.377). At times, the text cries out for hyphens, but there are none:

> how giddily a turnes about all the Hot-blouds, betweene, foureteene &
> fiue & thirtie, sometimes fashioning them like *Pharaoes* souldiours
>
> (*Ado.* 3.3.129)

It takes a moment to work out that Borachio means *fiue-&-thirtie*.

In all of this, we are not talking about many instances. The frequency of hyphens in *Err* is not great – just 28 line-breaks and 41 compound forms in a play of 1,919 Folio lines. That is the story throughout the Quartos and the Folio – only around 8,500 hyphens in all. If we have an impression to the contrary it is because they sometimes occur in clusters, as if the compositor was having a 'hyphen moment'.

needy-hollow-ey'd-sharpe-looking-wretch

(*Err.* 5.1.241)

or the writing requires it:

Pastoricall-Comicall-Historicall-Pastorall

(*Ham.* 2.2.397)

especially when there is a long sequence of premodifying adjectives:

base, proud, shallow, beggerly, three-suited-hundred pound, filthy woosted-stocking knaue, a Lilly-liuered, action-taking, whoreson glasse-gazing super-seruiceable finicall Rogue, one Trunke-inheriting slaue

(*Lear.* 2.2.13)

And sometimes, the characterization requires it. This is most notice-able in *The Merry Wives of Windsor*, where we find them used as an integral part of the speech of Evans (*Got-plesse, So got-udge me, Fery-well*) and especially of Dr Caius:

Peace-a-your tongue: speake-a-your Tale.

(1.4.79)

I be-gar, and de Maid is loue-a-me: my nursh-a-Quickly tell me so mush.

(3.2.58)

Here is an old abusing of the King's hyphens, indeed!

5 'Speak the speech': Shakespearean phonology

Phonology is the study of the sound system of a language – a system that consists of two dimensions. The 'segmental' dimension includes all the spoken vowels and consonants, and the rules governing the ways these combine to make syllables; the 'nonsegmental' dimension includes the patterns of pitch, loudness, tempo, rhythm, and tone of voice. A particular segmental sequence, such as the string of seven units which make up the words 'But soft', can be said in a variety of different ways – relatively high or low, loud or soft, fast or slow, urgent or hushed . . . There are over a hundred variants commonly encountered in everyday speech today, and actors in performance add significantly (and often idiosyncratically) to the phonological repertoire. A set of these variants (specifically, those to do with rhythm in versification) is traditionally studied under the heading of *prosody* (see further below).

There is a degree of correspondence with the graphological features identified in Chapters 3 and 4. The vowels and consonants of speech are written down using the vowels and consonants of writing. But as there are only twenty-six units of writing (letters, or *graphemes*) and forty-four spoken sounds (*phonemes*) in most accents of Modern English, clearly the correspondence cannot be a straightforward one – hence the complexities of English spelling. The nonsegmental features of speech are written down using the punctuation marks and other graphic conventions of writing, but only in a very approximate way – for example, there is no simple rule which makes questions always have a rising pitch pattern and statements a falling one. Some features of graphology have no corresponding features in speech at all (e.g. initial capital letters, paragraph indention); and some features of speech cannot be written down, other than by a vague description (e.g. 'she said caustically').

When used with reference to individuals, phonology refers to the way that we personally exploit the properties of the writing system. Having learned to speak, we each have a distinctive style of speech, with an individual voice quality (that is much easier to recognize than our handwriting) and often idiosyncratic adaptations of accent reflecting our personal background. My own accent is a mixture of sounds reflecting my geographical history in Wales, Liverpool, and the south of England, as well as my age, sex, and social position. In fact, it would be more exact to say a mixture of accents, for I do not speak in the same way all the time, but adapt my speech to the people I am talking to (a phenomenon which linguists call *accommodation*).

An old song relates the two dimensions of phonology, and hints at the special importance of nonsegmental features: 'It ain't what you say but the way that you say it'. No Shakespearean actor, director, voice-coach, or playgoer would disagree. But here lies a problem. For the unpalatable fact is that we have next to no information about 'the way that they said things' in Shakespeare's time. I explore this topic further in this chapter, and will return to the properties of Elizabethan segmental phonology in the next.

THE WAY THEY SAID IT

The sixteenth-century scholarly writers on English give us just tantalizing hints. As we have seen, they talk a lot about pauses in relation to punctuation (p. 67). But apart from that, there is only the occasional mention, usually just with reference to particular marks. John Hart, for instance, writing in *An Orthographie* (1569), says that the tone of voice associated with questions (at least, those beginning with a question-word, such as *What*) begins 'sharp, and so falleth lower, according to the length of the sentence'. There is no systematic description of 'the way people say things'. Not until 1775 do we find a first attempt at such a description: Joshua Steele's *The Melody and Measure of Speech*. And for really detailed accounts, we have to await the emergence of twentieth-century phonetics.

From the allusions to tone of voice in Shakespeare, we can sense that the way the language worked then was pretty much the same as it works now. No less than Caesar recognizes the distinction between segmental and nonsegmental phonology:

> I do not much dislike the matter, but
> The manner of his speech

(Ant. 2.117)

And all the parameters into which tone of voice can be analysed are given a mention somewhere or other in the canon. Speech can vary in pitch, both in the sense of being 'high/low pitched':

> *Cleo.* Didst heare her speake? Is she shrill tongu'd or low?'
> *Mes.* Madam, I heard her speake, she is low voic'd.

(Ant. 3.3.12)

and 'speaking at a high level':

> In clamours of all size both high and low

(Lover. 21).

It can vary in loudness, being either soft, as with Cordelia:

> Her voice was euer soft,
> Gentle, and low,

(Lear. 5.3.271)

or loud, as with the common people:

> Clapping their hands, and crying with loud voyce

(2H6. 1.1.158)

or very loud, as with some actors:

> to split the eares of the Groundlings

(Ham. 3.2.10)

or unbelievably loud, as with Antony:

> He was as ratling Thunder

(Ant. 5.2.86).

Speech can vary in speed, also, being either fast, as Rosalind wants Celia to be:

> I pre'thee tell me, who is it quickely, and speake apace
>
> (*AYLI.* 3.2.192)

or slow, as in Page's character-note for Nym:

> I neuer heard such a drawling-affecting rogue
>
> (*Wiv.* 2.1.132).

Rhythm is occasionally mentioned. Hamlet can produce a piece of metrical speech, as Polonius affirms:

> well spoken, with good accent, and good discretion
>
> (*Ham.* 2.2.464)

(*accent* here means 'accentuation', not regional speech); and Belarius is sure that the arhythmicality in a voice he has heard belongs to Cloten:

> the snatches in his voice, and burst of speaking were as his
>
> (*Cym.* 4.2.106).

A wide range of impressionistic tones of voice is mentioned, some of which allow several interpretations: Gratiano is 'to[o] rude, and bold of voyce' (*MV.* 2.2.168); Bottom says he can speak 'in a monstrous little voyce' (*MND.* 1.2.48); Sir Andrew describes the Clown as having a 'mellifluous voyce' (*TN.* 2.3.51), and is later advised to speak 'with a swaggering accent sharpely twang'd off' (*TN.* 3.4.174). All of these can be readily interpreted (albeit with variations) today.

Then, as now, people recognize each other's voices and notice changes in them, whether natural or contrived:

> Me thinkes thy voyce is alter'd, and thou speak'st
> In better phrase, and matter then thou did'st
>
> (blind Gloucester to disguised Edgar: *Lear.* 4.6.7)

> The trick of that voice I do well remember
>
> > (blind Gloucester of Lear: *Lear*. 4.6.106).

They are also aware that people speak in different 'keys', depending on their sex or occupation:

> Speak't in a woman's key
>
> > (*TNK* 1.1.94)

> in a bond-mans key
> With bated breath and whispring humblenesse
>
> > (*MV*. 1.3.120)

and they know that accents change over time. Mercutio pours scorn on Tybalt:

> The Pox of such antique lisping affecting phantacies, these new tuners of accent
>
> > (*Rom*. 2.3.26).

In one place there is even a firm affirmation of the present-day linguistic principle: be yourself:

> what neede I
> Affect anothers gate, which is not catching
> Where there is faith, or to be fond upon
> Anothers way of speech, when by mine owne
> I may be reasonably conceiv'd;
>
> > (*TNK*. 1.2.44)

Human linguistic nature, it seems, has not changed much over the past 400 years.

This conclusion, though obvious, is actually quite helpful, for it means we can use our knowledge of how spoken language works today as a way in to understanding how it must have worked in the past. The English language has not changed much during the past 400 years either (p. 11). So although there is very little direct or detailed information available about 'the way' that Elizabethans spoke, we can use our modern phonological intuitions to make some well-informed deductions about how it must have been, using as evidence the graphology of the texts, as well as the observations of those sixteenth-century authors who wrote about the 'art' of poetry and style. Much of the latter falls under the heading of what is today called *prosody*, the study of versification. In Greek, *prosodia* was originally a song sung to music; and, as we shall see, the notion of harmonious sound is a recurrent theme in Elizabethan poetic thinking.

PROSODY

If any property of phonology has to be taken as fundamental, it has to be rhythm – our auditory perception of regularity in the stream of speech. The rhythmical properties of the mother's speech can be heard by her foetus in the womb from around six months; language-specific rhythms are the first features to be heard in the phonetic output of an infant at about nine months of age; and they are the basis of a widely used classification of many languages into two broad types: *stress-timed* and *syllable-timed*. English is a stress-timed language: the beats of rhythm (*stresses*) fall at roughly regular intervals, producing an auditory effect best characterized as 'tum-te-tum-te-tum'. Some people have called it the 'heartbeat' of English. By contrast, French is a syllable-timed language: each syllable carries a stress, so that the auditory effect is more like 'rat-a-tat-a-tat'. English has been a stress-timed language, as far as we can tell, for at least a millennium (the presence of inflectional endings in Old English may have given the language a different rhythmical character in its earliest stages). Only in our present age, following the emergence of English as a global language, are we beginning to hear regional varieties spoken by millions in a syllable-timed way (as in the subcontinent of India).

Rhythm is an obligatory feature of *all* normal utterance, whether verse or prose, oratory or everyday speech. (I add 'normal' here to allow for the cases of arhythmical utterance heard in some types of speech disorder, such as stammering, or which accompanies states where the speakers are not in control over what they are saying, perhaps because of drink or drugs.) The pulses of stress-timed speech are always there, regardless of the melody (*intonation*), loudness, speed, and tone of voice of the speaker. It is possible to have a good rhythm without any intonation at all, as when we speak in a monotone; but it is not possible to have good intonation without a good rhythm. Rhythm is the organizing principle of utterance.

How does this organization operate? Because of our biological need to breathe, and our communicative need to make sense, we break our utterance up into rhythm-units. These units also display a pattern of intonation – a sequence of pitches (or *tones*) which fall, rise, or stay level in ways that are individual to a particular language. In the linguistics literature these units are usually called *tone-units* or *tone-groups*, but I am going to call them *rhythm/tone-units* in this book, to emphasize their twofold character. When someone says

Whither away so fast?

we hear a single rhythm/tone-unit, with the strongly stressed syllables shown by the underlining. Speech (including spoken poetry) is organized into a sequence of rhythm/tone-units, and writers do their best with the meagre resources of punctuation at their disposal to indicate what these are. Or, at least, some writers do. As we have seen, the author of the *More* text did not:

kill them cutt their throts possesse their howses

From our sense of what is being said, this would have to be three rhythm/tone-units:

kill them / cut their throts / possesse their howses /

and in print, we would expect to see commas representing the pauses.

The practice in literary study has long been to mark the strong and weak syllables within rhythm/tone-units, using diacritics over the vowels, such as:

Whíthĕr ăwáy sŏ fást?

The strong syllables are said to be *stressed* or *accented*; the weak syllables *unstressed* or *unaccented*. But this is to tell only half of the story. Just as important – indeed, more important, if we think about an actor's performance – is the associated intonation pattern. Nobody ever marks this. Is it a rising pitch, in this sentence, or a falling one, or a level one, or some combination of all three? If rising, just how far should the pitch rise? Should it start high, making the utterance sound like a casual query? Or should it start low, making it sound more ominous. Each intonation permits a different set of meanings, the exact effect conveyed depending on such other factors as the facial expression of the speaker or the loudness and speed with which it is spoken.

If all speech has rhythm, what then is the difference between ordinary speech (prose) and the kind of speech which people call poetry – or, more precisely, *verse*? It lies in the way the rhythm is organized. In everyday speech, we do not notice the rhythm, although it is there. Only very occasionally do we make the rhythm a noticeable part of our conversational expression, as when we might exclaim 'I really think we ought to go!' When we do this, we make our stress-timing – and remember that the definition above was 'roughly regular intervals' – more exact. We drop the 'roughly'. And as soon as we do that, our utterance acquires an extra meaning – impatience or irritation. Doll Tearsheet is very good at this sort of thing:

thou damn'd Tripe-visag'd Rascall

(2H4. 5.4.8)

Away you Bottle-Ale Rascall, you Basket-hilt stale Iugler, you

(2H4. 2.4.127)

This is prose, but from the point of view of rhythm it is moving in the direction of verse.

In verse, rhythm is there to be noticed. That is what it is for. And English poets make us notice it by imposing an extra discipline on the patterns of stress-timing that we find in everyday speech. The nature of this discipline varies greatly, from poetic age to age; but in the leading verse tradition, which dates from the Middle Ages, poets have tried to make the stress-timing as exact as they could, imposing limits upon it by working within verse *lines* and by privileging certain stress patterns. They would then introduce variations into these patterns to produce particular effects. It is this discipline which is called *metre*.

Metre is the term used to describe and analyse the rhythmical organization of lines of verse. In a tradition which dates back to Classical times, verse lines were evaluated to the extent that they conformed to rules governing the number of rhythmical units (or *feet*) allowed in a line, and the types of strong + weak syllable combinations allowed in these units. That kind of rhythmical censorship is out of fashion now (*vers libre*, 'free verse' meant essentially: 'verse in which the traditional metrical rules were disregarded'); but in Elizabethan times the Classical model held sway, and poets were scrupulous about paying attention to it. To break away from it was a feat of poetic daring.

We can see the Classical influence in George Puttenham's *Art of English Poesie* (1589). Chapter 1 of his second book is headed 'Of Proportion Poeticall', and it begins:

> It is said by such as professe the Mathematicall sciences, that all things stand by proportion, and that without it nothing could stand to be good or beautiful.

He then goes on to stress the importance of writing 'harmonically', by which he means 'a certaine congruitie in sounds pleasing the eare'. We see what he means by 'congruity' when he goes on to talk about metre (Chapter 3):

> his [its] shortest proportion is of foure sillables, and his longest of twelue, they that vse it aboue, passe the bounds of good proportion. And euery meeter may be aswel in the odde as in the euen sillable, but better in the euen, and one verse may begin in the euen, & another follow in the odde, and so keepe a commendable proportion.

A very detailed account follows. He acknowledges that English is a
very different language from Latin and Greek, and has different 'naturall' rhythms because it has far more monosyllabic words in it. But,
deep down, he thinks English poets could not do better than try to
follow the Classical model; and at the beginning of Chapter 12 he nails
his flag to the mast:

> Now neuerthelesse albeit we haue before alledged that our vulgar
> *Saxon English* standing most vpon wordes *monosillable*, and little
> vpon *polysillables* doth hardly admit the vse of those fine inuented
> feete of the Greeks & Latines ... if I should now say otherwise it
> would make me seeme contradictorie to my selfe, yet ... we will
> in this present chapter & by our own idle obseruations shew how
> one may easily and commodiously lead all those feete of the
> auncients into our vulgar language.

Shakespeare was well able to follow the pattern of 'ancient feet' when
he wanted to. And well able to depart from it when he didn't.

I said earlier that rhythm is there to be noticed. To be more
precise, it is the *contrasts* in rhythm which are there to be noticed. If
every line in a poem displayed an identical rhythm, the effect would
soon fade into the auditory background. It is when we are lulled into a
sense of auditory security by hearing one rhythm, and then are brought
up short with another, that we realize something powerful is going on
(*Ham.* 1.5.98):

> Yea, from the Table of my Memory,
> Ile wipe away all triuiall fond Records,
> All sawes of Bookes, all formes, all presures past,
> That youth and obseruation coppied there;
> And thy Commandment all alone shall liue
> Within the Booke and Volume of my Braine,
> Vnmixt with baser matter; yes yes, by Heauen:
> Oh most pernicious woman!
> Oh Villaine, Villaine, smiling damned Villaine!

The predictable rhythm of the first six lines sets up an auditory expectation that the seventh is going to be the same; but it is not. The rhythm stops short half way through. The new rhythm in the second half of the line is a warning shot that something is about to happen. The explosion happens in the next line, two beats shorter than anything before it. And then the rhythmical guns start to pound.

An example like this shows that there are two factors always involved in rhythm. Usually they interact, but occasionally we can see them working separately. Rhythm, firstly, is sometimes used for no other purpose than to produce a sound which is (for example) pleasant, harsh, funny, or urgent – a *phonetic* (more precisely, a *phonaesthetic*) purpose. The most obvious examples of this are when someone says something that is nonsensical but nonetheless effective, as in the first line of Caliban's excited rhyme (*Temp.* 2.2.180):

> Ban' ban' Cacalyban
> Has a new Master, get a new Man.

When Jasper Britton played Caliban in the Globe's production in 2000, he chanted these lines to the audience, who enthusiastically took up the rhythm, shouting and clapping along with him at top volume for over a minute. How do you follow that! By placing it next to the interval, to allow everyone a chance to get over it.

This was a purely phonetic use of rhythm. It added nothing to the meaning of the words in the line. It just provided an enjoyable auditory experience. By contrast, the second function of rhythm is to draw attention to particular words or phrases, so that the relationship between their meaning is highlit – a *phonological* purpose. The clearest examples here occur when a character is wanting to make a simple semantic contrast (such as 'good' vs 'bad') or semantic reinforcement (such as 'good' and 'wonderful') – or, as in the following speech by Miranda, a series of sometimes overlapping sense relations between the nouns and verbs (*Temp.* 3.1.76).

Fer. Wherefore weepe you?

Mir. At mine vnworthinesse, that dare not offer
   What I desire to giue; and much lesse take
   What I shall die to want: But this is trifling,
   And all the more it seekes to hide it selfe,
   The bigger bulke it shewes. Hence bashfull cunning,
   And prompt me plaine and holy innocence.
   I am your wife, if you will marrie me;
   If not, Ile die your maid: to be your fellow
   You may denie me, but Ile be your seruant
   Whether you will or no.

When we hear this speech read well, we cannot help but notice that *offer* contrasts with *give*, then *give* with *take*, then *take* with *want*. *Hide* then contrasts with *take*, and *cunning* with *innocence*. And the speech ends with a string of sense relationships: *wife* and *marry*, *marry* and *maid*, *wife* and *maid*, *marry* and *fellow*, *fellow* and *servant*. It is not difficult to understand what is being said, but it is only possible to understand it if the nouns and verbs are brought into a dynamic relationship through the use of rhythm. That is what I mean when I talk about rhythm having a phonological purpose. 'Phonological' always means 'semantically relevant'.

There is of course much more that could be said about the way sounds reinforce meaning in this speech. Apart from the (nonsegmental) relationships we perceive through rhythm, there are also (segmental) patterns relating some of the words. The most noticeable effect comes from the repeated initial consonants of stressed words (*alliteration*) in *dare, desire,* and *die, bigger, bulke* and *bashful, prompt* and *plaine, marrie* and *maid,* and then again *die* and *deny*. Alliteration has been a basic fact of school life for generations, with students taught to identify examples in passages. But the question of *why* it is there sometimes escapes them. It is an important feature of English poetry because English is not a language that naturally alliterates in everyday speech. So when someone uses a sequence of identical sounds (as in a television jingle, or a poem), we take notice. But what exactly are we noticing? As with rhythm, alliteration can just 'sound nice', making verse memorable; but it can also suggest relationships that are semantically interesting.

WHY PENTAMETERS?

Many books have been written exploring the various metrical patterns used by Shakespeare, classifying them into types, and noting regularities and irregularities.[1] At best, they can illuminate our understanding of the meaning or dramatic effect of a particular passage. At worst it can be a sterile numerical exercise, in which the acquisition of metrical terminology becomes an end in itself. We have the eighteenth-century grammarians to thank for this unfortunate outcome. Metre was seen as part of the study of grammar, in those days; and it was influenced by the ethos of the time, in which sentences (or metrical patterns) were viewed as 'correct' or 'incorrect', and where high marks were scored if pupils could recognize a particular construction in a sentence, or the particular shape of a poetic line, and knew what it was called. That was the end of the lesson. No extra marks would have been gained if they had explored the reasons for such uses, or the effects conveyed by them. That 'explanatory' perspective is something which has emerged but recently in educational linguistic thinking.

No subject can exist without terminology. It is a means of adding precision to thought, a communicative convenience between fellow practitioners, and a signpost offering increased illumination. The fear many people have of grammatical and prosodic terminology arises from the way teachers have focused on the first two of these aims and not on the third. But if we restore the third aim to its rightful place – as the top priority – then it does not take long to see that the fear is misplaced. It is, after all, no more difficult to use the term *pentameter* to mean 'a verse line consisting of five rhythmical units' than to say that a *pentathlon* is 'an athletic contest consisting of five events'. If we feel there is a difference between these two terms – and most people do – it is because something else is getting in the way. In the case of the pentathlon, we have no difficulty seeing the bridge between the term and what happens in the real world. In the case of books on the pentameter, the real world is often not there at all.

We are interested in pentathlons to see who wins. And likewise, we should be interested in pentameters to see how the poet wins – or, perhaps, helps us to win – by giving us verse which is insightful, attractive, dramatic, and memorable. If a term such as *pentameter* helps us to achieve these goals, then it is worth knowing about. And the same principle applies to the other types of line length that have been identified in the prosodic literature, as well as to the different rhythms used in a pentameter line. Chief amongst these is the *iambic pentameter* – the favourite pattern of the Elizabethan era – in which we hear a sequence of five feet, each foot consisting of a 'te-tum' (weak + strong, or *iambic*) unit of stress-timing. In Shakespeare's early work, there are speeches which consist of nothing else, as in this one from the Duke of Bedford (*1H6*. 1.1.148):

> His Ransome there is none but I shall pay.
> Ile hale the Dolphin headlong from his Throne,
> His Crowne shall be the Ransome of my friend:
> Foure of their Lords Ile change for one of ours.
> Farwell my Masters, to my Taske will I,
> Bonfires in France forthwith I am to make,
> To keepe our great Saint *Georges* Feast withall.
> Ten thousand Souldiers with me I will take,
> Whose bloody deeds shall make all Europe quake.

The most noticeable feature of this kind of writing is the way each line consists of the same rhythmical pattern followed by a pause. The only suggestion we get of a rhythmical contrast is the comma in the fifth line. Otherwise it is rhythmically pretty dull stuff, which an actor really has to work at to make the urgently dramatic content of the lines come across.

We might contrast at this point the extract from *The Tempest* above, which comes from the other end of Shakespeare's writing career. It is just not possible to superimpose a simple 'iambic pentameter' model on such mature writing. Miranda's lines are full of variations and surprises. There is an extra syllable at the ends of some lines (*offer*, *trifling*, *cunning*, *fellow*, *seruant*) – what is sometimes called a *feminine ending* (following the practice in French versification, where a final mute *e* was associated with the feminine gender). Four lines have no end punctuation, the sense running on into the next line (*run-on* lines, or *enjambment*). There we find an associated mid-line break – what Puttenham calls the 'Cesure' (modern *caesura*, a Latin word meaning 'cutting') – marked variously by a comma, semicolon, colon, or period, suggesting different degrees of pause. This is far more interesting, both phonetically and phonologically. From a rhythmical point of view, the *Henry VI* and *Tempest* extracts are worlds apart.

One of the most important signs of Shakespeare's development as a poet is the way he manipulates the rhythmical properties of lines. Table 1 shows one aspect of this: the sharing of a single rhythmical line between characters. Here is an example from the very beginning of *Henry V* (1.1.20):

ELY: This would drink deep.
CANTERBURY: 'Twould drink the cup and all.

This is from a modern edition, where the line-sharing is clearly shown by layout. In the First Folio, all we see is this:

Bish.Ely. This would drinke deepe.
Bish.Cant. 'Twould drinke the Cup and all.

Sometimes three or more people share a line – and in theory up to five could do so, with each assigned a single short utterance. In practice, the nearest we come to this is a sequence in *King John* (3.3.64), where a single metrical line is broken up four times. The contrast between the leisurely rhythm of the longer lines before and after this exchange is striking:

Iohn. Good *Hubert, Hubert, Hubert* throw thine eye
       On yon young boy: Ile tell thee what my friend,

> He is a very serpent in my way,
> And wheresoere this foot of mine doth tread,
> He lies before me: dost thou vnderstand me?
> Thou art his keeper.
> *Hub.* And Ile keepe him so,
> That he shall not offend your Maiesty.
> *Iohn.* Death.
> *Hub.* My Lord.
> *Iohn.* A Graue.
> *Hub.* He shall not liue.
> *Iohn.* Enough.
> I could be merry now, *Hubert,* I loue thee.
> Well, Ile not say what I intend for thee:

In the layout of a modern edition, we see the rhythmical consequences more clearly:

JOHN: **Death.**
HUBERT: My Lord.
JOHN: A grave.
HUBERT: He shall not live.
JOHN: Enough.

Sharing the lines gives a clear indication to the actors to increase the tempo of the interaction, which in turn conveys an increased sense of dramatic momentum (for further examples, see Chapter 9).

The plays do not use shared lines equally. As we see in Table 1, there is a noticeable trend to use them more frequently over time – an interesting index of Shakespeare's maturing control over the dramatic representation of a conversation. In the early plays, few characters swop part-lines in this way; but the proportion (column 3) steadily increases, with only a few exceptions. *Henry V* and *Pericles* have half the number we would expect, given their dates; and *The Two Gentlemen of Verona* and *The Taming of the Shrew* are ahead of their time.

Table 1: *Shared lines related to the number of verse lines in the plays*

Play	Date	A: No of part lines	B: No of lines of verse	% (A/B × 100)
3H6	1591	24	2,892	0.8
KE3	1594	28	2,488	1.1
1H6	1592	37	2,664	1.4
2H6	1590–1	43	2,580	1.7
Tit	1592	70	2,479	2.8
Err	1594	45	1,543	2.9
R2	1595	88	2,752	3.2
R3	1592–3	134	3,516	3.8
H5	1598–9	73	1,943	3.8
MND	1595	78	1,713	4.6
TGV	1589–91	80	1,613	5.0
AYLI	1599–1600	65	1,276	5.1
John	1596	143	2,569	5.6
2H4	1597–8	88	1,547	5.7
Shr	1590–1	122	2,075	5.9
1H4	1596–7	101	1,665	6.1
Wiv	1597–8	24	338	6.2
Rom	1595	186	2,610	7.1
MV	1596–7	170	2,025	8.4
LLL	1594–5	158	1,715	9.2
Ado	1598–9	75	739	10.1
TN	1601	102	949	10.8
Tro	1602	264	2,250	11.7
Per	1607	234	1,903	12.3
JC	1599	281	2,207	12.7
Ham	1600–1	424	2,742	15.5
Tim	1606	295	1,707	17.3
MM	1603–4	311	1,634	19.0
Lear	1610	516	2,345	22.0
AWW	1606–7	324	1,447	22.4

Table 1: (cont.)

Play	Date	A: No of part lines	B: No of lines of verse	% (A/B × 100)
Oth	1603–4	604	2,599	23.2
Mac	1606	545	1,948	28.0
Cym	1610–11	827	2,808	29.5
Temp	1610–11	464	1,568	29.6
H8	1613	820	2,735	30.0
Cor	1608	805	2,570	31.3
WT	1609–10	699	2,181	32.1
Ant	1606	1,004	3,017	33.3
TNK	1613	926	2,641	35.1

Note: Play dates after Wells & Taylor (2005). Totals derived from the *Shakespeare's Words* database (see Preface).

But what is it about the iambic pentameter which made it so popular, and which makes it feel such a natural and effective medium for dramatic poetry? To answer this, we must consider the nature of poetry in general. If an oral performance is to be perceived as special, it must contain formal features which listeners can readily identify and appreciate. Different cultures do it in different ways, but it all comes down to the same thing in the end: a special mode of oratory. We do not 'say' a poem; we 'recite' it. Listeners are thus not just expecting to hear some content, but to hear that content presented in a different way from how it would be if it were just 'said'. The more that the reciters can introduce special devices into their speech, the more we are impressed. It is a bit like going to the circus, and seeing the trapeze artist do not just one, but two, or three, but surely never four somersaults between the bars. However, unless they do at least one, we are not much impressed. It is the same with poetry: something different has to be done to the language to make it special. Robert Graves once said that this is achieved by poets 'bending and breaking' the rules of language.[2]

The nature of the bending varies greatly between different literary periods. In Old English poetry, the chief rule that made oral performance special involved a mixture of rhythm and alliteration: the rhythm/tone-units were typically organized into pairs, each linked by two strong stresses and repeated initial sounds. In Middle English, the fashion changed, especially under French influence, and *rhyme* became the normal index of poetic expression – the repetition of a syllable (sometimes more than one syllable) at the end of lines. The discipline of rhyming is itself a departure from the rules of English speech, where words do not normally rhyme. The inflectional endings of Old English words had produced a modicum of word-end repetition, but once these died away, there was no routine rhyming in everyday speech. Anyone who inadvertently rhymes today might easily receive the riposte of 'being a po-et and didn't know it'.

Rhyme, then, is an excellent way of telling listeners that something linguistically special is going on. It works by drawing attention to the *ends* of rhythm/tone-units – typically at the ends of lines, as they would appear in writing. And there is something permanent about its appeal. Young children love it, from as early as the second year, especially when linked with rhythm (hence: 'nursery rhymes'). And adults love it too, exploiting it in huge amounts of comic poetry. Throughout the Middle Ages, we see rhymes and rhyme-schemes of all kinds, and they continue to be used in the poetry of the Elizabethan period. Shakespeare's sonnets and narrative poems fall firmly within the rhyming tradition. Using the convention of identifying lines which rhyme by the same letter of the alphabet, we find such rhyme-schemes as:

- the six-line stanza, as used in *Venus and Adonis* and *The Rape of Lucrece*: ababcc
- the seven-line stanza, as used in *A Lover's Complaint*: ababbcc
- the fourteen-line sonnet: abab cdcd efef gg

There are some interesting exceptional cases, such as Sonnet 99, which has fifteen lines, with an unusual ababa opening:

a   The forward violet thus did I chide,
b   Sweet theefe whence didst thou steale thy sweet that smels
a   If not from my loues breath, the purple pride,
b   Which on thy soft cheeke for complexion dwells?
a   In my loues veines thou hast too grosely died,

But perhaps this is not really an exception. The opening line is outside the structure of the poem. This is the only sonnet to begin with a reporting clause introducing a piece of direct speech.

Rhyme stayed popular in a great deal of poetry, but from the mid-sixteenth century it fell out of fashion as a technique in poetic drama. It was replaced by *blank verse* – a term which means simply 'verse that does not rhyme' (*blank* is here being used in its sense of 'absent' or 'lacking' – as when we say that someone's face has a 'blank expression'). Rhyme did not disappear from plays entirely. It is a prominent feature in the dialogue between lovers and fairies in *A Midsummer Night's Dream*, for example, and it turns up from time to time in some of Shakespeare's other plays, such as *Romeo and Juliet*. But the general impression is that it is used sparingly and for special effects, such as in songs. It is also frequently used to signal the end of a scene, where the audience is given notice, as it were, that an end is approaching by being presented with a rhyming couplet or some similar device. Play-endings especially closed in this way.

> For neuer was a Storie of more Wo,
> Then this of *Iuliet*, and her *Romeo*.
>
> (*Rom.* 5.3.309)

However, only just over half of the 600 or so scenes which end in verse in the canon have this closing couplet; and there seems to be no particular pattern to it. In *Richard II* and *Twelfth Night*, virtually all the scenes do; in *Coriolanus* and *The Winter's Tale*, virtually all the scenes don't; and in *Richard III* and *Troilus and Cressida* they are pretty evenly split.

If rhymes are ruled out as a means of making dramatic poetry special, what alternative is left? Very little, in fact. There are only two of phonologically identifying a 'line' in speech. One is to signal where it begins or ends; the other is to specify its length. With rhyme out of fashion as an end-line marker, the appeal of the iambic pentameter was that it offered a natural alternative, focusing on length. If every line (or most lines) has five units of two syllables each, then listeners know where they are.

But why a *five*-unit line, a pentameter, and not a two-unit (*dimeter*), three-unit (*trimeter*), four-unit (*tetrameter*), six-unit (*hexameter*), or something longer? This is an intriguing question. My view is that it is probably because the pentameter comes closest to the way our brain actually processes everyday speech. If we examine the length of rhythm/tone-units in normal conversation, we find that 95 per cent of them have between one and five stressed syllables.[3] The average is 2.5 stressed syllables per rhythm/tone-unit. That seems to be the equivalent of a pentametric half-line. Two of them neatly make up one whole-line pentameter. No other metric unit fits so well.

It's also interesting that five stressed items also seems to be the most we can comfortably handle within a single rhythm/tone-unit without it becoming a strain on our working memory. Psychologist George Miller once established the rule of 'magic number seven plus or minus two'.[4] People can repeat a sequence of up to seven random items (e.g. single numerals, monosyllabic words) with relative ease, but they begin to feel the strain when the sequence contains more than five units of meaning. The rules of grammar, and the semantic associations between words, help us to remember longer strings of words, of course, but there are still limits to the strings that can be most comfortably and efficiently remembered – as every (working) actor knows.

By 'unit of meaning' I mean a single *content item* – a noun, verb, adjective, or adverb – often accompanied by one or more of the *grammatical items* which give a sentence its structure (such as *the, of, in, it, not, and*). Hence, *the earl* is a single unit, in this sense, and *the noble earl* contains two units – *noble* and *the earl* (with the word-order changed because of the rules of English grammar). But *the earl is noble* also has only two units of meaning, and so does *it is the earl who is noble.* Note that there is no simple correlation between units of meaning and number of words. *Romeo loves Juliet* is three units of meaning and three words. But *Romeo is the one who is in love with Juliet* also has only three units of meaning, despite being ten words. People sometimes get away with being wordy in this way. Polonius is one who doesn't:

Mad / call I it; / for to define / true / Madnesse,
What is't, but to be nothing else but mad. /
But let that go.
Qu. More matter, with lesse Art.

His first line is semantically respectable, with five units of meaning (shown here separated by /); but his next line is semantically 'short', with only one content word (*mad*) out of ten. And the Queen notices.

It is possible to virtually empty a line of content meaning, as in the Polonius example, or to pack meaning in, as when someone is reporting an event and mentions lots of proper names – in which case, the number of semantic units in a line might reach seven or eight. Here is Northumberland telling his fellows (*R2.* 2.1.277):

That *Harry* / Duke / of *Herford,* / *Rainald* / Lord / *Cobham,*	6
That late / broke / from the Duke / of *Exeter,*	4
His brother / Archbishop, / late / of *Canterbury,*	4
Sir / *Thomas* / *Erpingham,* / Sir / *Iohn* / *Rainston,*	6
Sir / *Iohn* / *Norberie,* / & Sir / *Robert* / *Waterton,* / & *Francis* / *Quoint,*	8
All these well furnish'd / by the Duke / of *Britaine,*	3
With eight / tall / ships, / three / thousand / men of warre	6
Are making / hither / with all / due / expedience,	5
And shortly / meane / to touch / our Northerne / shore:	5

The average number of units per line, in this passage, is 5.2. This is high. Usually lines tend to have four or five content items in them, occasionally fewer, but rarely more. Typically we find three, four or five (the Prologue to *H5,* printed in italics):

O For a Muse / of Fire, / that would ascend	3
The brightest / Heauen / of Inuention:	3
A Kingdome / for a Stage, / Princes / to Act,	4
And Monarchs / to behold / the swelling / Scene.	4
Then / should the Warlike / Harry, *like himselfe,*	3
Assume / the Port / of Mars, */ and at his heeles*	4
(*Leasht in, / like Hounds) should Famine, / Sword, / and Fire*	5
Crouch / for employment. / But pardon, / Gentles all:	4
The flat / vnraysed / Spirits, / that hath dar'd,	4
On this vnworthy / Scaffold, / to bring forth	3
So great / an Obiect. / Can this Cock-Pit / hold	4
The vastie / fields / of France? / Or may we cramme	4
Within this Woodden / O, / the very / Caskes	4
That did affright / the Ayre / at Agincourt?	3

Here the average is 3.7. In theory, there could be ten monosyllabic content items in a pentametric line. I cannot recall ever seeing such a case.

With the pentameter in place as the 'default option', it was then possible for Shakespeare to play with it, adapting it to suit the dramatic needs of the moment. If a thought proved too long for the line, it could run on into the next. If a mind in turmoil had to be portrayed, the line was long enough to be fragmented. If the pace of interaction between characters needed increasing, then the line could be shared. If a really emotional crisis had to be expressed, then the line could be stopped half way through. Varying the patterns of strong and weak syllables within the five units provides another parameter of variation – something that traditional books on Shakespearean prosody fully explored.

- the strong + weak pattern, or *trochee*: O **Ro**meo, **Ro**meo, **where**fore **art** thou **Ro**meo?

(*Rom.* 2.2.33)

- the strong + strong pattern, or *spondee*: **On, on**, you Noblish English,

(*H5.* 3.1.17)

- the strong + weak + weak pattern, or *dactyl*: **See** what a grace was seated on his Brow

(Ham. 3.4.56)

- the weak + weak + strong pattern, or *anapaest*: I am **more** an Antike Roman then a Dane:

(Ham. 5.2.335).

The terminology can be difficult to remember, but the rhythmical contrasts are clear and distinct. Why are they there? Because they reflect the main features of rhythmical variation in everyday speech, and thus convey the emphases and emotions that we hear there. Proper names, for example, can be (or include) iambs (*Berowne*), trochees (*Falstaff*), spondees (*Doll Tearsheet*), dactyls (*Antony*), and anapaests (*Roderigo*). The pentameter has to be able to cope with all of this, and its beauty is that it *does* cope, extremely well, incorporating the varied rhythms of natural speech while maintaining the required poetic discipline.

As has often been pointed out, as Shakespeare's writing matures we see an increasingly daring range of variations introduced into the line of verse, so much so that it sometimes proves impossible to work within the parameters of classical prosodic models. This is especially noticeable in the use of caesurae (p. 114). In the later plays, we see lines being split at any point, each break setting up a semantic contrast between what precedes and what follows. In a five-unit line there must be four possible breaks. All can be heard in this one speech (*Ham.* 3.3.74)

> And now Ile doo't, and so he goes to Heauen,
> And so am I reueng'd: that would be scann'd,

[break after the third unit]

> A Villaine killes my Father, and for that
> I his foule Sonne, do this same Villaine send
> To heauen. Oh this is hyre and Sallery, not Reuenge.

[break after the first unit]

> He tooke my Father grossely, full of bread,

> With all his Crimes broad blowne, as fresh as May,
> And how his Audit stands, who knowes, saue Heauen:
> But in our circumstance and course of thought
> 'Tis heauie with him: and am I then reueng'd,
>
> > [*break after the second unit*]
>
> To take him in the purging of his Soule,
> When he is fit and season'd for his passage? No.
> [*break before the final unit – here, the sixth unit in an extra-long line*]

Modern editions display great variations in the way they present such passages. Punctuation can vary, and so can lines. Editors who keep the canons of the prosodic tradition resounding in their ears will want to regularize the line-lengths to maintain a pentametric appearance. So, in this speech, the words 'To heaven' and 'No' are usually printed as separate lines in a modern edition. That merely substitutes one kind of rule-bending for another.

Once he had chosen the pentameter, Shakespeare rarely departed from it. We do find exceptions, such as the four-unit lines in the fairy speeches in Act 5 of *A Midsummer Night's Dream*:

> If we shadowes haue offended,
> Thinke but this (and all is mended)
>
> > (5.1.413)

but these are special cases, easily explained with reference to type of character or situation. The pentameter rules. Its power lies in its flexibility, its adaptability to meet the demands of the huge range of subject-matter encountered in the plays (p. 6). It is the optimal working unit for oral performance in English.

6 'Trippingly upon the tongue': Shakespearean pronunciation

The subject of phonology mainly deals with the segmental side of pronunciation: the vowels, the consonants, and the way vowels and consonants combine to make syllables and, ultimately, words. It is very much a rule-governed system. We cannot string sounds randomly together to make syllables. In English, certain sounds never appear at the beginnings of words: there are none beginning with the sound [ŋ]; that sound is heard in the middle and end only (as in *singing*). A *h* sound (as in *happy*) is never heard at the end of a word. A *sh* sound (as in *ship*) is heard very rarely before a *p*, *t*, or *k* – just in a few recent loan-words, such as *spiel*. And so on.

Differences in regional or social accent are mainly a matter of vowels and consonants (though tone of voice can be important too). The prestige British accent known as 'received pronunciation' (RP) pronounces *h* at the beginning of words, as in *hurt*, and avoids it in such words as *arm*. Cockney speakers do the reverse; *I 'urt my harm*. Most English accents around the world pronounce words like *car* and *heart* with an audible *r*; RP is one of the few accents which does not. In RP, words like *bath* are pronounced with a 'long *a*' ('bahth'); up north in England it is a 'short *a*'. Accent variations mainly affect the vowels of a language. They are easy to hear, but difficult to write down without mastering a phonetic transcription. Learning some phonetics might seem a bit off-topic for a student of Shakespeare, but it is well worth it. As novelist Anthony Burgess said in the epilogue to his memoir, *A Mouthful of Air*: 'Phonetics, phonetics, and again phonetics. There cannot be too much phonetics.' I think Shakespeare would have said the same thing. Orlando, at least, seems to have been a budding phonetician:

> Your accent is something finer, then you could purchase in so
> remoued a dwelling
>
> (to disguised Rosalind: *AYLI*. 3.2.331).

We need to know about the vowels and consonants and the variations in accent which were current in Shakespeare's time because without this knowledge our auditory experience of the plays and poems lacks an entire dimension. How did they sound, in those days? Hearing a play in a modern regional accent (some companies have specialized in productions in 'Yorkshire' or 'Scottish', for example) can be an exciting, moving, unsettling experience. But a play in which everyone speaks in a Yorkshire accent, for example, brings with it the 'baggage' of everything we associate with Yorkshire accents. It is to replace one set of modern values with another. Putting on a play in 'original pronunciation' (OP), as it is often called, is a very different matter. If we can reconstruct the way people spoke in Shakespeare's time, there will be no modern baggage. It will be an accent that is distant – 400 years distant – from anything heard in our times.

But not entirely unfamiliar. When Shakespeare's Globe mounted its first production in OP, in 2004 – *Romeo and Juliet* – I spent some time asking the audiences how they found it. Everyone, without exception, claimed to recognize it, and to own it. People from Lancashire felt it sounded northern. People from Scotland said it was close to Scottish. A group from Dublin identified it as basically Irish. A lady from Melbourne said she could hear some Australian in it. A man from Virginia said it was just like they speak in the mountains up his way (yeah, right: see p. 1). And a group of inner-city London kids said: 'They're speaking like us, innit!' Of course the accent was like none of these. But it was a *little* bit like each of them. What people were hearing was the occasional echo of their own speech. Which is not surprising, given that the accents which were around in Shakespeare's time travelled the globe soon after.

The phrasing in that last sentence is important: accent<u>s</u>. The England – and especially the London – of Elizabethan times was a salad-bowl of accents, with people from the country (Shakespeare among them) rubbing vocal organs with people from the city, and also with foreign visitors and immigrants. And when different accents come up against each other, they begin to influence each other (the notion of *accommodation*, p. 101). Then, as now, there would have been mixed accents. It is of course possible – again, then as now – that people kept their original accent after moving to London. Robert Armin, Shakespeare's clown, was from Lynn in Norfolk. Would he have kept his provincial accent, or modified it? We do not know. But mixed accents are the normal state of affairs.

The chief difference between then and now was the absence of any one prestige accent. There was nothing like RP in those days. RP evolved as an upper-class accent towards the end of the eighteenth century. In Elizabethan times, you could have a strongly regional accent and still reach the highest levels in the kingdom. Francis Drake and Walter Raleigh were from Devon. The judge Thomas Malet observed of the latter: 'he spoke broad Devonshire to his dying day'. And when James brought his court down from Scotland, suddenly Scottish accents were everywhere. Francis Bacon describes James' speech as 'swift and cursory, and in the full dialect of his country'.[1]

The lack of an upper-class accent is the single biggest barrier to thinking ourselves into the auditory mindset of the Elizabethans. Today, if actors want to portray someone with an upper-class background, or satirize such a person, all they need to do is put on a 'posh' voice – which means a variety of RP, perhaps a 'far-back' variety. That has been possible over the past hundred years or so. But there was nothing like it in Shakespeare's time. If members of his company wanted to play kings and nobles, or to poke fun at Osrics or Tybalts, they could not do it simply by switching accents. They would have to do it in other ways, by using a more elevated vocabulary (see p. 224 for an example of this in *King Lear*), or by their dress or props or the way they held themselves. By their acting, in short.

There is a limit to what we can access in OP. We shall never know the exact phonetic character of the accent-mix that was used on stage. We shall never know the exact phonetic nature of the *r* heard after vowels. Was it a sound with the tip of the tongue curled back towards the palate, as we hear in much American English? Was it a trilled sound, as we often hear in Welsh or Scottish? Was it a sound with noticeable friction? Was it at the back of the throat (a 'uvular' *r*), as is heard in some north-eastern British accents? We can get some hints from what contemporary writers say, as we shall see. But *some* sort of *r* sound there was, by all accounts. And that is what we need to know to give us an insight into the sound system (or phonology) of OP.

Who benefits from this insight? Linguists, obviously, for knowing about the phonological character of Early Modern English fills a gap in our understanding of the evolution of English pronunciation from Anglo-Saxon to modern times. But, for this book, I would stress the contribution a phonological perspective can make to our understanding of the texts and to their interpretation in performance. Why did Jaques, after listening to Touchstone, laugh 'sans intermission / An houre by his diall'? If we read what Touchstone says (*AYLI*. 2.7.20), it doesn't seem especially funny – not enough to keep someone giggling for an hour, anyway:

> And then he drew a diall from his poake,
> And looking on it, with lacke-lustre eye,
> Sayes, very wisely, it is ten a clocke:
> Thus we may see (quoth he) how the world wagges:
> 'Tis but an houre agoe, since it was nine,
> And after one houre more, 'twill be eleuen,
> And so from houre to houre, we ripe, and ripe,
> And then from houre to houre, we rot, and rot,
> And thereby hangs a tale.

But once we know that the pronunciation of *hour* in OP was [oːr] – something like *oar* in Modern English – and that this was also the pronunciation of *whore*, the speech takes on new life.

An awareness of how lines originally sounded can add a freshness, and occasionally semantic illumination, to our appreciation of the plays and poems. At the very least, it enables us to hear rhymes working which haven't worked for the last two hundred years. The effect of Oberon's mystical chant (*MND*. 3.2.102) is much enhanced when it is said with the vowels echoing each other, with the endings on *archery*, *gloriously*, and *remedy* having a greater degree of stress and sounding more like *rye*, *lie*, and *die* would today (but with a more central starting point to the diphthong in all cases, using the sound [ə] as in *the*):

> Flower of this purple die,
> Hit with *Cupids* archery,
> Sinke in apple of his eye,
> When his loue he doth espie,
> Let her shine as gloriously
> As the *Venus* of the sky.
> When thou wak'st if she be by,
> Beg of her for remedy.

A bad rhyme sometimes hits us between the ears. Both actors and audiences feel uncomfortable when they hear a crude lack of rhyme in a couplet which has an attention-seeking location in a play. The last lines of *The Taming of the Shrew* in a modern edition (Penguin, 5.2.187) read like this:

> HORTENSIO: Now go thy ways, thou hast tamed a curst shrew.
> LUCENTIO: 'Tis a wonder, by your leave, she will be tamed so.

It is a slightly awkward moment, which simply does not happen in OP (as the Folio spelling indicates):

> *Horten.* Now goe thy wayes, thou hast tam'd a curst Shrow.
> *Luc.* Tis a wonder, by your leaue, she wil be tam'd so.

Here, *Shrow* was pronounced with an [oː] vowel, to rhyme with *so*. An even more awkward case occurs at the end of *Macbeth*, where two sets of couplets rhyme, the first setting up the expectation that the second will also – and then it doesn't.

> That call's vpon vs, by the Grace of Grace,
> We will performe in measure, time, and place:
> So thankes to all at once, and to each one,
> Whom we inuite, to see vs Crown'd at Scone.

(Mac. 5.6.111)

I have heard actors try to get round this by pronouncing *Scone* with a short vowel to match *one* (as if it rhymed with *gone*) – doubtless to the ire of any Scottish members of the audience. The lines work fine in OP, where the vowel in both words would have been [oːn], rather like modern *own*.

THE EVIDENCE

How do we know? There are several sources of evidence. I treat them here separately; but it is important to appreciate that any conclusions about Shakespearean phonology come from a synthesis of information from all sources.

Contemporary accounts

The most important evidence is that provided by the contemporary writers, some of whom had made a detailed study of pronunciation as part of their interest in spelling reform (p. 58). Consider, for example, what we can learn from George Puttenham (in *The Art of Poesie*, 1589, Book 2, Chapter 8). This is part of a passage where he is rebuking any poet who tries to 'wrench his words to helpe his rime':

> as for example, if one should rime to this word *Restore* he may not match him with *Doore* or *Poore* for neither of both are of like terminant, either by good orthography or in naturall sound, therfore such rime is strained.

We do not know from this description exactly how these words sounded; but evidently the vowel in *door/poor* was different from that in *restore*. Likewise, he goes on, *came* should not be pronounced to rhyme with *ram*. These are just details, but the spelling-reform books of the time are full of such details, because there was great anxiety to try to make letters an accurate reflection of sounds. Gradually they provide us with a picture of how educated Elizabethans spoke.

Some of the accounts are very detailed. Ben Jonson's description of *r* as 'the dog's letter' (in his *English Grammar* – a translation of Latin *litera canina*) sounds a little vague (though think: *grrr*), but he then goes on to talk about 'the tongue striking the inner palate with a trembling about the teeth', and how it sounds 'more liquid' in the middle and end of words. It could have been a modern phonetician talking. And, vague or not, it evidently had some popular currency, according to the Nurse (*Rom.* 2.4.202):

> Doth not Rosemarie and *Romeo* begin both with a letter?
>
> *Rom.* I Nurse, what of that? Both with an *R*   [*I Nurse* = 'Ay, Nurse']
> *Nur.* A mocker that's the dogs name. *R.* [*A mocker* = 'Ah, mocker!']

We always have to be cautious, when reading contemporary accounts. People who talk about pronunciation in print – phoneticians aside – usually operate towards the pedantic end of the opinion spectrum, and often record what they would *like* to hear (or what they *used* to hear) rather than what is actual current practice – much as, today, we might read a book which tells us that *controversy* has the stress on the first syllable, and does not mention the fact that most of us put it on the second. Doubtless many conservative, idiosyncratic, or even archaic pronunciations are recorded in the Elizabethan writers on spelling. So we need to look for other evidence, to check what they say. And this is where the poets and dramatists come in.

Rhymes

Consider the following question: how was the name *Rosaline* pronounced in *Love's Labour's Lost*? Today some people say the name to rhyme with *pin* and some with *pine*. If we take its opening use in the First Folio (2.1.181 – in fact, here an error for *Katharine*), we might think 'pin':

> Dum.   Sir, I pray you a word: What Lady is that same?
>
> Boy.   The heire of *Alanson*, *Rosalin* her name.

but from the second use we might think 'pine'

> And *Rosaline* they call her, aske for her:
>
> (3.1.163)

All is resolved by Costard's rhyme:

> From my Lord *Berowne*, a good master of mine,
> To a Lady of *France*, that he call'd *Rosaline*.
>
> (4.1.106)

and this is reinforced by a further rhyme with *thine* later in the play.

Once again, we have to be cautious. The evidence does not actually tell us which of the words is like which. It is conceivable that *Rosaline* was pronounced like 'pin' and *mine* was pronounced like 'min'. We have to eliminate this possibility. And we do so by looking at all the cases where *mine* appears, and seeing whether there is any evidence to support the 'pin' type of pronunciation. If we found *mine* rhyming with such words as *kin* and *din*, then we would conclude that it did. And if we found it rhyming with such words as *fine* and *shine*, we would conclude that it didn't. This is what Helge Kökeritz found, in his influential *Shakespeare's Pronunciation* (1953), which examined all the rhymes in the Folio and Quarto texts:

> brine, christalline, Colatine, combine, confine, decline, define, designe, divine, eien, eine, eyne, fine, incline, line, nine, pine, resigne, shine, Valentine

and also some near-rhymes: *clyme*, *time*. A word like *kin*, on the other hand, he found rhymes with *begin*, *him*, *sin*, and *sinne*. There is no overlap. *Mine* must definitely have sounded like modern *mine*, and likewise the ending of *Rosaline*.

We especially have to be cautious over interpreting what in modern literature would be called *eye rhymes* – pairs of words which have the visual appearance of a rhyme but lack any corresponding sound, such as *love* and *prove*. These emerged in English as the spelling and pronunciation systems diverged in the fifteenth century, but the rate at which the divergence took place is by no means clear. Did *love* and *prove* have the same vowel in Shakespeare's time? Ben Jonson is one who claims they did, and if so, the evidence suggests that it would be *prove* sounding like *love* rather than the other way round ('loove'). It is not an unusual rhyme, even today: many Scottish people would make it, for instance.

However, the evidence is not always easy to interpret. *Love* evidently rhymes with *dove*:

> Not *Hermia*, but *Helena* now I loue;
> Who will not change a Rauen for a Doue?

> (*MND.* 2.2.113)

And *dove* is clearly intended to rhyme with *prove*, in this two-part line:

> His Doue will proue; his gold will hold,

> (*Wiv.* 1.3.90)

Love also rhymes with *prove*:

> Make me but like my thoughts, and I shall proue
> A louer of thy drumme, hater of loue.

> (*AWW.* 3.3.10)

That's settled, then? It would seem so, for most of the examples support this conclusion. But then we encounter *love* rhyming with *prove* in Sonnet 136.7, where it is spelled *prooue*! That really suggests a long 'oo' vowel, and thus a real eye-rhyme. The evidence, in other words, is mixed. Perhaps poets were happy to do this sort of thing as a literary convention in their sonnets, thinking of them as works to be read rather than read aloud. Or perhaps both pronunciations were current at the time.

134 Think on my words

Metre and stress

Knowing that Shakespeare was a master of metre allows us another kind of evidence. If we see polysyllabic words in a speech which is metrically regular, we can deduce from where the stress falls within the words at least one way in which those words could be pronounced. It is not immediately obvious how *contrite*, for example, should be spoken: was it *contrite* or *contrite* in the 1590s? The two instances in the canon indicate the former:

> And on it haue bestowed more contrite teares
>
> (*H5*. 4.1.289)

> Her contrite sighes vnto the clouds bequeathed
>
> (*Luc*. 1727)

And all fifteen instances of *antique* support the pronunciation *antique*:

> That old and Anticke song we heard last night;
>
> (*TN*. 2.4.3)

Many words have a stress pattern that is no longer current in English. In such words as *aspect*, the stress always fell on the second syllable (where today it falls on the first):

> Then lend the Eye a terrible aspect:
>
> (*H5*. 3.1.9)

and we hear the same type of shift in these trisyllabic words: *gallantly*, *canonize*, *illustrate*, *opportune*, *retinue*, and *sinister*. By contrast, in such words as *July* the stress fell on the first syllable (where today it falls on the second), as it did in *corrosive*, *horizon*, *pioner*, *enginer*, *acceptable*, and *detestable*.

July is an example that surprises people, because the modern stress pattern is so familiar. According to the *OED*, the stress on the first syllable remained in English until well into the eighteenth century (indeed, it can still be heard in some regional dialects, especially in Scotland, where it sounds like the name *Julie*). The shift to *July* is unusual (no other month-name has a final stress) and inexplicable. In the two Shakespearean verse uses, the stress pattern is unambiguously the earlier one:

> And proofes as cleere as Founts in *Iuly*, when
> Wee see each graine of grauell;
>
> (*H8*. 1.1.154)

> He makes a Iulyes day, short as December,
>
> (*WT*. 1.2.169)

This means, of course, that we must remember to stress the word appropriately in its third use, in a passage of prose, when Don Pedro concludes a piece of letter-writing repartee with Benedick:

> The sixt of Iuly. Your louing friend, *Benedick*.
>
> (*Ado*. 1.1.162)

This is actually one of the commonest sources of pronunciation inconsistency in productions. The actors remember the old stress pattern in the verse, for the metre reminds them; but they slip back into the modern pronunciation in prose. I don't think I have ever heard a Don Pedro say *July* in anything other than the modern pronunciation.

Several of the variations we find in Shakespeare are still present in modern English, such as *direct* vs *direct*, *entire* and *entire*, or *sincere* vs. *sincere*:

> Suppos'd sincere, and holy in his Thoughts:
>
> (*2H4*. 1.1.202)

> From sincere motions, by Intelligence,
>
> (*H8*. 1.1.183)

But often the variation has since disappeared, as in *consign* (which we still have) and *consign* (which we have lost), or *character* and *character*. Cases of verbs and adjectives ending in *-ed* raise an extra complication. *Distressed*, for example, appears in two stress patterns, one of which we have lost:

> Alas! you three, on me threefold dis<u>trest</u>:
>
> (*R3.* 2.2.86)

> O send some succour to the <u>dis</u>trest Lord.
>
> (*1H6.* 4.3.30)

But in addition we find examples such as this:

> The eldest Son of this dis<u>tress</u>ed Queene.
>
> (*Tit* 1.1.106)

where plainly the metre requires that we turn *distressed* from a two-syllable word into a three-syllable one. In editions which partly modernize the spelling, we will see such contrasts as the following:

> the distress'd Lord   or   the distressed Lord
> this distressed Queen   or   this distressèd Queen

In the First Folio, the difference between the two pronunciations is often clearly shown, using an *e* or an apostrophe, as in this line of Romeo's:

> Hence banished, is banisht from the world,
>
> (*Rom.* 3.3.19)

or the lines when Capulet wails over Juliet's supposed corpse:

> Despis'd, distressed, hated, martir'd, kil'd,
>
> (*Rom.* 4.5.59)

But, as we saw in Chapter 4, Folio graphology is never straightforward. When we look at Paris's corresponding wail in the previous speech, we find a typical uncertainty over the use of the apostrophe (p. 87):

> Beguild, diuorced, wronged, spighted, slaine,
> Most detestable death, by thee beguil'd,
>
> (*Rom.* 4.5.55)

And the contrast is not always represented. In this next extract, the regular metre indicates that the *e* of *unappeased* ought to have been replaced by an apostrophe:

> That so the shadows be not unappeased,
> Nor we disturb'd with prodigies on earth.

> (*Tit.* 1.1.103)

As a result, quite a few of the *-ed* endings in a modern edition are regularizations introduced by the editor.

Metre and contractions

Examining the metrical structure of the pentameter brings to light another feature of Elizabethan pronunciation: the use of colloquially contracted forms. These are cases where the full form of a word, as used in slow and careful speech, has been shortened by omitting one or more of its sounds. Thus today we say *I'll* for *I will*, *they're* for *they are*, and so on. This is one of the uses of the apostrophe in standard English (p. 83), and such forms are accepted as a legitimate way of representing informal speech. Other types of contraction have not been so lucky. When we drop a syllable in *library*, pronouncing it as *libry*, as most people do, this is considered to be 'sloppy' speech. And one of the techniques novelists have of showing that a character is using a regional or uneducated accent is to signal these omissions with an apostrophe. The character who says he has been *to the library* is plainly of a different background from one who says he has been *to the lib'ry*. A few polysyllabic words have lost a syllable and come to be accepted without quibble in modern English (such as *Wednesday*), but there is still a backlash against such pronunciations as *lib'ry* and *Feb'ry*, which do not follow the spelling, and rows still break out over whether the *t* should be pronounced in *often* or whether *difference* has three syllables or two. This is the legacy of Holofernes (p. 58).

The focus on spelling was beginning to make itself felt in Shakespeare's time. While there was nothing like RP, as we have seen, it *was* possible for people to make themselves sound more educated by articulating words – as Holofernes recommended – with every letter pronounced, showing that they knew how to spell. The practice – of 'spelling-pronunciation', as it would today be called – was evidently common enough to be satirized as an affectation. But affectations are informative, for they show that the users are aware of norms (from which they want to distance themselves). The everyday pronunciation of words would have been full of contractions.

Many of them are shown in the original texts. In some cases the contraction can be deduced simply by observing the omission of a letter; in others the omitted sound is marked by an apostrophe. Thus we see in Mercutio's Queen Mab speech (*Rom.* 1.4.65; see Figure 1, p. 28) *the Moonshines watry Beames*, and in one of Ulysses' speeches (*Tro.* 1.3.374), *make a Lott'ry*. There are many examples of words being reduced in this way: *batt'rie, eu'ry, mockrie, recou'ry, desprate, bach'-ler, gard'ner, wandrers, blistring, remembring, boystrous, med'cine.* Most of them have exactly the same informal pronunciation today.

Why do people shorten words in this way? It is partly for ease of articulation. It requires greater effort to articulate the sequence of two *r*s in *library*, and some consonant clusters are really quite difficult to say, such as the *sts* in *beasts*. But it is also to promote fluency, to maintain a comfortable, stress-timed speech rhythm (p. 105). A jerky, erratic speech rhythm can sound unpleasant and can interfere with our ability to understand what is being said. Contracted forms help maintain the rhythm, and allow the speech to flow. So this must be at least part of what Hamlet had in mind when he gave his famous advice to the company of players visiting Elsinore (*Ham.* 3.2.2):

> Speake the Speech I pray you, as I pronounc'd it to you trippingly on the Tongue: But if you mouth it, as many of your Players do, I had as liue [= lief] the Town-Cryer had spoke my Lines:

The mention of town criers suggests that an orotund tone of voice is part of 'mouthing'; and 'trippingly' suggests a degree of rapidity; but underlying both of these notions is a reference to a smooth flow of enunciation, and the avoidance of over-careful articulation. Plainly what many actors did then, as many do now, is artificially ar-tic-u-late, loudly and precisely, with especial attention given to sounding consonants and consonant clusters, especially at the ends of words. In such a style, every syllable of a polysyllabic word would be pronounced: Benedick's *Februarie face* (*Ado.* 5.4.41) would be articulated 'feb-roo-ah-ree'. And in this style, lines like Paulina's (*WT.* 3.2.173) would take an age, for every final *-t*, *-d*, *-ts* and *-ds* (15 instances in all – almost half the words in this extract) would be carefully released:

> What studied torments (Tyrant) hast for me?
> What Wheeles? Racks? Fires? What flaying? boyling?
> In Leads, or Oyles? What old, or newer Torture
> Must I receiue? whose euery word deserues
> To taste of thy most worst.

It is impossible to retain a coherent speech rhythm under such circumstances. Something has to give.

Anyone who has ever done any acting knows where this style comes from. If you want your voice to reach the back of the theatre and to have your words – words which an audience might find unfamiliar – clearly heard, then it makes sense to sound them out carefully. Recommendations about clear articulation thus abound in the actor-training manuals, as they do in training programmes for BBC announcers and courses for people going in for public speaking. And the authors all have a point. Hamlet is not saying 'Don't be clear'. He is saying 'Don't overdo it'. As voice coach Patsy Rodenburg puts it:[2]

> Over-enunciated and affected speaking encourages the audience to watch and listen to the actor's craft rather than the words spoken. Hamlet wants them interested in the play, not the actor's mouth.

And there are of course several strategies which can be taught to achieve the ideal blend of audibility and fluency.

The point is critical because contractions are so common. There are some thirty instances in the Folio page shown in Figure 1, for example – two in Mercutio's opening lines (*Rom.* 1.4.40):

> Tut, duns the Mouse, the Constables owne word, [= dun is]
> If thou art dun, weele draw thee from the mire. [= we will]

Six occur in these four lines of dialogue between the two old Capulets (*Rom.* 1.5.33):

> How long 'ist now since last your selfe and I [= is it]
> Were in a Maske?
> 2. *Capu.* Berlady thirty yeares. [= by Our Lady]
> 1. *Capu.* What man: 'tis not so much, 'tis not so much, [= it is]
> 'Tis since the Nuptiall of *Lucentio*,

These examples show one of the most noticeable orthographic features of the original texts: the way contractions affect 'small' grammatical words, such as *the, and, in* and *them.* Their frequency clearly indicates a norm of informal pronunciation which seems to have changed little over the past 400 years. Consider:

> she might a bin a Grandam ere she died.
>
> (*LLL.* 5.2.17)

The orthography reflects a pronunciation which is no different from what we would say today as *She might've been a grandmother.* It is just that modern English writes the contraction as *'ve* and not as *a.* Similarly, Hotspur's impatient *d'you* is spelled differently in the Folio from how we would write it now, but there is no spoken difference:

> In *Richards* time: What de'ye call the place?
> A plague vpon't, it is in Gloustershire:
>
> (*1H4.* 1.3.239).

Several other grammatical words contract in similar manner, such as dropping the final *d* of *and* (*an'*), the *th* of *them* (*'em*), and the initial *i* of *it is* (*'tis*).

Alongside these are the cases where Elizabethan contractions have no counterpart in Modern English. They include many prepositions, the definite article, and pronouns, as in the reduced *in the* and *at his* in these lines:

When thou hast hung thy aduanced sword i'th' ayre,

(*Tro.* 4.5.188)

To lay my Crowne at's feete, and there to kneele.

(*Ant.* 3.13.76)

The double contraction *Berlady* also falls into this category. These are all cases where 'trippingly' means what it says. Actors should never try to sound the syllables out with care. The spelling is simply an author's best effort at transcribing what we all know happens in everyday speech. And no creative writer has ever solved the problem. Modern representations of colloquial speech in plays are just as approximate as are those in the Folio. (Only when plays are written entirely in phonetic transcription will the problem disappear!)

The metrical regularity of the pentameter also tells us that some words will be pronounced in their unstressed form, regardless of the way in which they are written down. When the Chorus says that Harry will

Assume the Port of Mars, *and at his heeles*

(*H5.* Prologue.5)

we know from the regular iambic rhythm that the words *the, of, and,* and *his* are all unstressed. In colloquial English, the *f* of *of* would be dropped (as in *cuppa tea*), the *and* would become either *an'* or *'nd* or possibly *'n'* (as in *fish 'n' chips*), and the *his* would become *is.* If 'trippingly' means anything at all, it suggests an approximation to these values.

The use of contracted forms is motivated in verse by the need to make lines scan, and it does not always follow that a line containing a contraction will necessarily be spoken faster than one without. On the other hand, when several words are contracted, the pace inevitably quickens. There could be a difference of a second or two between a 'mouthed' version of Romeo's

It is my Lady, O it is my Loue, O that she knew she were,

(*Rom.* 2.2.10)

and a 'tripping' version of it, where *my* becomes 'mi' or 'm' (cf. the common *m'lady*) and *she* becomes 'shi' or even 'sh'. When this kind of pronunciation was adopted by the Shakespeare's Globe company for their OP version of *Romeo and Juliet* – a production that ran in tandem with the one in modern English – the OP production was ten minutes shorter overall.

Spellings

The last kind of evidence about how words were pronounced comes from the spellings in the First Folio and Quarto texts. As we saw in Chapter 3, English spelling was not fully standardized in Shakespeare's time; but that now turns out to be a blessing in disguise, for when there is flexibility in the system then people will very likely try to spell as they speak. We have to be cautious, once again, given that some idiosyncratic spellings reflect compositorial error. Isolated spellings prove very little. But when seen in relation to usage as a whole, some plausible suggestions emerge. Queen Mab, for example, has a whip whose lash is *of Philome* (*Rom.* 1.4.66): this suggests a pronunciation of *film* as two syllables, much as in modern Irish English. A little later (2.1.38), Mercutio talks of a *Poprin Peare*, which suggests that *poppering* (a type of pear, named after a Belgian town) was pronounced with two syllables, not three, and that the final sound was [n] and not [ŋ].

Here are three other examples of the way spelling can help us arrive at a sense of original pronunciation:

- *Quotha* appears as *ke-tha* in the *Pericles* Quarto (2.1.78), which along with *banket* for *banquet* (*AYLI.* 2.5.59), *coat* for *quote* (*LLL.* 5.2.781), and other such spellings indicates that the French pronunciation of *qu-* in loanwords (but not in native words, such as *queen*) was still current. The modern pronunciation of [kw] came later, influenced by the spelling.

- *Orthography* is spelled *ortagriphie* when Holofernes uses it (*LLL.* 5.1.19), which along with several variant forms of more common words suggests that *th* in the middle of a word was often pronounced [t]. We see it today, of course, in *Anthony*, but the double spelling is found in Shakespeare: it is *Anthonio* in the Folio text of *Antony and Cleopatra* (apart from in one line) and *Antonio* in *Julius Caesar*. The heroine in *The Taming of the Shrew* is both *Katherine* (twenty-three times) and *Katerina* (thirteen times).

- *Torturing* is spelled *tortering* in *Titus Andronicus* (Q1, 2.2.285), and a similar spelling is seen in dozens of words which we would today spell in *-ure*, such as *venter* for *venture* (*H5*. 1.2.192) and *ioynter* for *jointure* (*Shr*. 2.1.363), making it clear that, in cases where the *-ure* spelling is routine (as in *nature*), the older pronunciation should be used.

INSIGHTS

As the *Jaques* example in *As You Like It* showed, the reading of lines in OP can sometimes point to a meaning that is obscured when read in a modern English accent. Usually, it is a pun that is revealed, as seen in the prologue to *Romeo and Juliet*:

> From forth the fatall loynes of these two foes,
> A paire of starre-crost louers take their life.

Loins seems innocent enough. But when we realize that the sound of *oi* was at the time the same as the sound of the vowel in *lines*, an extra level of meaning suggests itself. Whether this was coincidental or deliberate, on the part of the author, is for others to debate. The linguistic facts remain.

The OP production of *Troilus and Cressida* at Shakespeare's Globe in 2005 made a great deal of another pun, which only an OP rendition allows. At one point (2.1.63) Thersites says this to Achilles about Ajax:

> But yet you looke not well vpon him: for who some euer you take him to be, he is *Aiax*.

This seems rather like stating the obvious. But once you know that the normal pronunciation of *Ajax* at the time was 'a jakes', and know that *jakes* in Elizabethan English meant 'lavatory' (as indeed it still does in Irish English), then the line takes on some force. The actor playing Thersites went out of his way to stress the 'jakes' pronunciation to Ajax, thrusting the pun into his face over the next lines, much to the delight of the audience, who – apart from the possible philologist standing in the yard – would never have encountered this joke before:

> This Lord (*Achilles*) *Aiax* who wears his wit in his belly, and his guttes in his head, Ile tell you what I say of him.
> *Achil.* What?
> *Ther.* I say this *Aiax* –

Once we are aware of an OP pun, of course, then we can keep our ears open for other instances of its use. *Ajax* turns up again in the last scene of *Love's Labour's Lost* (5.2.573), when Costard tells Nathaniel, who has been attempting to present Alexander, one of the Nine Worthies:

> your Lion that holds his Pollax sitting on a close stoole, will be giuen to Aiax. [*pollax* = battle-axe]

Ajax falls neatly into place here, as a *close stoole* was a 'chamber-pot'. We can also keep our ears open for places where the word is avoided. In *As You Like It* (3.3.67), why else does Touchstone greet Jaques in such a curious way?

> Good euen good Mr what ye cal't:

The fastidious euphemism is still used today. Although there are times when the metre demands that *Jaques* be pronounced with two syllables, the normal colloquial pronunciation of the name was 'jakes'.

Many of the OP puns in Shakespeare have already been identified by scholars such as Kökeritz,[3] who has a useful list of 226 of them.

But there is always the chance of finding more, which is why phonology is one of the most exciting areas of future exploration in Shakespearean studies. Until all the plays and poems are transcribed and performed in OP, it is difficult to predict what will happen. Most have yet to receive their first OP production (in 400 years).

7 'Think on my words': Shakespearean vocabulary

Vocabulary is the area of language least subject to generalization. Unlike the grammar, prosody, and discourse patterns of a language, which are subject to general rules that can be learned thoroughly in a relatively short period of time, the learning of vocabulary is largely ad hoc and of indefinite duration. By contrast with the few hundred points of pronunciation, grammar, and discourse structure which we need to consider when dealing with Shakespeare's language, the number of points of vocabulary run into several thousand. As a result, most books do little more than provide an alphabetical glossary of the items which pose a difficulty of comprehension.

The glossary-writers concentrate, as they should, on the difficult words, by which is usually meant words used in Shakespeare that are different from those used today. Either the words themselves have changed (e.g. we no longer use *finical*) or the meanings of the words have changed (e.g. *naughty* no longer means 'evil'). But difference and difficulty are not the same.

There are, firstly, some difficult words that are not different (see p. 13). Few students now are familiar with the mythology of Classical Greece or Rome, so the use of such names as *Phoebus* and *Phaeton* presents a difficulty. But this is an encyclopedic not a linguistic problem – a lack of knowledge of the world (as it existed in Classical times), rather than a lack of knowledge of how to talk about the world. There is no linguistic problem in the phrase Orsino uses to describe Antonio's face: 'As blacke as Vulcan, in the smoake of warre' (*TN.* 5.1.50), but it makes no sense until you know who Vulcan is. He turns out to be the same Roman god of fire, the gods' blacksmith, as he was 400 years ago. This is not a matter of language change. And the same educational point applies to those parts of Shakespeare's text which are indeed in a foreign language – French, Latin, Spanish, and Italian, along with some mock-foreign expressions. In the days when most people learned French and Latin in school, those passages (such as the scenes in *Henry V* where a great deal of French is used) would have posed no problem. Today, they often do.

Secondly, there are many different words which are not difficult. In fact, the notion of 'difficulty' turns out to represent a broad spectrum. At one extreme, there are words which hardly need to be glossed at all. At the other extreme, there are words where it is not possible to deduce from their form what they might mean, and a gloss is obligatory.

EASY WORDS

At the 'easy' end, we find words such as *oft, perchance, sup, morrow, visage, pate, knave, wench,* and *morn,* which are still used today in special contexts, such as poetry or comic archaism. A craven knight, such as Sir Coward de Custard (from the *Dandy*) would employ several. A number also still exist in regional usage, at least in Britain, such as *aye* 'always', *good morrow* – pronounced 'moruh' – and *sup* 'drink'. 'Eat all, sup all, say nowt', as they say in Yorkshire.

Then there are words where the formal difference is too small to obscure the meaning, such as *affright* ('frighten'), *afeard* ('afraid'), *scape* ('escape'), *ope* ('open'), *down-trod* ('down-trodden'), and *dog-weary* ('dog-tired'). In isolation, such words might seem obscure: *ope,* for instance. But words are never used in isolation. If someone says:

My teares will choake me, if I ope my mouth

(*Tit.* 5.3.174)

the context makes the meaning perfectly clear. Similarly, the context allows us to immediately interpret idioms such as *what cheer!* and *go your ways.*

Also into the 'easy' category we can place the many words whose elements are well known today but their combination is not, such as *bedazzle, dismasked, unpeople, rareness,* and *smilingly,* and such phrasal verbs as *press down* ('overburden'), *speak with* ('speak to'), and *shove by* ('push aside'). We say *unmasked* today, rather than *dismasked*, but because we know the prefix *dis-* in its sense of 'reverse the action' from hundreds of modern words (*disconnect, dishearten*...), we have no trouble working out that *dismask* must mean 'remove a mask'. Again, the context invariably provides a clue – often a clear lexical contrast, as here (*LLL.* 5.2.295):

> Faire Ladies maskt, are Roses in their bud:
> Dismaskt, their damaske sweet commixture showne,
> Are Angels vailing clouds, or Roses blowne.

Often the clue is situational:

> *Coriolanus rises, and offers to goe away.*
> *Senat.* Sit *Coriolanus*: neuer shame to heare
> What you have Nobly done.
> *Coriol.* Your Honors pardon:
> I had rather haue my Wounds to heale againe,
> Then heare say how I got them.
> *Brutus.* Sir, I hope my words dis-bench'd you not?

> (*Cor.* 2.2.64)

Innovative uses of this kind are not totally unfamiliar, because we do precisely the same thing today. If I jocularly said of someone who had just had his jacket taken from him, 'He's been disjacketed', you would know what I meant.

I would also place into my 'easy' category most of the cases of *conversion*, or *functional shift*, where a word belonging to one part-of-speech is used as a different part-of-speech. Most often, a common noun is used as a verb, as in the underlined cases below:

> Tut, tut, Grace me no Grace, nor Vnckle me,

> (*R2.* 2.3.86)

> Lord *Angelo* Dukes it well in his absence

> (*MM.* 3.2.90)

but there are several other possibilities, which Shakespeare exploits so much that lexical conversion has become one of the trademarks of his style. Here a proper name is verbed:

> I warrant him *Petruchio* is Kated.
>
> > (*Shr.* 3.2.244)

In this next case an adverb *askance* is used as a verb:

> frō their own misdeeds askaunce their eyes?
>
> > (*Luc.* 637)

And here the adjective *third* is used as a verb:

> Yet what man / Thirds his owne worth
>
> > (*TNK.* 1.2.96).

Here the verb *impair* is used as an adjective:

> Nor dignifies an impaire thought with breath:
>
> > (*Tro.* 4.5.103)

and here the noun *kingdom* is adjectived:

> Kingdom'd *Achilles* in commotion rages,
>
> > (*Tro.* 2.3.173).

In such cases, although the grammar is strikingly different from everyday usage, the lexical meaning is not. And because conversion continues to operate freely in Modern English:

> Child (at bedtime): Can I have another biscuit.
> Mother: I'll biscuit you if you don't get off to bed right now.

we should be able to feel immediately the dramatic effect of a new word function. I have used the process twice in the present paragraph – I trust without making my text unintelligible. And it is worth noting the effect of doing so: to say 'a proper name is verbed', for example, is more succinct than the alternative: 'a proper name is turned into a verb'. When there is a concern to fit language into the discipline of a metrical pattern, such options are hugely helpful to a writer (see further, pp. 189–90).

METRICAL CONSTRAINTS

Some words are different solely because Shakespeare needed an extra syllable to meet the demands of the metre, but these do not usually cause any great difficulty of interpretation. Here is Glendower:

> I can call Spirits from the vastie Deepe.

(1H4. 3.1.50)

Vast deep would have been possible. Timon talks about the 'vast sea' (*Tim.* 4.2.439) and Romeo the 'vast shore' (*Rom.* 2.2.83). But such a phrasing does not suit Glendower's style. His previous fifteen-line speech, in which he asserts 'I am not in the Roll of common men', is almost entirely regular iambic pentameter, as is his speech in general. *Vast deep*, with its two adjacent strong beats, is out of metrical character.

We can perform a thought experiment to understand Shakespeare's problem. Why did he have to invent a new word to fit the metre? Could he not have chosen an already existing word with the right two-beat rhythm with the meaning of 'vast'? The answer is no, because there was no such word. What words existed in Elizabethan English with the meaning of 'very big'? There was *large* and *huge*, which had both been in English since the thirteenth century, and *great*, which had been around since Anglo-Saxon times. But these were everyday words, which a creative writer might not think sufficiently expressive to express the enormity of the concept in Glendower's mind. Anyway, with just one syllable, they had the wrong rhythm. The words *immense* and *enormous* were available, but they had the wrong rhythm too. There was *massive*, which had the right rhythm, but unfortunately the wrong meaning. *Massive* expresses the idea of concrete size upwards (as in *a massive building*), not the idea of a flat expanse. *Vast* was the only word which had the right meaning and which was sufficiently novel (its first recorded usage is 1575) to make it poetically attractive. Shakespeare seemed to like the word: he uses it himself on another fifteen occasions. Giving *vast* a new ending was therefore an easy solution, for this kind of word creation was commonplace at the time. He seemed to like his creation, too, at least in the late 1590s, for he uses it three times in *Henry V* and again in *The Merchant of Venice*. And he uses the same -*y* device in other adjectival innovations, such as *steepy*, *brisky*, and *plumpy*. We know the basic meaning of the word in these cases (*vast*, *steep*, *brisk*, *plump*). We also know the meaning of the suffix: 'characterized by', as in Modern English *hairy*, *sandy*. We therefore should have no problem working out what such words mean. Metrically induced alternations of this kind do not usually have much semantic consequence.

The operation of metrical constraints on vocabulary is particularly clear when we see Shakespeare using alternative forms of the same word (as happens also in grammar: see p. 190). The choice between *vantage* and *advantage*, *scape* and *escape*, *shrew* and *beshrew* and many other such alternatives can be solely due to the location of the word in the line. Sometimes we can even see the alternative forms juxtaposed, as when both *oft* and *often* appear in *Julius Caesar* (3.1.115):

> Bru.   How many times shall *Caesar* bleed in sport,
>   That now on *Pompeyes* Basis lye along,
>   No worthier then the dust?
> Cassi. So oft as that shall be,
>   So often shall the knot of vs be call'd,
>   The Men that gaue their Country liberty.

Names can be altered too. At one point in *Pericles*, narrator Gower refers to Pericles' counsellor with his full name:

> In *Helycanus* may you well descrie,
>
> (22.114)

At another, he shortens it:

> Good *Helicon* that stayde at home,
>
> (5.17)

There may be a stylistic effect involved (cf. modern *David* and *Dave*), but there is no semantic issue here.

DIFFICULT WORDS

At the other extreme in the difficulty spectrum, there are words where it is not possible to deduce from their form what they might mean – such as *finical, fardel, grise,* and *incony*. There are around a thousand such items in Shakespeare, and in these cases we have no alternative but to learn them – steadily, over a period of time, handling the most frequent ones first – as we would new words in a foreign language. Traditional presentations of difficult vocabulary – notes at the foot of a page of text or at the back of an edition – are not the best way of building up our sense of Shakespeare's lexicon, because there is a natural tendency to see the word only in the context of the line in which it appears, as a literary or dramatic choice, and not to see it in its broader context – as a word in the language as a whole. In any case, no edition has space to explain all the linguistic points, and some editions (because of the thematic approach they have chosen) may actually give very limited information about the meaning of individual words. Also, because our study of individual plays and our theatre visits are usually separated by significant periods of time, it proves difficult to build up an intuition about what is normal in the vocabulary of the period in which Shakespeare was writing – Early Modern English.

Neither is an alphabetical glossary of synonyms the best way of carrying out the task of learning Shakespeare's difficult words. Such an arrangement does not display the words in context, and its A-to-Z structure does not allow the reader to develop a sense of the meaning relations involved: *aunt* is at one end of the alphabet and *uncle* at the other, yet their definitions complement each other. It therefore makes good sense to study their meanings at the same time. Clusters of difficult words can have their meanings mutually illuminated in this way.

It is also useful to explore the whole range of uses of a new word as soon as we come across it, for this can help comprehension in a number of ways. Not only does the exercise help us get to grips with the word when we next meet it, it can actually help us understand the word's force the first time we read it. A typical example is *fardels* in *Hamlet* (3.1.76):

Who would these Fardles beare
To grunt and sweat vnder a weary life,

The notes tell us that it means 'burden, load, bundle', and for many readers the story of *fardel* stops there. But the word is also used by Autolycus and others in *The Winter's Tale* (e.g. 4.4.750):

Aut. The Farthell there? What's i'th' Farthell? Wherefore that Box?

Shep. Sir, there lyes such Secrets in this Farthell and Box, which none must know but the King,

The *Hamlet* example occurs in the middle of his 'To be or not to be' speech, and the association with 'grunting and sweating', along with the general context of suicidal ruminations, can lead to the conclusion that the word must mean 'really heavy and depressing burdens'. That isn't the nuance required when Autolycus meets the Shepherd. And once we realize that fardels can actually be ordinary everyday things, it might make us look again at the force of the line as used by Hamlet.

I find it helpful to approach difficult words in the way that young children do when they acquire vocabulary. Children never learn words randomly, or alphabetically, but always in context and in pairs or small groups. 'That's not the cold tap, that's the hot one', says the parent. Something is 'safe or unsafe.' Things are 'tiny, small, large, huge'. The words define each other, and their meanings reinforce and illuminate each other in various ways. Pairs and clusters of words operate in Shakespearean vocabulary too.

If an instance of *beget* turns up in a play, the editor might well gloss it as 'conceive' (if it is glossed at all) and then make no reference to other words derived from this form. Yet an interesting cluster of derivatives exist. From the base form meaning 'conceive', either literally or metaphorically, we can derive *begotten*, then discuss people who are *first-begotten* or *true-begotten*, and talk about children as yet *unbegot*. Being *first-begotten* is important, as Mortimer says (*1H6*. 2.5.65)

> The first begotten, and the lawfull Heire
> Of *Edward* King,

By contrast, being *misbegotten* is not such good news, and readily becomes a term of insult, as we hear from Falstaff (*1H4*. 2.4.217):

> three mis-be-gotten Knaues, in Kendall Greene, came at my Back,

And we can note in passing that someone who begets is a *begetter* – though the only instance we have of such a person in the Shakespeare canon is the mysterious 'W. H.', named as 'the only begetter' of the *Sonnets*.

Word 'families' of this kind are always worth compiling and exploring, especially when words are really unfamiliar; and some are quite large. At the same time, we also often find pairs of words which define each other in very specific ways, and these need to be related too. For example, some words are opposite or complementary in meaning (*antonyms*), such as *curbed* and *uncurbed*, *fathered* and *unfathered*, *seeming* and *unseeming*. Here the antonymy is shown through the prefix *un-*. In other cases, the oppositeness requires that we know which words go together. What is the opposite of *meanest* in the sense of 'lowest ranking'? This example tells us:

> And rather comfort his distressed plight,
> Then prosecute the meanest or the best
> For these contempts.

(Tit. 4.4.33)

If an excavation under a fortress wall is called a *mine*, what is the counter-measure called? This example tells us:

the Mynes is not according to the disciplines of the Warre; the
concauities of it is not sufficient: for looke you, th' athuer-sarie
[= adversary], you may discusse vnto the Duke, looke you, is digt
himselfe foure yard vnder the Countermines:

(H5. 3.2.57).

There are several other types of semantic relationship linking
words, which can help us get to grips with their meaning. One is the
relationship of inclusion (*hyponymy*): 'an X is a kind of Y'. A *bass
viol* is a kind of *viol*. *Boot-hose* is a kind of *hose*. Another is the
relationship of similarity of meaning (*synonymy*): *advantage* and
vantage, *compter* and *counter*, *coz* and *cousin*. And a further example is the relationship of intensity of meaning, as seen in such pairs
as *lusty* and *over-lusty*, *rash* and *heady-rash*, *amazed* and *all-
amazed*.

The specific associations linking the words in a sentence (the
collocations) can also give clues when we are faced with a totally
opaque word. For example, what does *tray-trip* mean when Sir Toby
says to Maria (*TN*. 2.5.183):

Shall I play my freedome at tray-trip, and becom thy bondslaue?

It is impossible to work out much meaning by considering the word in
isolation; but the collocation with *play* indicates that it must be some
kind of game. Another example, from earlier in the same play, is when
Sir Toby defends Sir Andrew against his critics, calling them
substractors:

they are scoundrels and substractors that say so of him.

The collocation with *scoundrels* gives us a fairly clear indication
of the general sense of this word (see also Edgar's harangue of
Oswald, p. 11).

In many cases, it is sensible to group words into topics (*semantic
fields*), such as 'clothing', 'weapons', 'sailing ships', or 'money', so that
we can more clearly see the relationships between them. Under the

latter heading, for example, we can distinguish between domestic coins (such as *pennies*) and foreign coins (such as *ducats*), and within the former to relate items in terms of their increasing value: *obolus, halfpence, three farthings, penny, twopence, threepence, groat, sixpence, tester/testril, shilling, noble, angel, royal, pound*. That is how we learn a monetary system today, and it is how we can approach the one we find in Shakespeare.

FALSE FRIENDS

In between the extremes of lexical familiarity and unfamiliarity, we find the majority of Shakespeare's difficult words – difficult not because they are different in form from the vocabulary we know today but because they have changed their meaning. In many cases, the meaning change is very slight: *intent* means 'intention'; *glass* means 'looking-glass'. These would rarely cause a problem of understanding. And often the change in meaning, though important, has no real consequence, as when Jack Cade uses the word *meat* (*H6*. 4.9.37):

> Looke on mee well, I haue eate no meate these fiue dayes, yet
> come thou and thy fiue men, and if I doe not leaue you all as dead
> as a doore naile, I pray God I may neuer eate grasse more.

Meat is here being used in the general sense of 'food' (still present in the word *sweetmeat*) – but if we were to interpret it in the modern, restricted sense of 'flesh meat', the effect would not be greatly different.

By contrast, there are several hundred cases where the meaning has changed so much that it would be highly misleading to read in the modern sense. These are the 'false friends' (*faux amis*) of comparative semantics – words in a language which seem familiar but are not. The term comes from foreign-language teaching, where we often find examples such as French *demander*, which does not mean 'demand', but 'ask' (*demand* is translated by *requérir*). False friends in Shakespeare include *naughty* ('wicked'), *heavy* ('sorrowful'), *humorous* ('moody'), *sad* ('serious'), *ecstasy* ('madness'), *owe* ('own'), *merely* ('totally'), and *envious* ('malicious'). 'The Duke is humorous', we hear

Le Beau say about Duke Frederick (*AYLI*. 1.2.256) and wonder why such a jocular person should be treating Orlando so nastily. Only when we learn that *humorous* in this context means 'moody, temperamental, capricious' does the line begin to make some sense.

In all instances of false friends, we need to pay careful attention to the context, which usually helps to eliminate the intrusion of the irrelevant modern meaning. We can see this operating, for example, in *King Lear* (5.1.5):

> *Reg.* Our Sisters man is certainly miscarried.
> *Bast.* 'Tis to be doubted Madam.

If we were to read in the modern meaning of *doubt*, it would suggest that Edmond is disagreeing with Regan, but he is not, as the broader context makes clear. We need a different meaning of *doubt* – 'fear, suspect'. It is a quite frequent usage, occurring in twenty-seven instances across the plays and poems (that is about a fifth of all uses of the verb *doubt*). When Hamlet says

> I doubt some foule play
>
> (*Ham.* 1.2.256)

he thinks there will be, not thinks there won't be. And similarly when young Arthur reflects on his state (*John*. 4.1.19):

> I should be as merry as the day is long:
> And so I would be heere, but that I doubt
> My Vnckle practises more harme to me:

he believes his uncle will, not won't, harm him.

In a number of cases, the old and modern senses of a word were both active in Shakespeare's time. *Doubt* is a case in point. So is *miscarry*, in the above quotation. *Bootless* is another. It sounds as if it means 'without boots', and that was indeed one of its senses. But the more common usage in the plays has the meaning 'useless, pointless, unsuccessful' – it comes from the word *bōt*, which is an Anglo-Saxon word meaning 'good' (modern *better* derives from the same root).

When Miranda reminds her father that her earlier questions had been a 'bootless inquisition' (*Temp.* 1.2.35), she is not suggesting that she asked without any shoes on; she means simply that her questioning had no results. But both senses are needed to explain the repartee between Hotspur and Glendower (*1H4.* 3.1.60):

> *Glend.* Three times hath *Henry Bullingbrooke* made head
>   Against my Power: thrice from the Banks of Wye,
>   And sandy-bottom'd Seuerne, haue I hent him
>   Bootlesse home, and Weather-beaten backe.
> *Hotsp.* Home without Bootes,
>   And in foule Weather too,
>   How scapes he Agues in the Deuils name?

'How does he get away without fevers if he's in bare feet?' asks Hotspur. Glendower ignores the pun.

Directors and actors ignore false friends at their philological peril. There is a famous scene in *Twelfth Night*, when Malvolio falls into the trap laid for him by Sir Toby, Maria, and Fabian. He is reading the letter which he believes to be addressed to him from Olivia, and finds part of it written in prose. This section of the letter begins with the instruction (2.5.139):

> *If this fall into thy hands, reuolue.*

It is rare to find a production of the play which respects the meaning of *revolve*. Most directors and actors pander to the modern meaning, make the actor look puzzled, and then have him affectedly turn round. It gets a good laugh. But it must make Shakespeare turn in his linguistic grave. For *revolve* did not mean 'perform a circular motion' in Shakespeare's day. That sense developed in English a century later – the *OED* cites a first usage of 1713. For Shakespeare, the primary meaning was 'consider, ponder, meditate', and in this sense the usage is neologistic, for *Twelfth Night* is its first recorded instance. The letter-writer is simply saying to Malvolio: 'think very carefully about what this letter contains'. It wouldn't have made a Globe audience laugh at all.

The 'meditative' sense is clearer in two other plays – one of which actually predates the *OED* citation by about a decade. The first known reference to *Twelfth Night* is on 2 February 1602, when a law student at Middle Temple referred to a performance he attended. But in *Richard III*, written in the early 1590s, we find Queen Elizabeth asking Queen Margaret how to curse her enemies (4.4.123). She begins:

> Forbeare to sleepe the night, and fast the day:
> Compare dead happinesse, with liuing woe:

And a few lines later, concludes:

> Reuoluing this, will teach thee how to Curse.

No turning round in circles there. And we have a later example in *Cymbeline* (3.3.14). Belarius tells Guiderius and Arviragus to take themselves off to the top of a hill, and when they get there,

> you may then reuolue what Tales, I haue told you,
> Of Courts, of Princes; of the Tricks in Warre.

No circling movement likely there either.

There are still resonances of the 'meditative' sense of *revolve* in use today. 'All sorts of ideas revolved in his brain', we can still say. So it would be perfectly possible for linguistically aware actors to convey the right sense by using an expression or gesture to suggest Malvolio 'turning things over' in his mind – and to squeeze a laugh out of it too. Alternatively, I suppose, they could quote the young prince in *Richard III* (3.1.15).

> God keepe me from false Friends.

Some further examples of false friends are given in the Appendix (p. 234)

OLD AND NEW WORDS

When we study Shakespeare's vocabulary, it is important to recognize that his period of the language – as all other periods – is not linguistically homogeneous. In Modern English we sense that some words are current, some old, and some new. People refer to the older usages as 'obsolete words' or 'archaisms', the new usages as 'coinages' or 'neologisms'. It is easy to spot an arriving usage, because its novelty is noticed and usually attracts some degree of comment. Usages which are becoming obsolete are rarely commented upon, and tend to pass away in dignified silence.

Early Modern English was a period of extraordinarily dynamic change. The consequences of the Renaissance were sweeping through the language, and causing not a little consternation among people unsure of how they should react to the thousands of new words being introduced, especially from Latin and Greek. There was a great deal of self-consciousness about usage, and the period is remarkable for its lexical inventiveness and experimentation, to which Shakespeare made his own major contribution (see further, p. 161).

From a modern perspective, it is difficult to develop an intuition about the archaisms and neologisms of the past; but they are always there. In Shakespeare several can be found in the introductory remarks of Gower to the various scenes in *Pericles*, where we find *iwis* ('indeed') and *hight* ('called'), as well as such older verb forms as *speken* ('speak') and *y-clad* ('clothed'). Other examples include *eyne* ('eyes'), *shoon* ('shoes'), *wight* ('person'), and *eke* ('also'). All of these would have been considered old fashioned or archaic by the Shakespearean audience. Several take us all the way back to Middle English.

For neologisms, we are helped by the fact that some of Shakespeare's characters actually tell us that they are dealing with new words and usages. Berowne describes the Spanish visitor to court, Don Armado, as 'A man of fire-new words' (*LLL*. 1.1.176), and Armado himself is well aware of the way language is needed to keep the classes apart: 'the posteriors of this day, which the rude multitude call the afternoon' (5.2.84). Mercutio thinks of Tybalt in the same way. Tybalt's 'new tuning of accent' (see p. 104) is not only a matter of pronunciation, but of vocabulary as well (*Rom.* 2.3.26):

> The Pox of such antique lisping affecting phantacies, these new tuners of accent: Iesu a very good blade, a very tall man, a very good whore.

Evidently Mercutio is irritated by the use of *very* as an intensifying word with a positive adjective, a linguistic trend which was emerging at the end of the sixteenth century. Also coming into fashion at that time was *accommodate*, which makes Bardolph reflect (*2H4*. 3.2.72), the sexual sense of *occupy* ('fornicate') noticed by Doll Tearsheet in the same play (2.4.144, Quarto text), and various new senses of *humour* ('mood', 'whim') which are obsessively used by Nym in *The Merry Wives of Windsor* and elsewhere.

That there was a level of style in which 'hard words' were the norm is plain from the many mistaken attempts at these words – malapropisms – put into the mouths of ordinary people, such as Mistress Quickly/Hostess, Dogberry, and various clowns. Launcelot says to Bassanio, 'the suit is impertinent to myself' – by which he means 'pertinent' (*MV*. 2.2.126). Shakespeare seems not to have much liked pompous language, for several of his major characters poke fun at linguistic affectation – such as Hamlet at Osrick (*Ham*. 5.2), or Kent at Oswald (*Lear*. 2.2.103: see further, p. 223). A whole conversation can be summed up in a single parodic moment. After taking part in an erudite conversation with Armado and Nathaniel, the schoolteacher Holofernes turns to constable Anthony Dull (*LLL*. 5.1.144):

> *Via* good-man *Dull*, thou hast spoken no word all this while.
>
> [*Via* = 'Come']
>
> *Dull*. Nor vnderstood none neither sir.

COINAGES

People sometimes say they can always spot a Shakespearean coinage on sight, when reading one of the plays; and indeed distinctive words do sometimes leap off the page. Usages such as *exsufflicate* 'puffed up' (*Oth*. 3.3.186) or *anthropophaginian* 'cannibal' (*Wiv*. 4.5.8) are idiosyncratic by any standards. But we can be easily deceived. Which of the three words in this famous line would you rate as a Shakespearean coinage (*Ham.* 1.5.77)?

> Vnhouzzled, disappointed, vnnaneld, [= unhouseled ... unanealed]

People usually go for the first and third. If you thought this, then you were right about *unaneled* (meaning 'without having received the last sacraments'), but wrong about *unhouseled* ('without the Eucharist'), which was used by Thomas More seventy years before. And if you disregarded *disappointed*, you would have been wrong there too. For, in the sense of 'unfurnished, unprepared', this is indeed a first recorded use by Shakespeare (but note the caution on p. 8). Some editions actually print the word as *dis-appointed*, which more clearly suggests its link to other sixteenth- and seventeenth-century usages as *ill appointed* and *well appointed*. It is these less vivid or dramatic words, such as *accessible, domineering*, and *indistinguishable*, which are the ones usually missed when people go coinage-spotting.

Also missed are the many cases of conversion (p. 148). *Sepulchre* as a noun dates from around 1200. As a verb, however, its first recorded use is in Silvia's caustic instruction to Proteus about where to bury his love (*TGV.* 4.2.113):

> Goe to thy Ladies graue and call hers thence,
> Or at the least, in hers, sepulcher thine.

Shudder as a verb is fourteenth century. As a noun it is first recorded when Timon harangues the two bawds (*Tim.* 4.3.138):

> you'l sweare, terribly sweare
> Into strong shudders,

There are some 200 cases where a new use relates to a particular part-of-speech in this way.

Even more difficult is the spotting of a neologistic sense in a familiar word. Take *angel*. In its sense of 'divine messenger', this is Anglo-Saxon in origin, occurring in the tenth-century Lindisfarne

Gospels. But in the sense of 'lovely being' – a person resembling an angel – the *OED*'s first citation is in fact Romeo's reaction on hearing Juliet's first words: 'Oh speake againe bright Angell' (*Rom.* 2.1.68). Or take *wicked*. In its sense of 'bad in moral character or conduct', this is a usage from the early Middle Ages; but in a weaker sense, meaning 'mischievous' or 'sly', the first known use is Rosalind/Ganymede's description of Cupid as 'that same wicked Bastard of *Venus*' (*AYLI.* 4.1.201). Senses are much more important than words, but they have never been counted. I do not know how many new senses we might attribute to Shakespeare, using the *OED* data.

One of the most important features of Shakespeare's word-creation is its exploratory character. In at least one instance he invents the same word twice over, and at roughly the same time. For example, he wanted to use a noun derived from the verb *annex*, which had been in English since around 1425. Rosencrantz uses one form in *Hamlet* (3.3.21):

Each small annexment, pettie consequence

And the narrator uses another in *A Lover's Complaint* (l.208):

With th'annexions of faire gems inricht,

Choosing a word-form is one thing; choosing which meaning to assign to it is another. And with some coinages we can see the gradual way in which a new meaning slots into the existing semantic network. The use of *unfledged* is an example.

Fledge is from the same root as *fly*, and during the Middle Ages it emerged as an adjective describing the state of birds whose feathers were fully developed. In the second half of the sixteenth century it began to be used as a verb, referring to the 'acquiring of feathers'. Shakespeare early on saw the potential for development: if birds grow feathers, then why not an analogous process in humans? When Falstaff describes the Prince as one 'whose Chin is not yet fledg'd' (*2H4*. 1.2.20), this is the first recorded use of the word in that sense.

There are occasional uses of *unfledge* as a verb from the end of the sixteenth century, but the adjectival use, *unfledged*, is very largely Shakespearean. Of its four senses in the *OED*, he is cited first for three of them. There is the literal sense shown in *Cymbeline* (3.3.27): Guiderius describes the life-style of himself and his brother in ornithological terms; they do not yet have enough feathers to fly:

> we poore vnfledg'd,
> Haue neuer wing'd from view o'th' nest.

From birds, Shakespeare then applies the word to people, and develops the sense of 'immature' or 'inexperienced'. *Hamlet* (1.3.65) is the first example here, when Polonius advises Laertes:

> But doe not dull thy palme, with entertainment
> Of each vnhatch't, vnfledg'd Comrade.

And from there, it is a short step to the sense 'characteristic of youth', seen first in *The Winter's Tale* (1.2.78), when Polixenes says to Hermione:

> In those vnfledg'd dayes, was my Wife a Girle;

We see this kind of 'multiple invention' quite often. There are many examples where Shakespeare seems to be trying out a word in a number of different ways. They show the range of meanings in English being significantly extended. Moreover, examples of this kind tell us something important about how to think of linguistic creativity. People often see inventiveness in a language as just a matter of creating new words. But it is much more than this. It is also a matter of creating new senses from existing words. Shakespeare, evidently, does both – and the latter much more commonly than the former, judging by the citations in the *OED*. It is this readiness to engage in semantic exploration which is so characteristic of the vocabulary found in the plays – and it is an impression which would remain with us, even if future historical lexicological research were to find prior instances of the words in English.

CLUSTERS

We are used to thinking of coinages as isolated usages: we encounter them every now and then, as we read or listen. This is what we would expect. Coinages by their nature are sporadic. If an author uses too many, the language will become so unfamiliar that no one will understand it. Indeed, one of the common complaints about mid-sixteenth-century writers was that they introduced so many Latin and Greek coinages into their work that it became impenetrable. Thomas Wilson, in *The Arte of Rhetorique* (1553) was one who condemned 'straunge ynkehorne termes' – words which were so long and elaborate that they used up excessive amounts of ink from the ink-horn – to the extent that 'if some of their mothers were aliue, thei were not able to tell what they say'! We can imagine that dramatists would be the least likely people to fall into the ink-horn trap.

On the other hand, there is no linguistic rule which says that coinages must be restricted to single instances. And we can well imagine occasions when an original and intricate thought requires more than one invented word for its complete expression. Certainly, as we explore the way Shakespeare introduces his new words, we find them often appearing in clusters of two or three. There are none over the first eight lines of this next speech (*Ham.* 1.4.39): the words and their lexical associations (collocations: p. 155) are all fairly predictable. But in line 9, something different happens: we encounter *hearsed, cerements,* and *enurned,* as well as two distinctive collocations, *jaws* which are *ponderous* and *marble.*

> Angels and Ministers of Grace defend vs:
> Be thou a Spirit of health, or Goblin damn'd,
> Bring with thee ayres from Heauen, or blasts from Hell,
> Be thy euents wicked or charitable,
> Thou com'st in such a questionable shape
> That I will speake to thee. Ile call thee *Hamlet,*
> King, Father, Royall Dane: Oh, oh, answer me,
> Let me not burst in Ignorance; but tell

> Why thy Canoniz'd bones Hearsed in death,
>
> Haue burst their cerments, why the Sepulcher
>
> Wherein we saw thee quietly enurn'd,
>
> Hath op'd his ponderous and Marble iawes,
>
> To cast thee vp againe?

This is by no means an isolated case. A little later in the play (1.3.129) we find Polonius using conventional language before breaking out into two neologistic images in quick succession – *investments* and *implorators*:

> For Lord *Hamlet*,
>
> Beleeue so much in him, that he is young,
>
> And with a larger tether may he walke,
>
> Then may be giuen you. In few, *Ophelia*,
>
> Doe not beleeue his vowes; for they are Broakers,
>
> Not of the eye, which their Inuestments show:
>
> But meere implorators of vnholy Sutes,
>
> Breathing like sanctified and pious bonds,
>
> The better to beguile.

It is this tendency for coinages to cluster that is part of the reason why comprehension varies so dramatically: we suddenly encounter islands of difficulty which force us to the glossary or notes.

Sometimes the incomprehension island is larger than we expect – as in the Greek council scene in *Troilus and Cressida* (1.3). Agamemnon sets the tone of what follows in a speech remarkable for its linguistic ornateness, and editions of the play routinely comment on its elaborate character. Here are its opening lines, with possible coinages underlined:

> Princes:
>
> What greefe hath set the Iaundies on your cheekes?
>
> The ample <u>proposition</u> that hope makes
>
> In all <u>designes</u>, begun on earth below
>
> Fayles in the promist largenesse: checkes and <u>disasters</u>

Grow in the veines of actions highest rear'd.
As knots by the <u>conflux</u> of meeting sap,
Infect the sound Pine, and <u>diuerts</u> his Graine
<u>Tortiue</u> and erant from his course of growth.

The most obvious coinages are the unfamiliar words, such as *conflux* ('flowing together') and *tortive* ('twisted, tortuous'). There are more of these later in the speech, when he describes the Greek actions as 'the <u>protractiue</u> trials of great Ioue, / To finde <u>persistiue</u> constancie in men'. *Protractive* means 'lengthening out'; *persistive* means 'tending to persist'. The two words are close to tautology – but then, the whole of Agamemnon's speech is saying in many words what might be said in very few.

The other Greek leaders accommodate to him, so that throughout the rest of the scene our ears are bethumped by such new words as *untimbered* ('frail'), *importless* ('unimportant'), *insisture* ('constancy' – though the meaning is debated), *neglection* ('neglect'), *scaffoldage* ('stage platform'), and *exposure* ('vulnerability'). And the coinages continue later in the play: *rejoindure* ('reunion'), *embrasure* ('embrace'), *multipotent* ('most powerful'), *oppugnancy* ('opposition') … No other play has so many.

The classical vocabulary contributes greatly to the grandiose style, which has been variously interpreted. The epic characters need a suitably heroic way of talking, and this is appropriately reinforced by their grand words. On the other hand, the words are indeed *very* grand – so grandiloquent, indeed, that they draw attention to themselves, and thus to the gap between words and actions which lies at the heart of the Greek situation.

But it is not only the unfamiliar-looking words which give this speech its semantically novel character. Several well-established words are being used in new senses:

- Various general senses of *proposition*, such as 'proposal for discussion', had been in English since the fourteenth century, but here Shakespeare is using the word differently to mean 'something put forward for acceptance' – in short, an 'offer'. The *OED* gives just one other example of this use a few decades later (*the proposition of rewards*). It is a usage which never survived.

- *Design* counts as a neologism only if we see the word as being used here with a general meaning. In its sense of a specific mental structuring – a 'plan', 'scheme', 'project' – it was already in widespread use when Shakespeare was writing. But in the less specific sense of 'aim' or 'intention', the usage here is the earliest recorded.

- *Disaster* is a neologism in a different play – when Horatio talks about 'disasters in the sun' (*Hamlet*, 1.1.118, Q2). There it means an 'inauspicious sight'. In the more general sense of 'calamity', it was coming into the language in Shakespeare's day, and there are several other people who are known to have used it earlier. However, the word would have been sufficiently fresh in people's minds to add to the overall impression of lexical novelty.

- *Divert* was much older – a fifteenth-century import from French – and it developed a range of senses in the sixteenth century. Some of these are neologistic, including the sense of 'turn awry', which could be relevant here and also later in the scene (1.99) when Ulysses talks about the various horrors which 'diuert, and cracke' the peaceful state of countries.

'Words pay no debts; giue her deedes', says Pandarus to Troilus about Cressida (*Tro.* 3.2.54). The advice might have been addressed to the Greek commander too, who in Act 1 of the play is much better at words than deeds.

REPETITIONS

When authors consciously create words that they consider to be particularly apt, we can easily understand them wanting to use them a second time. It is therefore interesting to see Shakespeare sometimes using a coinage twice in fairly quick succession, and then never again. Here are three examples.

In *Cymbeline*, *outsell*, meaning 'exceed in value, surpass', is used in relation to Innogen. Iachimo reports his meeting with her to Posthumus, saying (2.4.102):

> Her pretty Action, did out-sell her guift

and in the next Act (3.5.75) Cloten reflects on her qualities in the same way:

> she hath all courtly parts more exquisite
> Then Lady, Ladies, Woman, from euery one
> The best she hath, and she of all compounded
> Out-selles them all.

Shakespeare doesn't use the word anywhere else.

Incony is another example, meaning 'fine, darling, rare'. This is one of those words which keep etymologists in business, for its origins are uncertain. It probably relates to *cony*, 'rabbit', which developed as a term of male-to-female endearment. It was pronounced 'cunny', rhyming with *money* and *honey*, and this pronunciation inevitably gave it an indecent association, which was also current around 1600. It seems to have been a popular word – Marlowe, Middleton, and Jonson all use it – but the earliest instances in the *OED* are ascribed to Shakespeare. It is a Costardism. Costard refers to Don Armado as (*LLL*. 3.1.133):

> My sweete ounce of mans flesh, my in-conie Iew:

and 200 lines later (4.1.143) describes the repartee as:

> O my troth most sweete iests, most inconie vulgar wit,

Here also, these two instances are the only Shakespearean ones.

A slightly different instance is *discandy*, meaning 'dissolve, liquefy, melt away'. Antony uses it when reflecting on those who have left him for Caesar (*Ant.* 4.12.22):

> The hearts
> That pannelled me at heeles, to whom I gaue
> Their wishes, do dis-Candie, melt their sweets
> On blossoming *Caesar*:

Is he recalling the same neologism used by Cleopatra a few scenes earlier (3.13.165)? Antony has seen her let Thidias kiss her hand, and accuses her of being cold-hearted. She responds with vehemence, calling down hail from heaven onto herself, to dissolve her completely, if the accusation be true:

> the next Caesarian smile,
> Till by degrees the memory of my wombe,
> Together with my braue Egyptians all,
> By the discandering of this pelleted storme,
> Lye grauelesse,

The new word evidently bemused the Folio compositor, who printed it as *discandering*.

Sometimes the double usage cuts across plays, and perhaps therefore adds a tiny note of confirmation to hypotheses about dating. *Dry-beat* is a case in point, meaning 'cudgel, thrash'. This isn't a Shakespearean neologism (though of course he might have coined it himself, unaware of earlier usage): it was being used around the time that he was born. But in the plays, it appears twice, in *Romeo and Juliet*. Mercutio tells Tybalt he means to take one of his nine lives (3.1.78):

> that I meane to make bold withall, and as you shall vse me hereafter dry beate the rest of the eight.

And later in the play, Peter harangues the Second Musician by saying (4.5.122):

> I will drie-beate you with an yron wit,

There is only one other related use, and that appears in *Love's Labour's Lost*, when Berowne reflects on the lords' defeat by the ladies (5.2.263):

By heauen, all drie beaten with pure scoffe.

According to Wells and Taylor, *Romeo and Juliet* is 1594–5. *Love's Labour's Lost* is 1593–5 – but, perhaps, more 1594 than earlier, if the lexical similarity is persuasive. The frequency and distribution of neologisms can be a possible source of evidence, not just about authorship, but also about the links between plays.

SIGNPOSTS

When Shakespeare's coinages are examined together, interesting patterns emerge, some of which point to conclusions of general literary or dramatic interest. His use of the prefix *un-* is illustrative. He seemed to have had a penchant for using *un-* in imaginative ways. There are 314 instances in the *OED* where he is the first citation for an *un-* word. Most of them are adjectives (e.g. *uncomfortable, uncompassionate, unearthly, uneducated*), and there are a few adverbs (e.g. *unaware, unheedfully*) and nouns (e.g. *an undeserver*), but there are no less than 62 instances where the prefix has been added to an already existing verb, such as *unshout, unspeak, uncurse, unswear*, and the remarkable *undeaf*:

> Againe vncurse their Soules;
>
> (R2. 3.2.137)
>
> Vn-sweare faith sworne,
>
> (John. 3.1.245)
>
> My deaths sad tale, may yet vndeafe his eare.
>
> (R2. 2.1.16)

There are other dramatic images: Lady Macbeth calls on the spirits to 'vnsex' her (*Mac.* 1.5.39). Bolingbroke castigates Bushy and the others for their misleading of Richard, 'By you vnhappied' (R2. 3.1.10). Iago, searching for a simile to show how appalled he is at the fight involving Cassio, opts for 'As if some Planet had vnwitted men' (*Oth.* 2.3.176). The First Senator, who seems to have a liking for the *un-* usage, worries that the inflammatory words of Sicinius will 'vnbuild the Citie' (*Cor.* 3.1.197). The tone is not always high drama. There is surely sarcasm in Agamemnon's question to Ulysses about Achilles (*Tro.* 2.3.166)

> Why, will he not vpon our faire request,
> Vntent his person, and share the ayre with vs?

And there is elegant beauty, too, when the First Lord reports Celia's absence (*AYLI.* 2.2.7):

> They found the bed vntreasur'd of their Mistris.

Are the repeated quotations from *Coriolanus*, *Richard II*, and *Macbeth* significant? If we check the novel uses of '*un-* + verb' against the dates of the plays as given in the *OED*, there is indeed a trend. Some 30 per cent of these coinages are in just four plays – *Richard II*, *Macbeth*, *Troilus*, and *Hamlet*. Some of the novel uses, of course, apply only to just one sense of a verb. For example, *unbend* in other meanings ('release, relax') is known from well before Shakespeare; but he is the first to use it in the sense of 'weaken', when Lady Macbeth says to her husband, 'You doe vnbend your Noble strength' (2.2.45). Here are the eighteen verbs:

- *Richard II*: uncurse, undeaf, undeck, unhappy
- *Hamlet*:   uncharge, unhand, unmask, unpeg
- *Troilus*:   unlock, untent, untie, unveil
- *Macbeth*:   unbend, unfix, unmake, unprovoke, unspeak, unsex.

The last three of these plays are all 1600 or later, that year felt to be so significant by, among others, Frank Kermode in *Shakespeare's Language*.[1] Is there any difference in Shakespeare's usage, pre- and post-1600? Indeed there is. Using the *OED*'s dates, there are twenty-four instances in the twenty plays pre-1600, with seven plays not containing any instance at all. Post-1600 there are thirty-eight instances in eighteen plays, with only four not having any examples (*H8*, *TNK*, *Ant*, *AWW*). Half the lexical creativity with this form, in fact, appears between 1600 and 1607. The odd one out, in this scenario, is *Richard II*. But what does Kermode say? Commenting on the famous 'I have been studying ...' speech (5.5), he observes: 'one might foretell, from this point of vantage, a hugely different style'. And Stanley Wells, in his Penguin edition, describes the language of *Richard II* as both 'immensely complex and unusually self-conscious'. *Un-*, in its tiny way, has a part to play in fuelling these grander linguistic intuitions.

COLLOCATIONS

The focus on individual words has led to an unfortunate neglect of Shakespeare's collocations (p. 155), which by their nature present us with more striking images than we find in individual words. Collocations are the formal expectancies that exist between words in a sequence. Most of the time we do not notice them, because they are so ordinary: in Modern English, *spick* is obligatorily followed by *span*, and *auspicious* is likely to be followed by a time/event word, such as *occasion*. The UK television game-show *Blankety-Blank* used to get people to guess what the likely collocations of a word were: 'He was green with –?' There are very few words that can be used to fill the blank in this sentence. *He was green with delight* is definitely wrong.

Poets especially love to break normal collocational rules (p. 165), and Shakespeare is one of the greatest rule-breakers the language has seen. In this example, four collocation expectations are disturbed in just two lines (*Ham.* 3.2.58):

> No, let the Candied tongue, like absurd pompe,
> And crooke the pregnant Hindges of the knee,
> Where thrift may follow faining? [usually emended to 'fawning',
>   which appears in Q2]

They are striking images: *tongues* being *candied*, 'sweet-talking speakers'; *pomp* being *absurd* – the complete reverse of the word's usual collocations; the *hinges of the knee* being *pregnant* – the adjective means 'well-disposed, ready'; and abstract *thrift* being animated by *fawning*. It is these juxtapositions of images which stay with us, and which provide us with much of Shakespeare's quotability.

A useful technique is to take a single word, such as *time*, and explore its collocational range. Many temporal metaphors of today were also around in Elizabethan English. There we will find people spending, losing, and wasting time, just as they do now. But Shakespeare revels in alternative images of time, going well beyond the everyday to metamorphose and personify time in different ways. 'A little time will melt her frozen thoughts', says the Duke in *The Two Gentlemen of Verona* (3.2.9). And in other plays we find time *untangling, reviving, sowing, blessing, conspiring, brawling, begetting, weeping, inviting, unfolding, ministering, expiring,* and much more. People in the plays also deal with time innovatively: they *hoodwink* it, *redeem* it, *persecute* it, *confound* it, *greet* it, *name* it, *obey* it, *mock* it, *weigh* it, *jump over* it, and a great deal else. The *locus classicus* for imaginative verb-use with *time* is the dialogue between the lovers Rosalind and Orlando in *As You Like It* (3.2.291).

> Time trauels in diuers paces, with diuers persons: Ile tel you who Time ambles withall, who Time trots withall, who Time gallops withall, and who he stands stil withall.

Collocations are especially interesting when they relate to a word which is itself a neologism, such as *auspicious*. Shakespeare is in fact responsible for both the first and the second citations for this word in the *OED*. The first is said to be in 1601 (in *All's Well That Ends Well*, where fortune is described as an 'auspicious mistris', 3.3.8), and the second is in 1610 (in *The Tempest*, 'auspicious gales', 5.1.318). Shakespeare used the word on four other occasions too:

- in *Hamlet* (1.2.11), in a usage which probably antedates the *OED* one:

  With one Auspicious, and one Dropping eye,
- in *The Winter's Tale* (4.4.52):

  O Lady Fortune,
  Stand you auspicious.
- in *King Lear* (2.1.39):

> Here stood he in the dark, his sharpe Sword out,
> Mumbling of wicked charmes, coniuring the Moone
> To stand auspicious Mistris.

- and again in *The Tempest* (1.2.183):

> I finde my *Zenith* doth depend vpon
> A most auspitious starre,

One imagines, given the freshness of the word *auspicious*, that each of these collocations would have made an impact on the audience. This suggestion is reinforced if we look at the other adjectives which were being used with these nouns around that time. The adjectives which are found in *OED* quotations, pre-Shakespeare, for *mistress* are *low*, *worthy*, *special*, *absolute*, *great* (twice), *noble*, *sovereign*, and *sweet* – all rather literal and predictable. Those for *fortune* – not very many (this word tended to be used as a solitary noun) – are *good* (twice), *fair*, *evil*, *extreme*, and *great* – again, not a very imaginative set. *Auspicious* does seem to be a somewhat more creative adjectival collocation for these nouns.

PERSPECTIVE

As I pointed out in Chapter 1 (p. 13), cases of lexical difficulty in Shakespeare amount to no more than 10 per cent of all the words in the canon. It is not difficult to find extracts where anyone who speaks Modern English would find no further linguistic study needed at all. Spelling and punctuation aside, long stretches of text are virtually the same as they would be if written today in an equivalent style. A case in point is this exchange from *Romeo and Juliet* (2.2.167):

> *Iul.* What a clock to morrow
> Shall I send to thee?
> *Rom.* By the houre of nine.
> *Iul.* I will not faile, 'tis twenty yeares till then,
> I haue forgot why I did call thee backe.
> *Rom.* Let me stand here till thou remember it.
> *Iul.* I shall forget, to haue thee still stand there,

> Remembring how I Loue thy company.
> Rom. And Ile still stay, to haue thee still forget,
> Forgetting any other home but this.
> Iul. 'Tis almost morning, I would haue thee gone,

The two recurrent features of difference, *'tis* and *thou/thee/thy*, still have resonance today: *'tis* may look strange in writing, but it is common in modern English colloquial speech; and *thou* forms are still encountered in some religious and regional expression (see further, p. 193). *Forgot* is used for modern standard English *forgotten*; but as the two forms are so close, and as *forgot* is still heard in several non-standard dialects today, there should be no problem. Likewise, though the phrasings *what o'clock* and *by the hour of nine* feel slightly old-fashioned, we can readily interpret them. The only possible difficulty in the passage is the sense of *still*, 'constantly'; but as this is so close to one of the modern meanings of the word, 'now as before' (the sense in which I used it two sentences ago), any potential for misinterpretation is minor. In sum, a modern intuition encountering this dialogue would understand it without special help.

At the opposite extreme, there are extracts such as the following, where the difficulty is evident. Friar Laurence is advising Juliet how to escape from her dilemma (*Rom.* 4.2.93). It is a crucial part of the plot, with the mood urgent, so the language needs to be grasped quickly; but the unfamiliar words and phrasing can produce a dip in the level of comprehension just when we do not want it.

> Take thou this Violl being then in bed,
> And this distilling liquor drinke thou off,
> When presently through all thy veines shall run,
> A cold and drowsie humour: for no pulse
> Shall keepe his natiue progresse, but surcease:

Every line has at least one word which needs some glossing, and the result is a temporary uncertainty – temporary, because later in the speech there are clearer passages which make it plain what is to happen.

And in this borrowed likenesse of shrunke death
Thou shalt continue two and forty houres,
And then awake, as from a pleasant sleepe.

People who argue that Shakespearean vocabulary is unintelligible and inaccessible tend to quote the hard words and ignore the easier ones. It is always a good practice to read the whole of a speech before worrying about the difficulties found in a part of it.

8 'Talk of a noun and a verb': Shakespearean grammar

Grammar makes sense of language. That is what it is for. Words by themselves do not make sense. Individual words are too ambiguous, because their multiple meanings compete for our attention. *Table*, for example, has half a dozen meanings in Early Modern English, and the only way we can determine which is which is by observing how the word is used in context – which means, in a sentence:

> My Tables, my Tables; meet it is I set it downe, (*Ham*. 1.5.107) – 'writing tablets'
> you are well vnderstood to bee a perfecter gyber for the Table, then a necessary Bencher in the Capitoll. (*Cor*. 2.1.77; *gyber* = 'joker') – 'dinner table'
> when he plaies at Tables, chides the Dice
> In honorable tearmes (*LLL*. 5.2.326) – 'backgammon'

If we want to 'make sense' of Shakespeare, we have to look to his grammar.

As with vocabulary (see Chapter 7), the grammatical rules of English have changed very little over the past 400 years: some 90 per cent of the word-orders and word formations used by Shakespeare are still in use today, as can be seen in this speech of Benedick's from *Much Ado About Nothing* (3.1.209), here shown in modern orthography:

> This can be no trick. The conference was sadly borne. They have the truth of this from Hero. They seem to pity the lady. It seems her affections have their full bent. Love me! Why, it must be requited. I hear how I am censured. They say I will bear myself proudly if I perceive the love come from her. They say too that she will rather die than give any sign of affection. I did never think to marry. I must not seem proud.

A grammatical parsing of this extract would bring to light over a hundred points of sentence, clause, phrase, and word structure. All of them are found in Modern English.

There is nonetheless a widespread impression that Shakespeare's grammar is very different from what we find today. The impression chiefly arises because of the way grammar operates within discourse, especially in verse speeches where the constraints of the metre complicate word-order. But even in prose it is not difficult to find speeches which look as difficult, from a grammatical point of view, as the above looks easy. This sentence from the unexpectedly articulate First Watch in *Coriolanus* (5.2.38) is so long and convoluted as to tax any actor's ability to convey the meaning, let alone to maintain breath control:

> Can you, when you have pushed out your gates the very defender of them, and in a violent popular ignorance given your enemy your shield, think to front his revenges with the easy groans of old women, the virginal palms of your daughters, or with the palsied intercession of such a decayed dotant as you seem to be?

But even here, it should be noted, there is nothing that could not appear in Modern English.

Grammar reflects the way we think – more precisely, the way we process our thoughts – and the main unit in which we organize our thoughts is the sentence. We need to organize our thoughts into sentence *sequences* too (into paragraphs, stanzas, speeches . . .) – something we will explore in Chapter 9 – but the basis of our self-expression lies in the way we combine words to make individual sentences. It is the sentence, as suggested above, which literally 'makes' sense of what we are saying. And it is the overall length of a sentence, the way we order the words within it, and the way we display its internal structure through punctuation (in writing) and prosody (in speech), which controls our impression of grammatical difficulty. The more complex the thing we want to say, the longer and more internally complex our sentence is likely to be. We can try to break our thought down into smaller elements, and keep the sentences short. This is what Benedick has successfully done, and what the First Watch is having some difficulty doing. Whether we consider the latter's problem to be a character note, a response to his situation (he is talking to Menenius), or just a piece of poor writing, goes beyond the remit of this book.

There are two branches to the study of grammar: syntax and morphology. *Syntax* – the word is from Greek *syntaxis*, 'arrangement' – is the study of sentence structure, and in particular (for a language like English) the analysis of word-order. *Morphology* is the study of word structure – of the way words vary their shape to express grammatical relationships, such as by adding inflectional endings (e.g. *think > think'st, thinketh, thinks, thinking*), and of the way they build up complex units out of simple elements (e.g. *witch > bewitch > bewitchment*). Traditional accounts of Shakespeare's grammar presented detailed accounts of morphology, listing all the irregular verbs, adjectives, and so on that differed from Modern English, and paid relatively little attention to word-order. This is the wrong way round. It is to study the few odd-looking trees at the expense of the forest as a whole.

Having said that, it is important to know what the odd-looking trees are, because they do appear rather frequently in the texts. There are only a few old pronoun uses, but some of them are very common – over 13,000 instances in the canon of *thou, thee, thy, thine*, and *thyself*, for instance. It therefore makes good sense to know about the forms and meanings of the words which have a distinctively Elizabethan morphology, so that they do not become a distraction when we have to deal with the syntactic factors which are fundamental to the expression of Shakespeare's meaning. A single morphological oddity can give a grammatical colouring to a speech which is out of all proportion to its linguistic significance, as in this extract from *Hamlet* (5.1.271):

Come show me what thou'lt doe.
Woo't weepe? Woo't fight? Woo't teare thy selfe?

Woo't drinke vp *Esile*, eate a Crocodile?
Ile doo't. Dost thou come heere to whine;
To outface me with leaping in her Graue?

Woo't is a colloquial form of *wilt* or *wouldst thou*. It is a rare literary usage, but here its repetition, along with the other contracted forms and the use of *thou*, dominates the impression we have of the grammar, and gives an alien appearance to a speech which in all other respects is grammatically identical with Modern English, as this 'translation' shows:

Show me what you will do.
Will you weep, will you fight, will you tear yourself,
Will you drink up eisel, eat a crocodile?
I'll do it. Do you come here to whine,
To outface me with leaping in her grave?

SIMILARITIES AND DIFFERENCES

A reference grammar of Shakespeare's usage – such as Norman Blake's *A Grammar of Shakespeare's Language* – is as important as a dictionary is for his vocabulary. Such a grammar, as its name suggests, provides information about *all* aspects of morphology and syntax, not just the irregular or stylistically distinctive features. This is important, as there are always three perspectives to take into account when studying Shakespearean grammar: forms or constructions used by him that we still use today; forms or constructions used by him that are not used today; and forms or constructions we use today which are not used by him at all.

We have to be particularly on our guard against reading into Shakespeare the grammatical norms from a later period, and especially the unreal prescriptions that eighteenth-century grammarians and their successors imposed onto English. For example, one of the basic rules of Modern English is the 'concord rule' in the present tense: a third-person singular subject takes a singular verb (*she walks*) and a third-person plural subject takes a plural verb (*they jump*). Even today there are arguments over what counts as 'correct English'. Is it *committee is* or *committee are*? Is it *bacon and eggs is* or *bacon and eggs are*? A lot depends on how the subject is being perceived: *committee* viewed as an aggregate of individuals prompts plural concord; *committee* viewed as a monolithic unit prompts singular. Generations of prescriptive grammarians worried about such sentences, failing to appreciate that in English both possibilities exist.

We have to adopt similar thinking when looking at Shakespearean usage, bearing in mind that the rules were not as tightly constrained as in later centuries. A plural subject with a singular verb requires no emendation:

> My old <u>bones akes</u>:
>
> (*Temp.* 3.3.2)

> what <u>cares these roarers</u> for the name of King?
>
> (*Temp.* 1.1.16)

> the Duke is comming from the Temple, and there <u>is two or three Lords & Ladies</u> more married
>
> (*MND.* 4.2.16)

Nor does a singular verb following a coordinated subject:

> Our Master and Mistresse seekes you:
>
> (*AYLI.* 5.1.59)

> all disquiet, horror, and perturbation followes her.
>
> (*Ado.* 2.1.238)

'Double negatives' provide another example of a usage affected by prescriptivism. Despite centuries of using multiple negative words to express increasing intensity of negation, sentences such as *I haven't got none neither* came to be banned from standard English, and are now considered to be a mark of uneducated speech and writing. The only ones permitted are those where there is a mathematical 'cancelling out' of the negative meaning. Thanks to Latin grammar, the grammatical issue was known in Shakespeare's time. As Feste puts it:

> so that conclusions to be as kisses, if your foure negatiues make your two affirmatiues, why then the worse for my friends, and the better for my foes.

(TN. 5.1.19)

There are indeed some cases where we have to apply this reasoning, especially when a negative word associates with a negative prefix, as when Hamlet says:

> Let me be cruell, not vnnaturall,

(Ham. 3.2.402)

And there are even some cases where the negatives pile up in this way (Ado. 3.1.71):

> Vrsu. Sure, sure, such carping is not commendable.
> Hero. No, not to be so odde, and from all fashions,
>   As Beatrice is, cannot be commendable,
>   But who dare tell her so?

The context makes it clear enough that Hero is saying that Beatrice is not to be praised for her behaviour – but working it out from the sequence of negatives is tricky. For the most part, though, double or triple negatives in Shakespeare do not involve such complications. The rule is simple: the more negatives in the clause, the more emphatic the negative meaning.

> I sawe Marke Antony offer him a Crowne, yet 'twas not a Crowne neyther, 'twas one of these Coronets:

(JC. 1.2.234)

> Nor vnderstood none neither sir.

(LLL. 5.1.144)

There is no mathematical cancelling out of meaning intended here. Nonetheless, this did not stop some nineteenth-century editors

emending texts to avoid the multiple negation – a practice which
I dearly hope would never take place today.

NOUNS

Nouns provide a simple illustration of the similarities and differences
between grammatical usage today and that which was the norm in Early
Modern English. Nouns vary for number: they can be singular (*boy*) or
plural (*boys*), regular (adding an -*s*) or irregular (*woman, women*). They
also vary for case, expressing possession (*boy, boy's, boys'; woman,
woman's, women's*). Some nouns are countable (*a crown, a crocodile*),
some are uncountable (*music, pomp*). Some are common (*boy, crown*),
some are proper (*Henry, London*). Most of these uses are the same today
as they were in Shakespeare's time. All variants can be seen in this extract
from Mercutio's Queen Mab speech (*Rom.* 1.4.70: see Figure 1, p. 28):

> in this state she gallops night by night, through Louers braines: and
> then they dreame of Loue. On Courtiers knees, that dreame on
> Cursies strait: ore Lawyers fingers, who strait dreampt on Fees, ore
> Ladies lips, who strait on kisses dreame, which oft the angry Mab
> with blisters plagues, because their breath with Sweet meats tainted
> are. Sometime she gallops ore a Courtiers nose, & then dreames he
> of smelling out a sute:

We find:

- singular nouns: *state, night, breath...*
- plural nouns: *brains, knees, fees, lips...*
- possessive noun singular: *a courtier's nose*
- possessive noun plural: *courtiers' knees, lawyers' fingers*
- countable nouns: *nose, fingers, suit...*
- uncountable nouns: *love*
- common nouns: *state, night, brains, love...*
- proper nouns: *Mab*

There are just two noticeable differences with Modern English: there
is no apostrophe marking possession (see p. 85), and capitalization

is used for some of the common nouns (see p. 50). Otherwise, the use of nouns in this passage is the same as today.

If we don noun-hunting kit, and start exploring the works as a whole, we will eventually encounter some nouns that behave differently – for example, with respect to number and countability – but these are not many, compared with the vast majority of nouns in Shakespeare. Most notable are nouns which are uncountable today but which had a countable use then, such as *music, courage,* and *information*:

> I haue assayl'd her with Musickes,
>
> > (*Cym.* 2.3.38)

> Their discipline, / (Now wing-led with their courages)
>
> > (*Cym.* 2.4.24)

> In seeking tales and Informations / Against this man,
>
> > (*H8.* 5.3.110)

And similarly, we find *kindreds, thunders, behalfs, moneys, revenges,* and a few more. Also notable are cases where two forms of a plural co-exist:

> You shew'd your teethes like Apes,
>
> > (*JC.* 5.1.41)

> Defiance Traitors, hurle we in your teeth.
>
> > (*JC.* 5.1.64)

and those where an associated word shows that a noun can be either singular or plural:

> Say, where, when, and how / Cam'st thou by this ill-tydings?
>
> > (*R2.* 3.4.80)

> Thou hast made me giddy / With these ill tydings:
>
> > (*John.* 4.2.132)

Just a few other nouns display the same kind of variation, such as *news, nuptials,* and *riches.* It isn't a very rich haul.

ADJECTIVES

We can go on a similar hunt to show the similarities and differences in the use of any other part-of-speech, and get similar results. An analysis of adjectives, for example, would focus chiefly on the way the two states of the language handle comparison. In modern standard English, to express a higher degree of an adjective, we can use either a word ending (an *inflected* form, as seen in *big, bigger, biggest*) or a form consisting of more than one word (a *periphrastic* form, such as *more beneficial, most beneficial*). Lower degree is always expressed periphrastically (*less interesting, least interesting*). The choice with higher degree depends chiefly on the length of the adjective. Adjectives of one syllable take an inflection; adjectives of three or more syllables appear periphrastically; and adjectives of two syllables sometimes go one way (*happier* is preferred to *more happy*) and sometimes the other (*most proper* is preferred to *properest*).

This system had been established by Shakespeare's time, as we can see from these examples from *Antony and Cleopatra:*

- short adjectives with *-er*: You shall be yet farre fairer than you are (1.2.18)
- long adjectives with *more*: A more vnhappie Lady (3.4.12)
- short adjectives with *-est*: The roughest Berry on the rudest Hedge (1.4.64)
- long adjectives with *most*: She's a most triumphant Lady (2.2.189)

But the same play shows that the system had not finished developing.

hee's more mad / Then *Telamon* (4.13.1) [*then* = 'than']

And from other plays we find occasional usages as *more great, more long,* and *more near,* where today we would expect to see *greater, longer*, and *nearer*. Conversely, we find such forms as *honester* and *honestest*, *oftener* and *perfectest*, where today we would use constructions with *more* and *most*. And a few other differences from Modern English can be seen:

> our worser thoughts
>
> (*Ant*. 1.2.63)

> a more larger List of Scepters
>
> (*Ant*. 3.6.76).

'Double comparatives' (as in this last example) and 'double superlatives', where an inflected and a periphrastic form occur together (*more larger*, *most bravest*), are quite common, usually producing a more emphatic effect than if only one had been used.

> This was the most vnkindest cut of all
>
> (*JC*. 3.2.184)

They turn up in prose as well as verse:

> for the more better assurance
>
> (*MND*. 3.1.18)

But of course, having the option of rhythmical alternatives can be a boon to a poet working within the constraints of a metrical line, as this sequence in *As You Like It* shows (3.5.51):

> You are a thousand times a <u>properer</u> man
> Then she a woman. 'Tis such fooles as you
> That makes the world full of ill-fauourd children:
> 'Tis not her glasse, but you that flatters her,
> And out of you she sees her selfe <u>more proper</u>
> Then any of her lineaments can show her:

An adjective hunt would also bring to light a few occasions when word-order is different from what is conventional in Modern

English. We sometimes see a sequence of adjectives in which some appear both before and after the noun they modify, as in the Nurse's description of Lady Capulet (*Rom.* 1.5.113):

> Her Mother is the Lady of the house,
> And a good Lady, and a wise, and Vertuous,

that is, 'she is a good, wise, and virtuous lady'. It is an unusual effect, to modern ears and eyes, but not one that causes any difficulty of understanding. Similarly transparent are such variations as the reversal of word-order in friendly greetings, such as *good my lord* and *good my friend*.

VERBS

Most of the distinctive features of Shakespearean verb usage relate to the way these forms are used to express time (*tenses*). There are two tenses in Modern English, present and past, illustrated by *I walk* and *I walked*. English of course has other ways of using verbs to express time, such as auxiliary verbs (*I will walk, I have walked*), and these often add other meanings, such as possibility (*I might walk*) or obligation (*I must walk*). But the basic system is the contrast between the use of a past-tense form of the verb (regular or irregular: *I walked, sat, went...*) and a present-tense form (regular or irregular: *I walk, say, do...*). There is no variation in the past-tense form, when we use verbs with different persons – *I, you, he, she, it, we,* and *they* all *walked*. In the present tense, *I, you, we,* and *they* all *walk; he, she,* and *it* (the third-person singular form) *walks*. Great changes in this system had taken place during the Middle English period, but by Shakespeare's day it had largely settled down, and was not far from the one we know today.

The most noticeable differences are the two Middle English verb-endings which were still being used in the Early Modern English period: *-est* for the second-person singular following *thou* (*thou goest, thou know'st*); and *-th* or *-eth* for the third-person singular (*she goeth, she hath*). The forms of the verb *to be* also included four older items: *art, beest, wert, wast*. All the earlier forms were reducing in frequency during the time Shakespeare was writing. In due course the *-est* form would disappear and the *-th* forms would be replaced by *-s*, apart from in some religious English and the occasional modern jokey usage (*the taxman cometh*). We can actually see the change in the language taking place if we order the plays chronologically and look at the distribution of verbs with a *-th* ending. Using the *Shakespeare's Words* corpus (see Preface), nothing much happens with *hath* and *doth*. *Hath* is the dominant form (2,137 instances, compared with 424 of *has*), and it stays frequent throughout the period. *Doth* is less common (1,130 instances, compared with 350 of *does*), but it too remains in use, though its incidence starts to drop in the early 1600s. It is in the other verbs – such as *standeth, seemeth, pleaseth* – where we see the fortunes of the *-th* ending change dramatically. Out of the 304 instances in the plays, 238 (78 per cent) occur in the 16 plays up to and including *Henry IV Part 1* (dated 1596–7). The incidence drops noticeably with *The Merry Wives of Windsor*, and thereafter the usage is sporadic.

Interpretation is not straightforward, given that collaborators had different usage preferences, compositors may have altered forms, and editors may have modernized; but the basic point stands: three hundred or so instances of *-th* is not a very large total, when we consider all the third-person forms in the plays. The *-s* ending is the dominant one throughout the whole period, and in some late plays, such as *The Winter's Tale*, we see nothing else. As the usage was clearly dying out in the language as a whole, the interesting question is: why do we see it used at all? Metrical constraints are the usual explanation. The *-eth* ending adds an extra unstressed syllable to a word (with just a few exceptions, such as *saith*), thus giving the poet a second option:

The Bird of Dawning singeth all night long:

(*Ham.* 1.1.161)

It is the Larke that sings so out of tune,

(*Rom.* 3.5.27)

Sometimes both forms are used in the same line or in quick succession, as here:

> For *Suffolke*, he that can doe all in all
> With her, that hateth thee and hates vs all,

> *(2H6.* 2.4.52)

> he yoaketh your rebellious Neckes,
> Razeth your Cities, and subuerts your Townes,

> *(1H6.* 2.3.63).

And in a few cases we have evidence of metrical alternatives competing with each other. In this line from Polonius (*Ham.* 1.3.77), the Folio text goes one way and the second Quarto goes another:

> (F)   And borrowing duls the edge of Husbandry.
> (Q2) And borrowing dulleth edge of Husbandry.

The metrical value of *-th* is also evident in the narrative poems, where we see a much greater frequency than in the plays – sixty instances in *Venus and Adonis* and thirty-nine in *The Rape of Lucrece*. Several cluster because of the rhyme – using one or two at a line-ending means you have to use two or four (*Ven.* 457–60):

> This ill presage advisedly she marketh:
> Even as the wind is hush'd before it raineth,
> Or as the wolf doth grin before he barketh,
> Or as the berry breaks before it staineth,

There are fewer instances in the *Sonnets* – just sixteen, leaving aside the greeting that the 'euer-liuing poet wisheth the well-wishing aduenturer in setting forth'. They are sporadic, apart from two cases of rhyme (in Sonnets 20 and 33).

Metrical factors cannot explain everything, however, for we see *-th/-s* alternation in prose too, even in stage directions. Here is an instance of prose variation (*2H4.* 2.4.85):

> Neighbour *Quickly* (sayes hee) receiue those that are Ciuill; for
> (sayth hee) you are in an ill Name: now hee said so, I can tell

whereupon: for (sayes hee) you are an honest Woman, and well thought on

And here is one such stage direction (*1H4*. 5.4.76):

Enter Dowglas, he fights with Falstaffe, who fals down as if he were dead. The Prince killeth Percie.

Not only is there variation between *fights/falls* and *killeth* in the First Folio version; in the various Quarto texts of the play we find *fighteth* as well. This rather suggests that the two forms were in 'free variation', much of the time. Only in a few very restricted circumstances can we see why the older form would outrank the newer. It would be a fixed usage in a folk song, for instance:

for the raine it raineth euery day.

(*TN*. 5.1.389):

We might expect it in formulaic (or mock-formulaic) language intended to impress:

He heareth not, he stirreth not, he moueth not,

(*Rom*. 2.1.15)

Who chooseth me, shall gaine what men desire

(*MV*. 2.7.5).

And we can readily imagine the older -*th* form being preferred in situations where a more conservative vocabulary is the norm. It is not surprising to hear it coming from the mouth of Holofernes, for example, who uses the ending no less than eight times, sometimes along with some suitably old-fashioned words (*LLL*. 5.1.22):

he clepeth a Calf, Caufe: [*clepeth*: 'calls']

What is more surprising is that other 'elder statesmen', serious or comic, do not use it more often.

There is little to say about the use of past-tense forms in Shakespeare. These forms have changed greatly since Old English, and continue to do so today, as seen in the occasional uncertainty in standard English (e.g. *burned* vs *burnt*) and the variations heard in regional dialects (e.g. *I was sat there for hours*). A dictionary provides a complete list. Most verbs are regular *-ed* formations, the same as today. The opening pages of *Macbeth*, for example, give us *supplied*, *showed*, *smoked*, *carved*, *faced*, *unseamed*, *fixed*, and many more. Most irregular verbs are also the same as today: *told*, *fought*, *saw/seen*, *gone/went*, and so on. About a quarter of all irregular verbs display differences from what we have today, but as few of them are at all frequent, the overall impression of difference is not great:

- some verbs are irregular in Shakespeare which have become regular today, e.g. *durst* (*dared*), *holp* (*helped*), *ought* (*owed*), *fretten* (*fretted*)
- some verbs are regular in Shakespeare which have become irregular today, e.g. *digged* (*dug*), *shaked* (*shook/shaken*), *builded* (*built*), *having quitted* (*quit*)
- some irregular Shakespeare verbs stay irregular, but in a different way, e.g. *was awaked* (*awoken*), *bestrid* (*bestrode*), *brake* (*broke*), *drave* (*drove*), *forsook* (*forsaken*), *situate* (*situated*), *spake* (*spoke*), *writ* (*wrote*)

As with all change, old forms co-exist for a while alongside new ones, and we can sometimes sense a subtle difference of meaning. An example is the Princess's observation that

> None are so surely caught, when they are catcht,
> As Wit turn'd foole, follie in Wisedome hatch'd:

(LLL. 5.2.69)

Plainly the availability of two forms of *catch* is a help to any rhymer, but *catcht* here also seems to convey a more dynamic sense than *caught*. (The *-t* spelling for *-ed* was a common variant at the time: see p. 136.)

PRONOUNS

Because of their frequency, if for no other reason (p. 180), the use of *thou*-forms and *you*-forms dominates any discussion of Shakespearean pronouns. The *thou*-forms are *thou, thee, thy, thine,* and *thy selfe.* The *you*-forms are *you, ye, your, yours,* and *your selfe.* (The First Folio compositors were in a muddle over how to print the reflexive pronouns: *itselfe* and *themselues* are always printed solid; *my selfe* is usually spaced, with just two exceptions (in *Lear, Oth*); *her selfe* is also usually spaced, with just ten exceptions (*Lear, Rom, Tit*); and *himselfe* is usually solid, with just one exception (*Ant*)). *You*-forms are more frequent than *thou*-forms, in a ratio of 3:2 (approximately 21,000 vs 14,000).

The forms for *thou* and *you* (usually abbreviated to *T*-/*V*-forms, after the *tu/vous* distinction in French) have attracted especial attention in the linguistics literature because they are important markers of social and attitudinal differences between people. In Old English, *thou* was singular and *you* was plural. But during the thirteenth century, *you* began to be used as a polite form of the singular – probably because people copied the French manner of talking, where *vous* was used in that way. English then became like French, which has *tu* and *vous* both possible for singulars. So now there was a choice. The usual thing was for *you* to be used by inferiors to superiors – such as children to parents, or servants to masters; and *thou* to be used in return. But people would also use *thou* when they wanted special intimacy, such as when addressing God; and *thou* was also normal when the lower classes talked to each other. The upper classes used *you* to each other, as a rule, even when they were closely related.

So when someone changes from *thou* to *you* (or vice versa) in a conversation, it must mean something. The change will convey a different emotion or mood. The new meaning could be virtually anything – affection, anger, distance, sarcasm, playfulness ... To say *thou* to someone could be an insult: in *Twelfth Night* (3.2.43), Toby Belch actually advises Andrew Aguecheek to put down his enemy by calling him *thou* a few times. The way in which characters switch from one pronoun to the other therefore acts as a barometer of their evolving attitudes and relationships.

We find a good illustration in the opening scene of *King Lear* (1.1.55,ff.), where the king sets about dividing his kingdom among his daughters. We would expect Lear to use *thou* to them, and they to use *you* in return, which is how the interaction with Goneril begins:

> *Gon.* Sir, I loue <u>you</u> more then word can weild y matter, . . .
> *Lear.* Of all these bounds euen from this Line, to this, . . .
> We make <u>thee</u> Lady. To <u>thine</u> and *Albanies* issues
> Be this perpetuall.

Regan speaks in the same way, and receives the same pronoun response:

> I am alone felicitate
> In <u>your</u> deere Highnesse loue.
> *Lear.* To <u>thee</u>, and <u>thine</u> hereditarie euer,
> Remaine this ample third of our faire Kingdome,

But when Lear turns to his 'joy', Cordelia, he uses *you*:

> What can <u>you</u> say, to draw
> A third, more opilent then your Sisters? speake. [*opilent* = 'opulent']

Plainly, if *thou* is for 'ordinary' daughters, *you* must here be a special marker of affection. But when Cordelia does not reply in the way he was expecting ('Nothing'), Lear abruptly changes back:

> *Lear.* But goes <u>thy</u> heart with this?
> *Cor.* I my good Lord . . .. [*I* = 'Ay', a common printed spelling]
> *Lear.* Let it be so, <u>thy</u> truth then be <u>thy</u> dowre:

Now the *thou* forms are being used not as a marker of fatherly affection, but of anger: '<u>thou</u> my sometime Daughter.'

A little later in the play, we see *T*-forms being used in the opposite direction. Regan is trying to persuade Oswald to let her see

Goneril's letter (4.4.19). She begins with the expected *you*, but switches to *thee* when she tries to use her charm:

> *Reg.* Why should she write to *Edmund*?
> Might not you transport her purposes by word? Belike,
> Some things, I know not what. Ile loue thee much
> Let me vnseale the Letter.
> *Stew.* Madam, I had rather –
> *Reg.* I know your Lady do's not loue her Husband,

Oswald's hesitation makes her return to *you* again, and she soon dismisses him in an abrupt short line with this pronoun; but when he responds enthusiastically to her next request she opts again for *thee*:

> So fare you well:
> If you do chance to heare of that blinde Traitor,
> Preferment fals on him, that cuts him off.
> *Stew.* Would I could meet Madam, I should shew
> What party I do follow.
> *Reg.* Fare thee well.

Here we have *thee* being used as an index of warmth of feeling – quite the reverse of the insulting use of *thou* between nobles noted earlier.[1]

The old grammatical distinction between *ye* (as the subject of a clause) and *you* (as the object) had long gone by Shakespeare's time, as had any trace of a distinction between singular and plural. The hugely dominant form was *you* – over 13,000 instances in the plays, compared with just 342 of *ye*. And the two forms at times seem interchangeable. We see *Fare you well* (75 times) and *Fare ye well* (10 times). There are several examples like this one (*Ant.* 3.3.103):

> If it might please you, to enforce no further
> The griefes betweene ye: to forget them quite,
> Were to remember: that the present neede,
> Speakes to attone you.

And different texts sometimes use one and sometimes the other. Mercutio's line *'Tis no lesse I tell you* (*Rom.* 2.4.109) has *you* in the Folio but *ye* in the second Quarto.

The interesting question is: with such dominance of *you*, why was any use still made of *ye* at all? Metrical factors are irrelevant, with two monosyllabic words. And also unlike the *-eth* forms, there is no chronological progression: the five most common uses are in *Henry VIII* (72) and *The Two Noble Kinsmen* (39), at one end of the period, *Henry IV Part 1* (29) in the middle, and *Henry VI Part 1* (23), *Titus Andronicus* (21), and *Henry VI Part 2* (20), at the other. When we see distributions like this, other factors have to be at work.

Stylistic factors suggest themselves. Plainly, ye was not a poetic form: it does not appear in the long narrative poems, and only twice in the *Sonnets* (42, 111), both times there to provide a rhyme for *me*. It is partly related to character: Falstaff uses over half the instances in *Henry IV Part 1*; and Mercutio seems to mock the Nurse's usage (*Rom.* 2.4.107):

> *Nur.* God ye good morrow Gentlemen.
> *Mer.* God ye gooden faire Gentlewoman. [*gooden* = 'good-e'en']

On the other hand, everyone uses it, high or low, formally and colloquially, in *Henry VIII*, so it cannot solely be a matter of character idiosyncrasy. Situational informality plays a part, especially in *Henry IV Part 1*, where twenty seven of the thirty-four instances are used by the Falstaff circle (*ye fat-guts, ye rogue...*). Grammatical factors also have a role to play: it is likely to be used in vocatives (*ye people, ye citizens*) and certain fixed attention-getting phrases (*hark ye, beseech ye*); seven of the ten uses in *Julius Caesar* are *ye gods*. We can find instances of it reflecting an older high style, as when Pucelle invokes her spirits (*1H6.* 5.3.2):

> Now helpe ye charming Spelles and Periapts,
> And ye choise spirits that admonish me,

But she switches to *you* immediately after: *You speedy helpers...*

There is only one explanation which can account for such startling discrepancies, and that is multiple authorship. Four plays (*Tit*, *1H6*, *H8*, *TNK*) account for nearly half the instances (45 per cent), and they are all collaborations. If *Sir Thomas More* is added, this percentage rises to 63 per cent. (There are no *ye*s in the portion thought to have been written by Shakespeare: see p. 35.) John Fletcher was presumably responsible for the relatively heavy usage in *H8* and *TNK* (32 per cent of instances). He was certainly a *ye*-user: there are eighty-five instances in his *The Tamer Tamed* (thought to have been written in the early 1600s).

The focus on *T-* and *V*-forms has rather taken attention away from the many other ways in which pronouns are used differently in Shakespeare, compared with today. In particular, the system of relative pronouns (as in *the table which was broken ...*) was in a somewhat unstable state – as indeed it still is, for the choice between *which* and *that* is not entirely systematic today. But at least today there is no uncertainty over animateness: a human noun is followed by a human pronoun (*the man who ...*); an inanimate noun is followed by an inanimate pronoun (*the book which ...*). This distinction was not entirely systematic in Early Modern English either. It operates most of the time, but there are exceptions. Ferdinand talks about

> The Mistris which I serue,
>
> (*Temp.* 3.1.6)

and Posthumus of

> that most venerable man, which I
> Did call my Father,
>
> (*Cym.* 2.4.55)

and there are few other such uses, such as after *husband* and *gentleman*. By contrast, *who* is occasionally used after a non-human noun, usually in a clearly personifying context, such as referring to Nature or a country as *who*:

the hot breath of Spaine, who sent whole Armadoes of Carrects to
be ballast at her nose [*Carrects* = 'carracks', i.e. large merchant ships]

(*CE*. 3.2.143).

We can see the vacillation in this sequence (*MV*. 2.7.4):

The first of gold, who this inscription beares,
Who chooseth me, shall gaine what men desire.
The second siluer, which this promise carries,

Most pronoun differences do not make much impact, if any, on comprehension. When we encounter such uses as:

Aniou and *Maine*? My selfe did win them both:

(*2H6*. 1.1.117)

we have no trouble seeing that *myself* is an emphatic subject (and we
may indeed even have heard it so used in Irish English). Similarly, we
readily understand the reflexive meaning in cases where we would use
a reflexive pronoun today:

I will buy me a sonne in Law in a faire,

(*AWW*. 5.3.148)

Again, the usage has some currency in regional speech. And when we
sense that a relative pronoun has been omitted in places where today
we would expect to find one, we simply 'read it in':

I haue a brother is condemn'd to die, [= 'a brother who is . . .']

(*MM*. 2.2.34)

But this I thinke, there's no man is so vaine, [= 'no man who is . . .']
That would refuse so faire an offer'd Chaine.

(*CE*. 3.2.188)

But there is one type of pronoun usage which is so far removed from
Modern English norms that, without special study, we are likely to
miss the meaning of the sentence altogether. This is the so-called
ethical dative. Early Modern English allowed a personal pronoun

after a verb to express such notions as 'to', 'for', 'by', 'with' or 'from' (notions which traditional grammars would subsume under the headings of the *dative* and *ablative* cases). The usage can be seen in such sentences as:

but heare me this (*TN*. 5.1.118)   [= 'But hear this from me']
Iohn layes you plots (*John*.   [= 'John lays plots for you to fall
3.4.146)   into']

It is an unfamiliar construction, to modern eyes and ears (though it does turn up occasionally, as in the song title 'Cry me a river'), and it can confuse – as a Shakespearean character himself evidences. In *The Taming of the Shrew* (1.2.8), Petruchio and Grumio arrive at Hortensio's house:

> *Petr.* Villaine I say, knocke me heere soundly.
> *Gru.* Knocke you heere sir? Why sir, what am I sir, that I should
> knocke you heere sir.
> *Petr.* Villaine I say, knocke me at this gate,
> And rap me well, or Ile knocke your knaues pate.
> *Gru.* My Mr is growne quarrelsome:
> I should knocke you first,
> And then I know after who comes by the worst.

Petruchio means 'Knock on the door for me', but Grumio interprets it to mean (as it would in Modern English) 'hit me'. If we do not recognize the ethical dative in Petruchio's sentence in the first place, we will miss the point of the joke entirely. But the fact that Grumio can be presented as confused suggests that the usage was probably already dying out in Shakespeare's time.

WORD ORDER

Most of the really unfamiliar deviations from Modern English grammatical norms which we encounter in Shakespeare arise in his verse, where he bends the construction to suit the demands of the metre. The basic form of the pentameter, as we have seen (p. 120) consisted of five metrical units, the whole line ending in a natural pause and containing no internal break. Accordingly, the least amount of grammatical 'bending' takes place when a line coincides with the major unit of grammar, the sentence. This is a characteristic of much of Shakespeare's early writing, as in this example from the Duke of Bedford (*1H6*. 1.1.148):

> His Ransome there is none but I shall pay.
> Ile hale the Dolphin headlong from his Throne,
> His Crowne shall be the Ransome of my friend:
> Foure of their Lords Ile change for one of ours.
> Farwell my Masters, to my Taske will I,

'Sentence per line' is the simplest kind of relationship between metre and grammar. 'Sentence per two lines' is a step forward. Bedford's speech continues with two two-line sentences.

> Bonfires in France forthwith I am to make,
> To keepe our great Saint *Georges* Feast withall.
> Ten thousand Souldiers with me I will take,
> Whose bloody deeds shall make all Europe quake.

'Clause per line' is not very different. Such grammatically regular lines are often seen in the *Sonnets*, where they convey a measured rhythmical pace:

> So oft haue I inuok'd thee for my Muse,
> And found such faire assistance in my verse,
> As euery *Alien* pen hath got my vse,
> And vnder thee their poesie disperse.
> Thine eyes, that taught the dumbe on high to sing,
> And heauie ignorance aloft to flee,
> Haue added fethers to the learneds wing,
> And giuen grace a double Maiestie.

> (*Sonn.* 78)

The pace of reading increases when the line-breaks coincide with a major point of grammatical junction within a clause, such as between a subject and verb, verb and object, or noun and relative clause. In this next example (*H5*. 4.3.64), because the first line contains only the clause subject, there is a dynamic tension at the end which propels us onwards to reach the verb:

> And Gentlemen in England, now a bed,
> Shall thinke themselues accurst they were not here;

We can feel this tension if we stop our reading at the end of the first line. A subject alone is like an unresolved chord, calling out for the rest of the clause to provide semantic coherence.

Even when a sentence stretches over several lines, the relationship between metre and grammar can be regular, as we can see in this speech from the deposed king in *Richard II* (5.5.1):

> I haue bin studying, how to compare [Q1: how I may compare]
> This Prison where I liue, vnto the World:
> And for because the world is populous,
> And heere is not a Creature, but my selfe,
> I cannot do it: yet Ile hammer't out.
> My Braine, Ile proue the Female to my Soule,
> My Soule, the Father: and these two beget
> A generation of still breeding Thoughts;
> And these same Thoughts, people this Little World
> In humors, like the people of this world,
> For no thought is contented.

The line endings are all major points of grammatical junction, so that each line makes a separate semantic point. By keeping the lines coherent, in this way, the meaning proceeds in a series of smooth, regular steps – very appropriate for a speech whose unique properties have been repeatedly praised: 'No other speech in Shakespeare much resembles this one' for its 'quietly meditative' tone, says Frank Kermode (see also p. 172). The effect would be totally lost if the lines did not coincide with these major units of grammar, as in this rewriting:

> Today I have been studying how to [Q1: how I may]
> Compare this prison where I live unto
> The world, and for because the world is

Such lines no longer have a semantic coherence. Grammatical structures are begun but broken awkwardly at the ends of lines: the particle *to* [Q1: *may*] is split off from its main verb *compare;* the preposition *unto* is split off from its noun phrase *the world*. This is not the metrical syntax of quiet meditation. On the other hand, it is precisely this sort of disruption which is needed when portraying a confused mind – in this case, Cloten's (*Cym.* 2.3.64):

> If she be vp, Ile speake with her: if not
> Let her lye still, and dreame: by your leaue hoa,
> I know her women are about her: what
> If I do line one of their hands, 'tis Gold
> Which buyes admittance (oft it doth) yea, and makes
> *Diana's* Rangers false themselues, yeeld vp
> Their Deere to'th' stand o'th' Stealer: and 'tis Gold
> Which makes the True-man kill'd, and saues the Theefe:
> Nay, sometime hangs both Theefe, and True-man: what
> Can it not do, and vndoo? I will make
> One of her women Lawyer to me, for
> I yet not vnderstand the case my selfe.

Here several lines break in unexpected places (an effect partly captured by the traditional notion of *caesura*) – in the middle of a two-part conjunction (*what / if*), after an interrogative word (*what*), and between a conjunction and its clause (*for / I*) – and clauses begin at the end of lines instead of at the beginning. Cloten comments: 'I yet not understand the case myself.' The disruption between metre and grammar suggests as much.

The more the metre forces grammatical deviations within a line, the more difficult the line will be to understand. If just one element of clause structure is affected, the problem is small. Here is the Queen Mab speech again (*Rom.* 1.4.70), this time with the Folio text given a verse setting (see p. 216), and with all the unusual word-order variations underlined:

> & in this state she gallops night by night,
> through Louers braines: and then they dreame of Loue.
> On Courtiers knees, that dreame on Cursies strait:
> [Cursies = 'curtsies']
> ore Lawyers fingers, who strait dreampt on Fees,
> ore Ladies lips, who strait <u>on kisses dreame</u>,
> which oft the angry Mab <u>with blisters plagues</u>,
> because their breath with Sweet meats <u>tainted are</u>.
> Sometime she gallops ore a Courtiers nose,
> & then <u>dreames he</u> of smelling out a sute:
> & somtime comes she with Tith pigs tale, [*Tith* = 'tithe']
> tickling a Parsons nose as a lies asleepe,
> then he dreames of another Benefice. [<u>dreams he</u> in Q1]
> Sometime she driueth ore a Souldiers necke,
> & then <u>dreames he</u> of cutting Forraine throats,

These variations present us with little or no difficulty, because we are used to a certain amount of word-order flexibility in English, especially in the use of adverbs and adverbial constructions (p. 16). This kind of thing is as common today as it was in Early Modern English:

- at the end of a clause: *We went home quickly*
- at the beginning of a clause: *Quickly we went home*
- between subject and verb: *We quickly went home*
- between auxiliary verb and main verb: *They have quickly gone home*
- between verb and adverbial: *We went quickly home*
- but not between verb and object: *We kicked quickly the ball*

Likewise:

- at the end of a clause: *God send her quickly!* (*AWW.* 2.4.12)
- at the beginning of a clause: *Quickly send – be brief* (*Lear.* 5.3.242)
- between subject and verb: *I quickly were dissolved from my hive* (*AWW.* 1.2.66)
- between auxiliary verb and main verb: *And I shall quickly draw out of my command* (*Cor.* 1.6.84)
- between verb and adverbial: *I am quickly ill and well* (*Ant.* 1.3.72)
- but not between verb and object: no example of the type *I struck quickly the man*

So there is no reason to be concerned about the comprehension of the adverb movements in the Queen Mab speech: *strait* (= straight away) is operating like *quickly*, and the fronting of *on kisses* and *with blisters* is only unusual because we are not used to seeing these expressions that way round: we normally 'dream about something', or 'plague someone with something', with the verb first.

The verb/subject reversal of order is a little different (*he dreames > dreames he*), as is the reversal between the verb and its following verblike adjective (*are tainted > tainted are*). These are word-orders which have long disappeared from standard English, and we therefore need to be on our guard. The primary point of word-order is to make the relationships between parts of the clause clear. Because we are aware of the rule governing Subject + Verb + Object, we can interpret the difference between:

The girl saw the boy
The boy saw the girl

but as soon as we deviate from this order of elements:

The boy the girl saw

it is no longer clear who saw whom, and – if we want to change our emphasis – we have to adopt a different construction:

It was the boy that the girl saw.

We can see several instances of this type of word-order variation in Shakespeare, though the construction was by no means as common then as it is today:

It was our selfe thou didst abuse.

(*H5*. 4.8.49)

[= 'Thou didst abuse ourself']

'Tis but an houre agoe, since it was nine,

(*AYLI*. 2.7.24)

[= 'It was nine but an hour ago']

A simple reversal, such as Subject + Verb > Verb + Subject, is unlikely to cause a problem of comprehension; but when several things happen at once, we can be in difficulty. In the second line of this next example (*R2*. 1.1.123), three unexpected word-order variations occur simultaneously:

He is our subiect (*Mowbray*) so art thou,
Free speech, and fearelesse, I to thee allow.

The line means 'I allow to thee free and fearless speech', but the direct object *free speech* is placed at the front, the indirect object *to thee* comes before the verb, and an adjective is coordinated after the noun (see p. 188). The gloss is much clearer, but it is unmetrical. Modern punctuation will not help the original version, which is metrically regular but at the expense of the syntax. Some might consider this to be an example of Shakespeare not at his best.

Sometimes the change in word-order can catch us off guard, as in this example from *Henry VI Part 2* (5.2.51), spoken by Young Clifford after seeing his dead father, and vowing revenge. Nothing, he says, will escape his wrath:

> Yorke, not our old men spares:
> No more will I their Babes, Teares Virginall,
> Shall be to me, euen as the Dew to Fire,
> And Beautie, that the Tyrant oft reclaimes,
> Shall to my flaming wrath, be Oyle and Flax:

A modern editor will try to make the sense clearer by substituting modern spelling and punctuation, perhaps as follows (this is the Penguin version):

> York not our old men spares;
> No more will I their babes; tears virginal
> Shall be to me even as the dew to fire;
> And beauty, that the tyrant oft reclaims,
> Shall to my flaming wrath be oil and flax.

Line four is still a problem. A casual reading would suggest that 'a tyrant often reclaims (i.e. tames, subdues) beauty' – but this makes no sense. Rather, the meaning is 'beauty, that often tames the tyrant, will act as fuel to my wrath'. *Tyrant* is not the grammatical subject of *reclaims*, but its object. Only by paying careful attention to the meaning can we work this out, and for this we need to think of the speech as a whole, and see it in its discourse context. Metre is often thought of simply as a phonetic phenomenon – an aesthetic sound effect, either heard directly or imagined when reading. In fact it is much more. Metrical choices always have grammatical, semantic, and pragmatic – as well as dramatic – consequences.

9 'Hear sweet discourse': Shakespearean conversation

The aim of stylistic analysis is ultimately to explain the choices that a person makes, in speaking or writing. If I want to express the thought that 'I have two loves', there are many ways in which I can do it in addition to that particular version. I can alter the sentence structure (*It's two loves that I have*), the word structure (*I've two loves*), the word-order (*Two loves I have*), or the vocabulary (*I've got two loves, I love two people*), or opt for a more radical rephrasing (*There are two loves in my life*). The choice will be motivated by my sense of the different nuances, emphases, rhythms, and sound patterns carried by the words. In casual usage, I will give little thought to the merits of the alternatives: conveying the 'gist' is enough. But in an artistic construct, each linguistic decision counts, for it affects the structure and interpretation of the whole.

It is rhythm and emphasis that govern the choice made for the opening line of Sonnet 144:

Two loues I haue of comfort and dispaire,

As the aim is to write a sonnet, it is critical that the choice satisfies the demands of the metre; but there is more to the choice than rhythm, for *I have two loves* would also work. The inverted word-order conveys two other effects: it places the theme of the poem in the forefront of our attention, and it gives the line a semantic balance, locating the specific words at the beginning and the end.

Evaluating the literary or dramatic impact of the effects conveyed by the various alternatives can take up many hours of discussion; but the first step in stylistic analysis is to establish that there are effects to be explained. The clearest answers emerge when there is a frequent and perceptible contrast between pairs of options, and this is the best way of approaching the analysis of discourse in the plays. By *discourse* I mean the way in which we use sentences in interaction, when speaking and writing to each other. The 'each other' might be other characters in the play or a character and the audience (as in the case of soliloquies and asides). A discourse study looks at language from a different perspective to that used in the earlier chapters of this book. The study of sounds, letters, prosodies, punctuation marks, words, and grammatical constructions are ways in which we can develop an understanding of language from the 'bottom up'. A discourse perspective makes us look at language from the 'top down'. Both perspectives are necessary if we are to arrive at the fullest possible understanding of the language of Shakespeare.

VERSE AND PROSE

Any 'top down' approach confronts us straight away with the difference between verse and prose. Shakespeare's practice in using verse or prose varied greatly at different stages in his career (see Table 2). There are plays written entirely in verse (*R2, John, KE3*) and others almost entirely in prose (*Wiv*), but most plays display a mixture of the two modes, with certain types of situation or character prompting one or the other. Verse – whether rhymed or unrhymed (see p. 118) – is typically associated with a 'high style' of language, prose with a 'low style'. This is partly a matter of class distinction. High-status people, such as nobles and generals, tend to use the former; low-status people, such as clowns and tavern-frequenters, tend to use the latter (though in a 'verse play', such as *R2*, even the gardeners talk verse). Upper-class people also have an ability to accommodate to those of lower class, using prose, should occasion arise. Prince Harry is a case in point. He tells Poins (*1H4*. 2.5.18):

> I am so good a proficient in one quarter of an houre, that I can
> drinke with any Tinker in his owne Language during my life.

And lower-class people who move in court circles, such as messengers and guards, are able to use a poetic style when talking to their betters.

This lower-class ability to accommodate upwards can take their listeners by surprise. The riotous citizens at the beginning of *Coriolanus* all use prose, but when Menenius reasons with them, in elegant verse, their spokesman gradually slips into verse too – much to Menenius' amazement:

> Your Bellies answer: What
> The Kingly crown'd head, the vigilant eye,
> The Counsailor Heart, the Arme our Souldier,
> Our Steed the Legge, the Tongue our Trumpeter,
> With other Muniments and petty helpes
> In this our Fabricke, if that they –
> *Men.* What then? Fore me, this Fellow speakes.
>
> (1.1.112):

The distinction between 'high' and 'low' style is also associated with subject-matter. For example, expressions of romantic love are made in verse, regardless of the speaker's social class.

> If thou remembrest not the slightest folly,
> That euer loue did make thee run into,
> Thou hast not lou'd.
> Or if thou hast not sat as I doe now,
> Wearing thy hearer in thy Mistris praise,
> Thou hast not lou'd.
> Or if thou hast not broke from companie,
> Abruptly as my passion now makes me,
> Thou hast not lou'd.

This elegant plaint is from Silvius, a shepherd (*AYLI.* 2.4.31), but it could have come from any princely lover. Conversely, 'low' subject-matter, such as ribaldry or teasing, tends to motivate prose, even when spoken by upper-class people. Hotspur and his wife are conversing in verse, but when he starts to tease, they switch into prose (*2H4.* 3.1.224):

Table 2: *Proportions of verse and prose in the plays*

Play	Verse		Prose	
	%	No. of lines	%	No. of lines
R2	100	2,752	0	0
John	100	2,569	0	0
KE3	100	2,493	0	0
3H6	99.7	2,892	0.3	8
1H6	99.5	2,664	0.5	14
Tit	98.6	2,479	1.4	35
R3	97.6	3,517	2.4	85
H8	97.4	2,735	2.6	74
TNK	94.5	2,641	5.5	154
Mac	93.5	1,948	6.5	135
JC	90.1	2,208	9.9	244
Ant	89.8	2,718	10.2	308
Rom	86.9	2,610	13.1	393
Err	86.6	1,543	13.4	239
Cym	85.2	2,808	14.5	487
2H6	83.7	2,580	16.3	503
Per	81.2	1,903	18.8	441
Shr	80.6	2,076	19.4	498
MND	80.6	1,713	19.4	413
Oth	80.4	2,599	19.6	633
MV	78.6	2,025	21.4	551
Cor	77.2	2,571	22.8	760
Temp	76.5	1,569	23.5	481
WT	73.2	2,181	26.8	800
Lear	73.1	2,345	26.9	865
Tim	73.1	1,707	26.9	627
TGV	73.1	1,613	26.9	595
Ham	71.5	2,742	28.5	1,092
Tro	66.4	2,250	33.6	1,137
LLL	64.2	1,716	35.8	955

Table 2: (*cont.*)

Play	Verse		Prose	
	%	No. of lines	%	No. of lines
MM	60.6	1,634	39.4	1,062
H5	60.5	1,943	39.5	1,269
1H4	55.6	1,666	44.4	1,332
AWW	51.6	1,447	48.4	1,356
2H4	47.6	1,547	52.4	1,700
AYLI	47.4	1,276	52.6	1,415
TN	38.2	949	61.8	1,532
Ado	28.3	739	71.7	1,871
Wiv	12.5	338	87.5	2,370

Note: Totals derived from the *Shakespeare's Words* database (see Preface).

> *Hotsp.* Now I perceiue the Deuill vnderstands Welsh,
> And 'tis no maruell he is so humorous:
> Byrlady hee's a good Musitian.
> *Lady.* Then would you be nothing but Musicall,
> For you are altogether gouerned by humors:
> Lye still ye Theefe, and heare the Lady sing in Welsh.
> *Hotsp.* I had rather heare (Lady) my Brach howle in Irish. [*Brach* =
> 'hound, bitch']
> *Lady.* Would'st haue thy Head broken?
> *Hotsp.* No.
> *Lady.* Then be still.
> *Hotsp.* Neyther, 'tis a Womans fault.
> *Lady.* Now God helpe thee.
> *Hotsp.* To the Welsh Ladies Bed.
> *Lady.* What's that?
> *Hotsp.* Peace, shee sings.

In a play where the upper-class protagonists tend to speak prose, it takes moments of special drama to motivate a switch to

verse, as in the scene when Claudio accuses Hero of being unfaithful
(*Ado.* 4.1.10).

> *Frier.* If either of you know any inward impediment why you
> should not be conioyned, I charge you on your soules to
> vtter it.
>
> *Claud.* Know you anie, *Hero*?
>
> *Hero.* None my Lord.
>
> *Frier.* Know you anie, Count?
>
> *Leon.* I dare make his answer, None.
>
> *Clau.* O what men dare do! what men may do! what men daily do!
>
> *Bene.* How now! interiections? why then, some be of laughing, as
> ha, ha, he.
>
> *Clau.* Stand thee by Frier, father, by your leaue,
> Will you with free and vnconstrained soule
> Giue me this maid your daughter?

The confrontation then continues in verse. In the same play we see a
switch in the other direction. Beatrice uses nothing but prose in the
first half of the play, but, left alone after overhearing the news that
Benedick loves her, she expresses her newly heightened sensibilities
in ten lines of rhyming verse (3.1.107 – which includes, incidentally,
her only use of *T*-forms in the whole play: see p. 193). In *Othello* (1.3),
the Duke of Venice speaks only verse in debating the question of
Othello's love for Desdemona, but when he has to recount the affairs
of state, he resorts to prose (1.3.220).

These norms explain only a proportion of the ways that verse and
prose are used in the plays. There are many instances where people
switch between one and the other, and when they do we must assume it
is for a reason. Sane adults do not change their style randomly. For
example, Benedick is tricked into thinking that Beatrice loves him, so
when he next meets her he uses verse as a sign of the new relationship
(*Ado.* 2.3.235). Beatrice, however, at this point unaware of any such
thing, rejects the stylistic overture, and her rebuttal forces Benedick to
retreat into prose:

> *Beat.* Against my wil I am sent to bid you come in to dinner.
>
> *Bene.* Faire *Beatrice*, I thanke you for your paines.
>
> *Beat.* I tooke no more paines for those thankes, then you take paines to thanke me, if it had been painefull, I would not haue come.
>
> *Bene.* You take pleasure then in the message.

We see a similar effect in the opening scene of *Timon of Athens* (1.1.179), where Timon and his merchant and jeweller flatterers have been engaged in a genteel conversation in verse about social and artistic matters.

> Things of like valew differing in the Owners,
> Are prized by their Masters. Beleeu't deere Lord,
> You mend the Iewell by the wearing it.

The arrival of the cynical Apemantus lowers the tone, and – anticipating trouble – the speakers switch into prose:

> *Tim.* Looke who comes heere, will you be chid?
>
> *Iewel.* Wee'l beare with your Lordship.
>
> *Mer.* Hee'l spare none.

Timon tries to maintain the high tone by addressing Apemantus in verse, and Apemantus shows he is capable of the high style by responding in kind; but his acerbic comments introduce a low tone which forces all to retreat into prose:

> *Tim.* Good morrow to thee,
> Gentle *Apermantus.*
>
> *Ape.* Till I be gentle, stay thou for thy good morrow.
> When thou art *Timons* dogge, and these Knaues honest.
>
> *Tim.* Why dost thou call them Knaues, thou know'st them not?
>
> *Ape.* Are they not Athenians?
>
> *Tim.* Yes.
>
> *Ape.* Then I repent not.

> *Iew.* You know me, *Apemantus*?
>
> *Ape.* Thou know'st I do, I call'd thee by thy name.

The one-line poetic riposte to the jeweller, under the circumstances, has to be seen as a mocking adoption of the high style.

If verse is a sign of high style, then we will expect those aspiring to power to use it to make their case, and disguised nobility to use it when their true character needs to appear. An example of the first is in *Henry VI Part 2*, where Jack Cade is claiming to be one of Mortimer's two sons, and thus the heir to the throne. He and his fellow rebels speak to each other in prose. When Stafford and his brother arrive, they show their social distance by addressing the rebels in verse. But Cade is playing his part well, and responds in verse, as would befit someone with breeding. His rhetoric is so impressive, indeed, that it even influences the Butcher, who responds uncharacteristically with a line of verse of his own (4.2.140):

> The elder of them being put to nurse,
> Was by a begger-woman stolne away,
> And ignorant of his birth and parentage,
> Became a Bricklayer, when he came to age.
> His sonne am I, deny it if you can.
>
> *But.* Nay, 'tis too true, therefore he shall be King.

An example of disguised nobility is the scene in *Henry V* when the king speaks to his soldiers. The long conversation between Williams and Bates is entirely in prose; but when the soldiers leave, we see the transition from other-directed to self-directed speech in the switch from prose to verse:

> *Bates.* Be friends you English fooles, be friends, wee haue French
> Quarrels enow, if you could tell how to reckon.
>
> *Exit Souldiers.*
>
> *King.* Indeede the French may lay twentie French Crownes to one,
> they will beat vs, for they beare them on their shoulders: but

> it is no English Treason to cut French Crownes, and to
> morrow the King himselfe will a Clipper.
> Vpon the King, let vs our Liues, our Soules,
> Our Debts, our carefull Wiues,
> Our Children, and our Sinnes, lay on the King:

The switch from verse to prose, or vice versa, can also give us insight into the state of mind of a speaker. In the case of Pandarus (*Troilus and Cressida*, 4.1.51), the switch to prose signals confusion. Aeneas calls on Pandarus early one morning, urgently needing to talk to Troilus, who has secretly spent the night with Cressida. The formal encounter and serious subject-matter motivate verse. But Aeneas' directness catches Pandarus off guard, who confusedly lapses into prose:

> *Aene.* Is not Prince *Troylus* here?
> *Pan.* Here? what should he doe here?
> *Aene.* Come he is here, my Lord, doe not deny him:
> It doth import him much to speake with me.
> *Pan.* Is he here say you? 'tis more then I know, Ile be sworne:
> For my owne part I came in late: what should he doe here?

People were evidently very sensitive to these modality changes, and sometimes the text explicitly recognizes the contrasts involved. In *Antony and Cleopatra* (2.2.112), the summit meeting between Caesar, Antony, and their advisors is carried on in formal verse. But when Enobarbus intervenes with a down-to-earth comment in prose, he receives a sharp rebuke from Antony:

> Thou art a Souldier, onely speake no more.

And in *As You Like it* (4.1.29), Orlando arrives in the middle of a prose conversation in which Jaques is happily expounding his melancholy to Ganymede (= Rosalind). Orlando addresses Ganymede with a line of verse, which immediately upsets Jaques:

> *Ros.*   And your experience makes you sad: I had rather haue a foole
> to make me merrie, then experience to make me sad, and to
> trauaile for it too.
>
> *Orl.*   Good day, and happinesse, deere *Rosalind*.
>
> *Iaq.*   Nay then God buy you, and you talke in blanke verse.

And Jaques promptly leaves.

In all this, it is important to appreciate that the distinction
between verse and prose is not always clear. The Folio compositors
did not always understand it, and there is a famous case (page 57 of
Romeo and Juliet, shown in Figure 1, p. 28) where a piece of verse –
most of the Queen Mab speech, which on metrical, grammatical, and
semantic grounds should undoubtedly be printed as lines of poetry –
is set as prose. Doubtless there was an error in the printing process
(p. 29). Page 58 must already have been typeset when the compositor
working on page 57 realized that he had too much text to fit into the
page. He rescued the situation by cramming thirty-eight lines of verse
into thirty lines of tightly packed prose.

It is a widespread modern editorial practice to print prose lines
immediately after the speaker's name, and verse lines beneath it, as in
these two examples from the above conversation between the
Hotspurs (from the Penguin edition):

HOTSPUR
>   Now I perceive the devil understands Welsh ... [verse]
> HOTSPUR I had rather hear Lady my brach howl in Irish. [prose]

However, discrepancies between different editions show that the distinction is not always easy to draw. And sometimes it is a problem for
editors to decide when to return to a verse layout. The Hotspur conversation continues like this in the Folio, with the whole of Hotspur's
speech set as verse:

> *Hotsp.*   Come, Ile haue your Song too.
>
> *Lady.*   Not mine, in good sooth.
>
> *Hotsp.*   Not yours, in good sooth?

> You sweare like a Comfit-makers Wife:
> Not you, in good sooth; and, as true as I liue;
> And, as God shall mend me; and, as sure as day:
> And giuest such Sarcenet suretie for thy Oathes,
> As if thou neuer walk'st further then Finsbury.
> Sweare me, *Kate*, like a Lady, as thou art,
> A good mouth-filling Oath: and leaue in sooth,
> And such protest of Pepper Ginger-bread,
> To Veluet-Guards, and Sunday-Citizens.

However, modern editions print the opening four lines of Hotspur's speech as prose, presumably because of its weak metrical structure.

There is at least general editorial agreement about that example. By contrast, there is divided practice in *Pericles* (4.6), when governor Lysimachus arrives at a brothel with the intent of seducing Marina, whom he thinks to be a prostitute. The entire scene in the 1609 Quarto text between him, Marina, and the brothel-keepers is in prose. He is then left alone with her, and continues – but in what, verse or prose?

> *Li.* Now prittie one, how long haue you beene at this trade?
> *Ma.* What trade Sir?
> *Li.* Why, I cannot name but I shall offend.
> *Ma.* I cannot be offended with my trade, please you to name it.
> *Li.* How long haue you bene of this profession?
> *Ma.* Ere since I can remember.

Some editors print this as prose (e.g. Penguin); some as a transition into verse (e.g. Oxford), the latter as follows:

LYSIMACHUS
Fair one, how long have you been at this trade?
MARINA What trade, sir?
LYSIMACHUS
I cannot name it but I shall offend.

MARINA

I cannot be offended with my trade

Please you to name it.

Some twenty lines on, when Lysimachus, losing patience, tells her to take him 'to some private place', Marina replies in a high style, showing she is not what she seems:

If you were borne to honour, shew it now, if put vpon you, make the iudgement good, that thought you worthie of it.

In the reconstructed text of Wells & Taylor, this is part of a speech of over twenty lines. All editions set the text as verse:

MARINA

If you were born to honour, show it now;

If put upon you, make the judgement good

That thought you worthy of it.

Lysimachus recognizes the new style of language straight away.

LYSIMACHUS

How's this? How's this? Some more. Be sage.

And the effect of Marina's switch from prose to verse is dramatic:

LYSIMACHUS

I did not think thou couldst have spoke so well,

Ne'er dreamt thou couldst.

Had I brought hither a corrupted mind,

Thy speeche had altered it.

Marina evidently knows the power of verse, and uses it again later in the scene to persuade Boult to take her side.

This example shows that the distinction between verse and prose is by no means always clear. Individual editorial decisions are being made all the time, each one adding a stylistic nuance to the text. Lysimachus's reaction ('How's this?...') is set as poetry in the Penguin edition; it is set as prose in Arden. Does it matter? I think it does: if the examples of Polonius and Pandarus are anything to go by, a prose response shows a man knocked off balance. And Lysimachus has certainly been bowled over, at this point.

METRE IN DISCOURSE

As we saw in earlier chapters, metrical patterns are identified with reference to verse lines, and their constraining force used to explain some choices of words and grammatical forms (see especially pp. 150, 190). But the effect of using a metrical structure extends into the area of discourse too, especially in the way it can be used to capture the dynamism of an interaction. The dramatic effect of even a brief pause can be considerable. In the following extract from *Macbeth* (4.3.177), shown here in a modern layout, Ross knows that Macduff's family has been killed, and he has to break the news. Faced with Macduff's direct questions, a pair of lies leap into his mouth. But there is a pause (conveyed by the missing metrical beat) before his second reply. We can almost hear his silent gulp.

MACDUFF   How does my wife?

ROSS   Why, well.

MACDUFF   And all my children?

ROSS   Well too.

By contrast, the extra-long line which results from this intervention of Hotspur's, interrupting a sequence of regular ten-syllable lines, reinforces our impression of his impatient character, and in its urgency contrasts with the measured tones of Worcester's stratagem (*1H4*. 1.3.261).

WORCESTER

Your son in Scotland being thus employed,

Shall secretly into the bosom creep

Of that same noble prelate well-beloved,

The Archbishop

```
HOTSPUR      Of York is it not?
WORCESTER                       True, who bears hard
      His brother's death at Bristol, the Lord Scrope.
```

On several occasions, these shared lines (see p. 114) identify a critical point in the development of the plot, as in this example from *The Winter's Tale* (1.2.412):

```
CAMILLO
      I am appointed him to murder you.
POLIXENES
      By whom, Camillo?
CAMILLO                       By the King.
POLIXENES                               For what?
```

Sometimes, the switching raises the emotional temperature of the interaction. In this *Hamlet* example (4.5.126) we see the increased tempo conveying one person's anger, immediately followed by another person's anxiety:

```
KING CLAUDIUS
      Speak, man.
LAERTES   Where is my father?
KING CLAUDIUS                       Dead.
QUEEN GERTRUDE
      But not by him.
KING CLAUDIUS
                       Let him demand his fill.
```

An increase in tempo is also an ideal mechanism for carrying repartee. There are several examples in *The Taming of the Shrew*, when Petruchio and Katherine first meet, as here (2.1.234):

```
KATHERINE   Yet you are withered.
PETRUCHIO                       'Tis with cares.
KATHERINE                               I care not.
```

In a sequence like the following (*Lear*, 2.2.194) there is more than one tempo change:

> LEAR   What's he that hath so much thy place mistook
>   To set thee here?
> KENT   It is both he and she:
>   Your son and daughter.
> LEAR   No.
> KENT   Yes.
> LEAR   No, I say.
> KENT
>   I say yea.
> LEAR   By Jupiter, I swear no.
> KENT
>   By Juno, I swear ay.
> LEAR   They durst not do't.

Here, if we extend the musical analogy, we have a relatively lento two-part exchange, then an allegrissimo four-part exchange, then a two-part allegro, and finally a two-part rallentando, leading into Lear's next speech. The metrical discipline, in such cases, is doing far more than providing an auditory rhythm: it is motivating the dynamic of the interaction between the characters.

VARIETIES OF LANGUAGE

It is a commonplace that Shakespeare gives us a remarkable picture of the range of social situations in Elizabethan England (p. 6). What is less often remarked is that each of these situations would have been linguistically distinctive. Just as today we have scientific, advertising, and broadcasting English, so then there was legal, religious, and courtly English – to name just a few of the domains which are exploited. In addition to archaisms and neologisms, hard words and easy words, there is speech representing different degrees of formality, intimacy, social class, and regional origins. In short, we encounter in the plays most of the language *varieties* of Early Modern English.

Because we are totally reliant on the written language, apart from the occasional observation by a contemporary commentator, we shall never achieve a complete picture of the spoken stylistic variation of the past. But the plays quite often give us clues from the way in which characters are portrayed. We need to note, for example, that when Fluellen (in *H5*) and Evans (in *Wiv*) are talking, utterances such as *how melancholies I am* are not normal Early Modern English, but a humorous representation of Welsh dialect speech. A distinctive pronunciation is seen in the spellings: *pless* for *bless* and *falorous* for *valorous*. And the famous stereotype of Welsh speech, *look you*, is also used – though whether it had any greater reality then than now (Welsh people do not actually say *look you* very much) is a moot point. There is certainly a strong element of pastiche in the way these speakers persistently get their grammar wrong – *this is lunatics, a joyful resurrections*.

In these two plays we also hear hints of Scottish in Macmorris and Irish in Jamy, as well as foreign (French) accents in Caius and Katherine; disguised Edgar slips into West Country speech in *King Lear*. But regional variation is not as strongly represented in Shakespeare as social variation, especially distinctions in class. People may hide their faces but not their voices (see p. 103). Orlando, encountering disguised Rosalind in the forest, notices her speech (*AYLI*. 3.2.331):

> Your accent is something finer, then you could purchase in so remoued a dwelling.

> *Ros.* I haue bin told so of many: but indeed, an olde religious Vnckle of mine taught me to speake, who was in his youth an inland man,

The upper classes had their own vocabulary, too, 'With many Holiday and Lady tearme [terms]', as Hotspur puts it (*1H4*. 1.3.45).

Many of the markers of class difference are to be found in the way people address each other – the titles they use, their terms of endearment, their insults, and their oaths. Such forms as *sirrah*, *wench*, *master*, and *gentle* are a sensitive index of personal temperaments and relationships. Variations in swearing habits, for example, are identified by Hotspur in the 'in good sooth' sequence quoted above. He prefers 'A good mouth-filling Oath', with expressions like *in sooth* left 'To Veluet-Guards, and Sunday-Citizens'.

As we have seen with Prince Hal, and also with Marina and Lysimachus, it is possible for someone high-born to manipulate varieties of language to suit their purpose. The point is explicitly recognized in *King Lear*, when disguised Kent attacks Oswald and gets into trouble with the Duke of Cornwall (2.2.79). His condemnation of Oswald is in bold, insulting, down-to-earth terms:

> A plague vpon your Epilepticke visage,
> Smoile you my speeches, as I were a Foole? [smoile = 'smile']
> Goose, if I had you vpon *Sarum* Plaine,
> I'ld driue ye cackling home to *Camelot*.
> *Corn.* What art thou mad old Fellow?
> *Glost.* How fell you out, say that?
> *Kent.* No contraries hold more antipathy,
> Then I, and such a knaue.
> *Corn.* Why do'st thou call him Knaue?
> What is his fault?
> *Kent.* His countenance likes me not.
> *Cor.* No more perchance do's mine, nor his, nor hers.

Kent then decides to be rude about everybody, and this makes Cornwall angry, who homes in immediately on his 'plain' style of speech:

> *Kent.* Sir, 'tis my occupation to be plaine,
> I haue seene better faces in my Time,
> Then stands on any shoulder that I see
> Before me, at this instant.
> *Corn.* This is some Fellow,

> Who hauing beene prais'd for bluntnesse, doth affect
> A saucy roughnes, and constraines the garb
> Quite from his Nature. He cannot flatter he,
> An honest mind and plaine, he must speake truth,
> And they will take it so, if not, hee's plaine.
> These kind of Knaues I know, which in this plainnesse
> Harbour more craft, and more corrupter ends,
> Then twenty silly-ducking obseruants,
> That stretch their duties nicely.

Perhaps realizing that he has gone too far, or perhaps merely wanting to score a point, Kent demonstrates he can speak in high style – a dangerous manoeuvre for someone wanting to remain incognito – but its effect is to take Cornwall aback:

> Kent. Sir, in good faith, in sincere verity,
>   Vnder th' allowance of your great aspect,
>   Whose influence like the wreath of radient fire
>   On flickring *Phoebus* front.
> Corn. What mean'st by this?

Kent then switches into prose, evidently fully aware of his bidialectal abilities:

> Kent. To go out of my dialect, which you discommend so much; I know Sir, I am no flatterer, he that beguild you in a plaine accent, was a plaine Knaue, which for my part I will not be, though I should win your displeasure to entreat me too't.

However, plain prose does not save him. He ends up in the stocks anyway.

A LEGAL EXAMPLE

Language varieties are defined by the totality of their distinctive linguistic features. Legal English, for example, is the result of a large number of phonological (in speech), graphological (in writing), grammatical, and lexical conventions which combine to make the spoken or written discourses we recognize as depositions, statements, contracts, acts, deeds, and so on. When these varieties are used in literature, to present characters or situations, only some of these conventions are used. A novel, poem, or play is not a legal document. If authors wish to portray a legal situation, or to introduce a legal theme, it is enough that the world of law is identifiable. Thanks largely to a stream of courtroom dramas, today we have a fairly good intuition about 'the language of the law' – or at least, those aspects of it selected for portrayal by the script-writers – and we can recognize a legal parody when presented by, for example, the Monty Python team. When we are faced with the legal language of past generations, this immediate level of recognition is largely missing. An important aspect of discourse analysis, accordingly, is to identify usages as being possible candidates for a variety. For the most part, in Shakespeare, this means putting his vocabulary under a specialist microscope.[1]

It is not surprising to find legal vocabulary used in legal situations, such as the trial scene in *The Merchant of Venice*. Almost every speech refers to the standing of the law, either the word *law* itself, or using a legal term – *justice, plea, court, sentence, penalty, forfeit, discharge* ... – as this dialogue between Portia, Shylock, and Bassanio illustrates (4.1.199):

> I haue spoke thus much
> To mittigate the iustice of thy plea:
> Which if thou follow, this strict course of Venice
> Must needes giue sentence 'gainst the Merchant there.
> *Shy.* My deeds vpon my head, I craue the Law,
> The penaltie and forfeite of my bond.
> *Por.* Is he not able to discharge the money?
> *Bas.* Yes, heere I tender it for him in the Court,
> Yea, twice the summe, if that will not suffice,
> I will be bound to pay it ten times ore,
> On forfeit of my hands, my head, my heart:

Over thirty terms with a legal resonance appear here and in the following lines, and they are used with confidence and accuracy. Indeed, Shakespeare's mastery of legal terminology is one of the main features of his writing. Words like *accusation, sentence,* and *execution* belong to criminal law. Words like *statute, franchise,* and *counsellor* belong to civil law. Words like *surety, indenture,* and *audit* belong to commercial law. The plays illustrate a large vocabulary to do with the hearing of a case: *cause, party, petition, suit, hearing, warrant, charge, redress, oath, resolution, action, witness.* Some of these words are used often: for example, *suit* and *witness* turn up over a hundred times each in the plays.

We would expect legal words to turn up when the subject-matter is to do with law. There is no particular surprise if Portia uses legal language so efficiently in her persona as Balthasar. What is stylistically important is to note that the use of legal vocabulary extends well beyond the courtoom. It is not only lawyers, or people well versed in legal affairs, who use it. All kinds of characters, from highest to lowest, sprinkle their speech with legalisms. Launce, one of the clowns in *The Two Gentlemen of Verona* (3.1.271), has written out all the attributes of his milkmaid lady-love on a piece of paper, and he does so in the manner of a lawyer's clerk:

> Heere is the Cate-log of her Condition. *Inprimis.* Shee can fetch
> and carry: why a horse can doe no more; nay, a horse cannot fetch,
> but onely carry, therefore is shee better then a Iade. *Item.* She
> can milke, looke you, a sweet vertue in a maid with cleane hands.

And Launce's friend Speed then lists a further six virtues and eleven vices, each solemnly introduced by *Item.* Terms such as *in primis* ('firstly') and *item* (a particular point) are straight out of the lawyer's lexicon.

So it is not that Shakespeare just uses legal terms when they are needed – as in the Portia scene, or when people are debating legal issues in the history plays. He uses them when they are not needed.

Hamlet need not have speculated about a lawyer's skull in the grave-digger scene. It might have been a doctor's or a soldier's or a clergy-man's. But having chosen a lawyer, we then get a ludic celebration of legal language, with pun piling on top of pun. Several of the individual words may mean little to us now (indeed they would have meant little to the groundlings then; they are part of the mystique of the law), but the cumulative effect produces a perfectly clear dramatic impact:

> why might not that bee the Scull of a Lawyer? where be his Quiddits now? his Quillets? his Cases? his Tenures, and his Tricks? why doe's he suffer this rude knaue now to knocke him about the Sconce with a dirty Shouell, and will not tell him of his Action of Battery? hum. This fellow might be in's time a great buyer of Land, with his Statutes, his Recognizances, his Fines, his double Vouchers, his Recoueries: Is this the fine of his Fines, and the recouery of his Recoueries, to haue his fine Pate full of fine Dirt? will his Vouchers vouch him no more of his Purchases, and double ones too, then the length and breadth of a paire of Indentures? the very Conueyances of his Lands will hardly lye in this Boxe; and must the Inheritor himselfe haue no more? ha?

Coriolanus is a play which revolves around matters of state, the legality of popular protest, the technicalities of election procedures, and much more.[2] Legal terms are therefore very frequent – *tribune, magistrate, court, edict, statute, treaty, justice* – and they are there, though less obviously, from the opening lines of the play:

> *1. Citizen.* Before we <u>proceed</u> any further, heare me <u>speake</u>.
> *All.*   Speake, speake.
> *1.Cit.*   You are all <u>resolu'd</u> rather to dy then to famish?
> *All.*   Resolu'd, resolu'd.

The dialogue is already sounding just like a legal procedure – but this is a street rabble. These are rioters speaking, not lawyers.

> *1.Cit.* First you know, *Caius Martius* is chiefe enemy to the people.
> *All.*   We know't, we know't.

> *1.Cit.* Let vs kill him, and wee'l haue Corne at our own price. Is't a
> <u>Verdict</u>?

A few seconds later, Menenius arrives and tries to persuade the crowd
that their course of action is wrong, using an analogy of how the parts
of the body rebelled against the belly, accusing it of being idle and
cupboarding up food while they did all the real work. We are not likely
to miss the clear legal terms, such as *muniments* – a legal document
defending a person's rights, but here, in the plural, and with a concrete
sense foremost, with the meaning of 'means of support'; but terms
such as *complaine* and *answer* are less obvious (as with *speake* above),
because of their common everyday use. Here is the Citizen's speech,
omitting Menenius' interpolations:

> The Kingly crown'd head, the vigilant eye,
> The <u>Counsailor</u> Heart, the Arme our Souldier,
> Our Steed the Legge, the Tongue our Trumpeter,
> With other <u>Muniments</u> and petty helpes
> In this our Fabricke, if that they …
> Should by the Cormorant belly be <u>restrain'd</u>,
> Who is the sinke a th' body. …
> The former <u>Agents</u>, if they did <u>complaine</u>,
> What could the Belly <u>answer</u>?

Counsellor heart is a warm and effective image. The meaning may be
obvious, but the impact of the collocation arises from its unusual-
ness. It is the only occasion that Shakespeare uses *counsellor* as
an adjective – a usage that is so rare in English that even the *OED*
doesn't mention it. When Menenius answers, he trades legalism
for legalism. The belly calls the other parts of the body 'my incorporate friends'. *Incorporate*, a highly technical legalism. It means they
are all united in one body, 'incorporated', just as if they had received
a corporate franchise. The same thing happened to Hermia and
Helena, when they were children, and is to happen to Romeo and
Juliet:

Both warbling of one song, both in one key:
As if our hands, our sides, voices, and mindes
Had beene incorporate.

(*MND*. 3.2.208)

For by your leaues, you shall not stay alone,
Till holy Church incorporate two in one.

(*Rom*. 2.6.37)

Iago, Casca, Portia, and Tamora are among others who use it.

In Shakespeare, legal language is never very far away. And it provides a great source of figurative expression, turning up in many unexpected contexts. When Menenius returns to Rome having failed to persuade Coriolanus to cease his plans for revenge, he gloomily tells the tribunes, 'there is no hope in't, our throats are sentenced and stay upon execution' (5.4.5). To my mind, one of his best images.

Epilogue – 'Your daring tongue': Shakespearean creativity

Shakespeare was writing in the middle of a period of English linguistic history called Early Modern English, which runs from around 1500 to around 1750. It was an age when the language was beginning to settle down after a turbulent few centuries when its structure radically altered from its Anglo-Saxon character. Old English (used until the twelfth century) is so different from Modern English that it has to be approached as we would a foreign language. Middle English (used until the fifteenth century) is very much more familiar to modern eyes and ears, but we still feel that a considerable linguistic distance separates us from those who wrote in it – Chaucer and his contemporaries.

During the fifteenth century, a huge amount of change affected English pronunciation, spelling, grammar, and vocabulary, so that Shakespeare would have found Chaucer almost as difficult to read as we do. But between Jacobethan times and today the changes have been very limited. Although we must not underestimate the problems posed by such words as *buff jerkin*, *finical*, and *thou*, we must not exaggerate them either. Most of Early Modern English is the same as Modern English. The evidence lies in the fact that there are many lines of Shakespeare where we feel little or no linguistic distance at all. That is why we call the period 'Early Modern' English rather than, say, 'Late Middle' English. The name suggests a closeness to the language of the present day.

There is an intimate relationship between Early Modern English and Shakespeare. The more we understand the linguistic norms of his age, the more we will be able to appreciate his departures from these norms; at the same time, his linguistic ear is so sharp, and his character portrayal so wide ranging, that much of what we know about the norms comes from the plays themselves. We therefore always need to focus on the interaction between these two dimensions. We should not try to study Early Modern English and *then* study Shakespeare. Rather, we should study Early Modern English alongside and through the medium of Shakespeare. Examining the way an author manipulates ('bends and breaks', p. 117) linguistic rules gives us insights into the nature of the rules themselves.

The examples in this book show that in order to develop our understanding of Shakespeare's use of language we need to work through a three-stage process:

- we first notice a linguistic feature – something which strikes us as particularly interesting, effective, unusual, or problematic (often because it differs from what we would expect in Modern English);
- we then have to describe the feature, in order to talk about it and to classify it as a feature of a particular type; the more precisely we are able to do this, by developing an awareness of phonetic, grammatical, and other terminology, the more we will be able to reach clear and stateable conclusions;
- we have to explain why the feature is there.

It is the last stage which is the most important, and which is still surprisingly neglected. If language work is to be illuminating, we must go beyond 'feature-spotting'. To say, 'I spy an instance of neologism (metaphor, alliteration, etc) in this line' is only a first step. We have to take a second step and ask: 'What is the neologism (metaphor, alliteration, etc) doing there?' This is much more interesting, for it makes us reflect on the issue as it must have presented to Shakespeare himself. Why did he choose to do what he did? What effect would have been conveyed if he had made a different choice? It is always a matter of choice: to use or not to use a linguistic form – that is the crucial stylistic question.

It is, of course, by no means the whole story. Language in turn must be placed within a wider literary, dramatic, historical, psychological, and social frame of reference. Establishing that a particular variety of language is a major theme of a play, for example, is only a first step; interpreting it is another. At this point linguistics hands the baton over to literary criticism for further investigation. We must also expect there to be many occasions when meaning and effect cannot be precisely determined. There will always be a range of interpretive possibilities in the language that offer the individual reader, actor, director, or playgoer a personal choice. But the linguistic stage in our study of Shakespeare should never be minimized or neglected, for it is an essential step in increasing our insight into his dramatic and poetic artistry. I like to think that the First Outlaw's words in *The Two Gentlemen of Verona* (4.1.57) have some contemporary relevance:

> A Linguist, and a man of such perfection,
> As we doe in our quality much want.

This use of *linguist*, incidentally, is a first recorded instance in the *OED*.

People talk a lot about Shakespeare's 'linguistic legacy', saying that he was a major influence on the present-day English language, and citing as evidence his coining of new words (such as *assassination* and *courtship*) and idiomatic phrases (such as *salad days* and *cold comfort*). But when we add all of the coinages up, we do not get very large numbers. As we have seen, the Shakespearean words that still exist in modern English can be counted in hundreds, not thousands, and there are only a few dozen popular idioms. Those who assert that huge numbers of words in modern English come from Shakespeare are seriously mistaken.

His real legacy is very different. From Shakespeare we learn how it is possible to explore and exploit the resources of a language in original ways, displaying its range and variety in the service of the poetic imagination. Was there ever anyone who could give us a better lesson in how to achieve economy of expression? Consider the compression achieved when Mowbray complains about his sentence of banishment (*R2*. 1.3.160)

> Within my mouth you haue engaol'd my tongue,
> Doubly percullist with my teeth and lippes, [*percullist* =
> 'portcullised']

And dull, vnfeeling, barren ignorance,
Is made my Gaoler to attend on me:

It is possible to express the same meaning by de-verbing *engaol'd*:

Within my mouth you've put my tongue in jail

It is the same metre, and the same sense, but not at all the same dramatic impact. We could try the same exercise with *portcullised*. If we want to say that our tongue has been shut in behind our teeth and lips like a portcullis, we have the option of using a simile ('like a'), but similes are wordy things. Economy of expression, the result always of a trading relationship between lexicon and grammar, is the hallmark of Shakespeare's linguistic creativity.

In his best writing, we see how to make a language work so that it conveys the effects we want it to. Above all, Shakespeare shows us how to dare to do things with language. Dare we invent words to express the inexpressible? We dare. *Unshout, unspeak, uncurse,* and *unsex* are all actions that exist only in the imagination. Dare we manipulate parts-of-speech as if they were pieces of plasticine? We dare. We can learn how *to lethargy, to dialogue, to word,* and *to joy.* Dare we take the norms of metre or word-order and make them do our bidding? We dare. *Musicke do I heare? / Ha, ha! keepe time.* In a Shakespearean master-class, we would receive an object-lesson in the effective bending and breaking of rules.

Appendix: An A-to-Z of Shakespeare's false friends

Some instances of *false friends* in Shakespeare were discussed in Chapter 7 (p. 156). This Appendix provides a further selection. Many more will be found on the Cambridge University Press website for this book, at www.cambridge.org/ 9780521700351. References to 'first recorded user' are to the citations in the *Oxford English Dictionary*.

awful (*adjective*) modern meaning: exceedingly bad, terrible

Since the eighteenth-century, the meaning of *awful* has weakened to that of a negative intensifier: we say such things as *You've been an awful time* and *I'm an awful duffer*. As an adverb, especially in American English, it can even be positive: *That dinner was awful good*. In Shakespeare, it was used only in its original Anglo-Saxon sense of 'awe-inspiring, worthy of respect'. In *Pericles*, Gower describes Pericles as a 'benign lord / That will prove awful both in deed and word' (2.Chorus.4). This meaning is easy to spot when *awful* goes with words denoting power, such as sceptre, rule, and bench (of justice). It is a little more distracting when we see it used with general words, as when one of the outlaws in *The Two Gentlemen of Verona* tells Valentine that they have been 'Thrust from the company of awful men' (4.1.46).

belch (*verb*) modern meaning: noisily expel wind from the stomach

This word, in its modern meaning, has been in English since Anglo-Saxon times, and it early developed a figurative usage, describing the way people can give vent to their feelings as a cannon or volcano 'belches' fire. The sense of 'vomit', literally or metaphorically, was common too, and we find this in Shakespeare when Emilia describes women as filling men's stomachs: 'when they are full, / They belch us' (*Oth*. 3.4.102), or when Ariel describes the 'three men of sin' as being 'belched up' by the sea (*Temp*. 3.3.57). It must also be the character-note for Sir Toby Belch in *Twelfth Night*. The more general sense is also found in Shakespeare, where the stomach is not involved. Cloten, talking of Innogen's rebuff, says 'the bitterness of it I now belch from my heart' (*Cym*. 3.5.135). Here it means simply 'discharge, emit'. Similarly, with the adjective, *belching*. When Pericles (*Per*. 3.1.62) and Nestor (*Tro*. 5.5.23) talk about the 'belching whale' they mean 'spouting'. We must dismiss any notion of a noisy burp.

catastrophe (*noun*) modern meaning: sudden disaster

The modern sense is relatively recent, recorded since the mid-eighteenth-century. In Shakespeare's time it had a much more neutral meaning, of 'conclusion, end-point'. Shakespeare is in fact the first recorded user of the word in this sense, when the King of France talks about someone whose 'good melancholy oft began / On the catastrophe and heel of pastime' (*AWW*. 1.2.57). This is the sense hiding within the catch-phrase 'I'll tickle your catastrophe!', used by the Page in *Henry IV Part 2* (2.1.58) – meaning 'smack your end-point – i.e. behind'. The word also had a more technical meaning, referring to the denouement or final event in a drama. This is the sense used by Edmund when he refers to Edgar's approach as being 'like the catastrophe of the old comedy' (*Lear*. 1.2.133). However, there is ambiguity between this meaning and the more general one when Boyet reads from Don Armado's letter to Jaquenetta, describing the encounter between King Cophetua and a beggar: 'The catastrophe is a nuptial' (*LLL*. 4.1.78).

dainty (*adjective*) modern meanings: delicately pretty; attractively presented; fastidious

All the modern senses were available to Shakespeare, but we must be careful not to read them into every use of the word. It would be possible to find the 'delicate' sense in Prospero's description of 'dainty Ariel' (*Temp*. 5.1.95), for example, but hardly when the schoolmaster addresses the powerful Duke Theseus as a 'dainty Duke' (*TNK*. 3.5.113). Here the word means 'excellent, splendid'. The collocations (p. 173) have also changed over the centuries. In its sense of 'refined, fastidious' we find Costard's description of Don Armado as 'a most dainty man' (*LLL*. 4.1.145) and a countryman's description of a schoolmaster as a 'dainty dominie' (*TNK*. 2.2.40) – neither likely associations today. And we need to be on the lookout for ambiguity. When Richard tells Joan la Pucelle, talking about Charles the Dauphin, 'No shape but his can please your dainty eye' (*1H6*. 5.3.38), he is not being nice about her eyes, but scoffing at what she has seen with them.

ecstasy (*noun*) modern meaning: intense delight, rapture

The modern meaning was emerging in the sixteenth century; but it was long preceded by a much wider range of senses, and these are the ones found in Shakespeare. It expressed any point on a scale of emotional intensity. The 'weak' end can be illustrated by the description of Venus, 'Thus stands she in a trembling ecstasy' (*Ven*. 895), where it means little more than 'emotion' or 'feeling'. In the middle we have the notion of 'mental fit' or 'frenzy', well illustrated by the Courtesan's description of the increasingly confused and angry Antipholus of

Ephesus: 'Mark how he trembles in his ecstasy' (*Err.* 4.4.49). And at the 'strong' end we have the various references to Hamlet by Ophelia and Gertrude, such as the latter's 'This bodiless creation ecstasy / Is very cunning in', to which Hamlet immediately replies 'Ecstasy?' and denies it, making the older sense perfectly clear: 'It is not madness that I have uttered' (*Ham.* 3.4.142).

fancy (*noun*) modern meaning: inclination, liking

The feeling expressed by the noun today is not especially strong – things 'take our fancy', or 'tickle our fancy'. This sense of 'whim' was available in Shakespeare's time – Don Pedro says of Benedick 'a fancy that he hath to strange disguises' (*Ado.* 3.2.30) – but more usually, when talking about the emotions, the word referred to a much more profound feeling of love, or even infatuation. Five lines later, in the same play, Don Pedro says Benedick 'is no fool for fancy', which would be confusing if we did not appreciate that here the word means 'love'. And similarly, when Silvius tells Phebe of 'the power of fancy' (*AYLI.* 3.5.29), or Demetrius talks of 'Fair Helena in fancy following me' (*MND.* 4.1.162), or Orsino describes Viola as 'his fancy's queen' (*TN.* 5.1.385), they are all saying much more than simply 'I fancy her'.

generous (*adjective*) modern meanings: free in giving; ample; magnanimous

Shakespeare is in fact the first recorded user of this adjective, but the modern meanings all developed after his death, and the commonest modern usage (the financial one) does not emerge until towards the end of the seventeenth century. So we must forget all about money when we hear Claudius describing Hamlet as being 'most generous' (*Ham.* 4.7.134) or Holofernes addressing Armado as 'most generous sir' (*LLL.* 5.1.86). In such uses, the word means 'well-bred, mannerly, noble-minded'. It is the same when Edmund describes his mind as being 'as generous' as his brother's (*Lear.* 1.2.8) or Desdemona tells Othello that the 'generous islanders' have invited him to dinner (*Oth.* 3.3.277). A particularly dangerous instance is in *Troilus and Cressida* (2.2.156), where we have to forget the modern collocation of *generous bosoms* (i.e. 'large breasts'). This is where Paris is reacting to the suggestion that the Trojans give up Helen: 'Can it be / That so degenerate a strain as this / Should once set footing in your generous bosoms?' He is not suggesting that Priam, Hector, *et al.* are fat.

honest (*adjective*) modern meaning: truthful, upright

When *honest* came into the language from French, in the fourteenth century, it had the general meaning of 'held in honour, honourable, respectable'. A century later it had developed its modern sense, which is often to be found in Shakespeare. But the older meanings were still very much around. The meaning of 'honourable' can be heard when Hamlet describes himself to Ophelia as 'indifferent honest' (*Ham.* 3.1.122) or Antony describes Brutus as 'noble, wise, valiant, and honest' (*JC.* 3.1.126). The word means 'genuine, real' when Hamlet describes what he has seen as 'an honest ghost' (*Ham.* 1.5.138). And it means 'innocent, well-intentioned' when Hero talks about devising 'some honest slanders / To stain my cousin with' (*Ado.* 3.1.84). But the most important difference from modern English is the sense of 'chaste, pure'. When Touchstone says to Audrey, 'thou swearest to me thou art honest' (*AYLI.* 3.3.23), or Othello says to Iago, 'I think my wife be honest' (*Oth.* 3.3.381), they are not inquiring into their women's truthfulness, but their morals.

injury (*noun*) modern meaning: hurt, damage, especially to the body

This word came into English from Latin at the end of the fourteenth century with a very broad meaning, referring to any kind of wrongful act. Most of Shakespeare's usage reflects this breadth, keeping well away from the modern sense of physical injury. When Worcester talks about 'the injuries of a wanton time' (*1H4.* 5.1.50) he means 'wrongs' or 'grievances'. When Oberon tells Titania 'Thou shalt not from this grove / Till I torment thee for this injury' (*MND.* 2.1.147) he means 'insult' or 'slight'. There is no suggestion that Titania has physically hurt him! The nearest we get to the modern physical sense is when Montjoy reports the words of the French king to Henry V (*H5.* 3.6.120): 'we thought not good to bruise an injury till it were full ripe'. This might mean simply 'hit back at a wrong', but the context suggests a more physical sense. *Injury* here more likely means a 'sore' or 'abscess'. The Second Quarto of *Romeo and Juliet* also has the word as a verb: 'I never injuried thee', says Romeo to Tybalt (3.1.67). If it is a genuine usage (the First Quarto and the Folio both have 'injured') it must mean 'do [you] an injustice'.

jog (*noun/verb*) modern meanings: nudge; moderate run or ride

The word *jog* appeared in the sixteenth century. Its etymology is uncertain: it may well be an adaptation of *shog*, a Germanic word with similar meaning which had been in English since the late fourteenth century, and which is a favourite expression of Nym in *Henry V* (2.1.42, 2.3.42). 'Shall we shog?' (= 'Let's go') has since become something of a catchphrase for bardaholics. Alternatively, it might have been a fresh onomatopoeic coinage, the sounds of the word reflecting the jerky movements involved. The basic sense is 'move along', especially with the idea of 'moving off or away'. This is the meaning we need when we hear Autolycus sing: 'Jog on, jog on, the footpath way' (*WT.* 4.3.121). The modern sense might well apply here without being at all misleading, of course. But when Katherina tells Petruchio: 'You may be jogging whiles your boots are green' (*Shr.* 3.2.210), she is telling him to go away, not advising him to take an early-morning gentle run.

keen (*adjective*) modern meaning: eager, ardent, intense (especially in UK)

Most of the original senses of this word ('wise, brave, mighty, fierce') had disappeared from English by Shakespeare's time. But the notion of sharpness was common, used especially with reference to weapons, and also metaphorically to talk about winds, thoughts, words, and senses, where it expressed such notions as 'biting, piercing, penetrating'. What has especially to be avoided is the modern sense of 'eager' in the sense of 'sexually attracted'. This is not what Ophelia means when she tells Hamlet 'You are keen' (*Ham.* 3.2.257) or when Helena refers to an angry Hermia as 'keen and shrewd' (*MND.* 3.2.323). Here the ladies are using the word in its older meaning: 'sharp, cutting, severe'. A milder sense is heard when Escalus says to Angelo 'Let us be keen and rather cut a little / Than fall, and bruise to death' (*MM.* 2.1.5), where the primary nuance is 'perceptive, shrewd'.

lover (*noun*) modern meaning: someone with whom one has a
sexual relationship, especially illicit in character

When *lover* came into English, in the thirteenth century, it developed several senses, but the illicit sexual sense appeared only 300 years later. Today, it has virtually taken over. So we have to be especially careful not to read it in when Shakespeare uses *lover* in the earlier sense of 'companion, comrade, dear friend'. This is the sense we need when Menenius refers to Coriolanus as 'my lover' (*Cor.* 5.2.14) or Ulysses says to Achilles 'I as your lover speak' (*Tro.* 3.3.214). And in *Julius Caesar* we need to interpret the characters correctly when Artemidorus closes his letter to Caesar with the words, 'Thy lover' (2.3.8), Cassius refers to himself and Brutus as 'Lovers in peace' (5.1.94), and Brutus harangues the crowd with ' Romans, countrymen, and lovers, hear me for my cause' (3.2.13). The plots could get very confusing, otherwise.

merely (*adverb*) modern meaning: only [and nothing more]

The modern usage is dismissive, often suggesting an unimportant or trivial context, and this sense was beginning to be used in Shakespeare's time, as in Jaques' famous line 'All the world's a stage, / And all the men and women merely players' (*AYLI.* 2.7.141). But there was an earlier sense, which died out in the eighteenth century, and this has a much stronger meaning of 'utterly, entirely'. To miss the strength of feeling can result in a seriously misleading interpretation. When Rosalind, in the same play (3.2.383), describes love as 'merely a madness', she is not playing it down: on the contrary. And when Hamlet compares the world to an unweeded garden, saying that 'Things rank and gross in nature / Possess it merely' (*Ham.* 1.2.137), he means that the weeds are everywhere. The nuance needs a positive tone of voice to be clearly conveyed – an important acting note.

> **naughty** (*adjective*) modern meanings: badly behaved [of children], improper [playfully, of adults], sexually suggestive [of objects, words, etc]

We have totally lost the grave implications of the word that were normal in Shakespeare's day. When Gloucester describes Regan as a 'naughty lady' (*Lear.* 3.7.37) or Leonato calls Borachio a 'naughty man' (*Ado.* 5.1.284) we cannot now avoid the impression that these are mild, 'smack-hand' rebukes. It is all the more important, therefore, to stress the strong sense the word had in Early Modern English when referring to people: 'wicked, evil, vile'. This is especially relevant in contexts where the jocular sense might seem acceptable, as when Falstaff (pretending to be King Henry) calls Prince Hal a 'naughty varlet' (*1H4.* 2.4.420). Concepts – such as the world, the times, and the earth – can also be 'naughty', and here too we need to note that the tone is serious not playful, as in Portia's description of a candle flame in the darkness: 'So shines a good deed in a naughty world' (*MV.* 5.1.91). And where a sexual sense would be relevant, there is always a note of real moral impropriety, as in Elbow's description of Mistress Overdone's abode as 'a naughty house' (*MM.* 2.1.74).

> **obscene** (*adjective*) modern meaning: sexually offensive, indecent, lewd

The sexual meaning dominates the modern use of the word, and was indeed present from the time when it first came into English, during the 1590s. Shakespeare is actually the first recorded user, but he employs it in a more general sense, as an intensifier of disgust – 'repulsive, offensive'. There are just three quotations. Prince Hal calls Falstaff a 'whoreson, obscene, greasy tallow-catch' (*1H4.* 2.4.224). The Bishop of Carlisle talks of Richard's overthrow by Bolingbroke as 'so heinous, black, obscene a deed' (*R2.* 4.1.131). And the King of Navarre reads Don Armado's letter describing an 'obscene and most preposterous event' (*LLL.* 1.1.236) – referring to no more than Costard's meeting with Jacquenetta within the court precinct, from which women have been banned. In modern English there are signs of a return to this intensifying sense. When we say 'he was paid an obscene amount of money', we mean 'disgusting', but without the sexual connotation.

portly (*adjective*) modern meaning: stout, corpulent

This rather elegant way of referring to someone as 'fat' is with one exception not recorded in the language until the 1720s. When the word first arrived, in the early sixteenth century, it meant 'stately, majestic, dignified'. This is the only possible sense when it is applied to ships, as when Salerio describes Antonio's argosies as having 'portly sail' (*MV*. 1.1.9) or a Lord tells Creon they have seen a 'portly sail of ships' (*Per*. 1.4.61), and to abstract nouns, as when Worcester talks of 'greatness' as being 'portly' (*1H4*. 1.3.13). The exception is Falstaff's description of himself as a 'goodly portly man' (*1H4*. 2.4.412), and as having a 'portly belly' (*Wiv*. 1.3.57). Achilles, too, is described as being of 'large and portly size' (*Tro*. 4.5.162). It is an unusual use, not recorded in English again for a century. For the most part, it is the sense of 'dignity' which is to be borne in mind in encountering Shakespeare. When Capulet tells Tybalt that Romeo 'bears him like a portly gentleman' (*Rom*. 1.5.66), he is not suggesting that the great lover is overweight.

queasy (*adjective*) modern meanings: unsettled, easily upset [especially of stomachs]; uneasy; scrupulous [especially of consciences]

We should think of Shakespeare whenever we feel nauseous, because Agrippa's reference to Rome being 'queasy' with Antony's insolence is the first recorded use of the modern sense (*Ant*. 3.6.20). There's a similar use when Don Pedro describes Benedick's 'quick wit and his queasy stomach' (*Ado*. 2.1.355); the gloss here is 'delicate, fastidious'. The sense of 'unease' is present in the noun, too, in Shakespeare's only use, when Morton describes Hotspur and the other rebels as fighting 'with queasiness' (*2H4*. 1.1.196). With such uses all familiar, it would be easy to assume that Shakespeare's remaining use would be the same – but we would be wrong. When Edmund reflects 'I have one thing of a queasy question / Which I must act' (*Lear*. 2.1.17), it means 'uncertain, hazardous', or possibly 'ticklish'. He isn't feeling unwell at all.

rude (*adjective*) modern meanings: impolite, offensive; mildly obscene

Of the two chief modern senses, it is the sexual one which is most likely to mislead. This is *never* the sense of the word in Shakespeare. The impoliteness sense is there, as when Duke Senior tells off Orlando for being 'a rude despiser of good manners' (*AYLI.* 2.7.93). But the word has a wide range of other uses. It often means 'violent', as when Ulysses says 'the rude son should strike his father dead' (*Tro.* 1.3.115) – the son is hardly being just impolite! Peasants, rebels, and brawls can all be *rude* in this sense. Applied to things, it means 'rough' and 'wild': hedges, walls, and castles can all be *rude*. When the wind and waves are *rude*, they are stormy. And anyone uncultured or ignorant could be called rude. Puck calls the rustics 'rude mechanicals' (*MND.* 3.2.9) and Prince Hal, according to his father, has been frequenting 'rude society' (*1H4.* 3.2.14).

silly (*adjective*) modern meaning: foolish, stupid

The modern sense was coming into the language in Shakespeare's time – 'This is the silliest stuff that ever I heard' says Hippolyta to Theseus (*MND.* 5.1.207) – but an older set of senses dominate in the plays. When Henry VI's Queen calls herself a 'silly woman' (*3H6.* 1.1.243), or Lodowick describes the Countess in the same way (*KE3.* 2.1.18), the word means 'helpless, defenceless'. Males can be silly too – Edward III describes a group of Frenchmen as 'poor silly men, much wronged' (*KE3.* 4.2.29) – and so can sheep and lambs: 'shepherds looking on their silly sheep' says Henry VI a little later in the play (*3H6.* 2.5.43). But when a captain describes the disguised Posthumus as being 'in a silly habit' (*Cym.* 5.3.86), a different sense emerges, of 'lowly, humble'. It is there again when Orsino reflects to Viola/Cesario that Feste's sad song is 'silly sooth' – the simple truth (*TN.* 2.4.46). We can sense the modern meaning waiting in the wings.

teen (*adjective/noun*) modern meaning: teenage; teenager

This modern-sounding word in fact dates from the mid-seventeenth century – but not as far back as Shakespeare. He knew a much older usage, deriving from an Old English word meaning 'hurt' or 'trouble', and it is this, in an extended group of senses, including 'distress' and 'suffering', which is found in the plays and poems. We hear it from the Nurse, when she talks about her (lack of) teeth: 'to my teen be it spoken, I have but four' (*Rom.* 1.3.14); and from Miranda to her father: 'To think o'th' teen I have turned you to' (*Temp.* 1.2.64). And in the poems, Adonis complains to Venus: 'My face is full of shame, my heart of teen' (*Ven.* 808). The old usage is so different from the modern one that there is unlikely to be any ambiguity; but the present-day meaning can nonetheless interfere, unless we consciously put it aside. Having said that, when the Duchess of York complains of 'each hour's joy wracked with a week of teen' (*R3.* 4.1.96), some parents might wonder whether there is any difference after all!

umpire (*noun*) modern meaning: arbitrator in certain games and contests

The sporting sense of 'umpire' seems to have arrived in English in the early eighteenth century. Before that it referred to someone who helped to resolve a dispute of any kind. So it is important to rid the mind of the sporting connotation when we encounter the word in Shakespeare, where it always has a general meaning of 'arbitrator, mediator'. For example, Mortimer refers to death as a 'kind umpire of men's miseries' (*1H6*. 2.5.29), and later in the play the King asks: 'Let me be umpire in this doubtful strife' (4.1.151). It is not a question of our misunderstanding the meaning of the word in these cases, but of misinterpreting its force. To think of 'umpire' in its modern sense would be to treat the conflict referred to by the king as if it were a game – and it is manifestly not that. Nor is Juliet thinking of a game when she tells the Friar, 'this bloody knife / Shall play the umpire' (*Rom*. 4.1.63), for her thought is of suicide.

vicious (*adjective*) modern meanings: unpleasantly fierce, nasty; dangerous; malicious

When the word came into English, in the fourteenth century from French, it preserved the literal sense of 'relating to vice', and generally meant 'immoral, depraved'. There is just one use of this in Shakespeare, when Cordelia asks her father to make it clear that his displeasure at her is not because of any 'vicious blot, murder, or foulness' (*Lear*. 1.1.227). Otherwise we get two derived senses. One is 'defective, bad, wrong', as when Hamlet talks of men who have 'some vicious mole of nature in them' (*Ham*. 1.4.24) or Iago says 'I perchance am vicious in my guess' (*Oth*. 3.3.144). The other is 'blameworthy, shameful', as when Cymbeline says, of his Queen, 'It had been vicious / To have mistrusted her' (*Cym*. 5.5.65). The modern sense of 'nasty to the point of physical attack' began in relation to animals, especially horses, in the eighteenth century. There is no hint of this in Shakespeare. When we hear Adriana talking of her husband as 'vicious, ungentle, foolish, blunt, unkind' (*Err*. 4.2.21), she is not suggesting that he beats her.

want (*verb*) modern meanings: desire, wish, need, require

Most of the meanings of *want* found in Shakespeare are still in use today; but there is an inevitable tendency to read in the primary modern meaning – the positive sense of 'desire' – in contexts where it does not work. It is the negative sense, of 'lack, be without' which is required when Cordelia says to Lear, 'I want that glib and oily art / To speak and purpose not' (*Lear*. 1.1.225). This could not possibly mean that Cordelia desires to be glib: she is distancing herself from her two sisters, whom she has just heard speaking in that way. Similarly, in the Epilogue to *The Tempest* (line 14), when Prospero says 'Now I want / Spirits to enforce, art to enchant' he does not mean that he desires spirits, for he has just sent them all away. He is reflecting on their absence. Over half of Shakespeare's uses of *want* are like this.

x

There are no false friends beginning with x, because the only words in Shakespeare beginning with that letter are two proper names – *Xerxes* and *Xanthippe* – and proper names do not usually display the kind of language change that we see in common nouns, even when they come into everyday use, as today with *Cupid* and *Hercules*. However, we do sometimes need to beware, as modern products and characters can be given classical names, with consequent semantic interference when they turn up in Shakespeare. I do not personally have any problems with *Adonis* or *Ajax*, or with *Pluto* or *Vulcan* (think *Star Trek*), but some might.

young (*adjective*) modern meaning: early aged

Most uses of this word today relate to the age of a person, animal, or plant, and that is how it has been since Anglo-Saxon times. Extensions to the meaning arrived in the Middle Ages, so that things and abstract notions could be described as young, with a range of senses such as 'recent' and 'vigorous'. All of these appear in Shakespeare, where we find references to *young ambition, affection,* and *conception,* as well as to *young nerves* and *enterprises,* and *young hours, days,* and *times.* We can readily understand the figurative uses; but we can easily miss a nuance when the meaning moves in the direction of 'immature' or 'inexperienced', as when Orlando tells Oliver 'you are too young in this' (i.e. wrestling, *AYLI.* 1.1.51). When Petruchio tells a Frenchman 'I was then a young traveller' (*Cym.* 1.5.41), he does not necessarily mean he was youthful. And the repartee between Katherina and Petruchio (*Shr.* 2.1.231) relies on a pun of two unfamiliar senses: the 'immature' meaning is strongest in her quip, 'Well aimed of such a young one'. But when Petruchio replies 'I am too young for you', he means 'strong, in good condition'.

zany (*adjective*) modern meaning: absurdly ludicrous

Shakespeare is the first recorded user of this word (*LLL.* 5.3.463), when Berowne describes Boyet as a 'slight zany'. The origin is Italian, where *zani* were the servants who acted as clowns in the *Commedia dell' arte* – ultimately a derivative from *Gianni* (= *Giovanni* = 'John'). Shakespeare uses it twice with the meaning 'stooge, clown's assistant', the other occasion being when Malvolio talks dismissively of people who laugh at clowns like Feste (*TN*. 1.5.83): 'I take these wise men, that crow so at these set kind of fools, no better than the fools' zanies'. In both cases, the context makes it perfectly clear that it is not a term of approbation – 'Some carry-tale, some please-man, some slight zany, / Some mumble-news . . .', says Berowne – and this is the major difference with modern usage, where to describe humour or a TV programme as 'zany' would be to suggest we liked it.

Notes

Chapter 1
Title quotation: *WT*. 3.2.79.

Chapter 2
Title quotation: *TN*. 1.5.211.
1. The 51 texts are itemized in Laurie Maguire's summary: 'Shakespeare published', in Wells and Orlin (2003), pp. 587–8; the quotation below is on p. 589.
2. Kathman (1996) at http://shakespeareauthorship.com/name1.html
3. For a paleographic account of this text, see Petti (1977), p. 87.

Chapter 3
Title quotation: *TGV*. 2.1.160.
1. Philip Voss on Prospero, in Smallwood (2003) pp. 17–18.
2. In Partridge (1964), p. 77.
3. In Bateson (1975), p. 3.
4. In Partridge (1964), p. 62.

Chapter 4
Title quotation: *Ham*. 3.2.373.

Chapter 5
Title quotation: *Ham*. 3.2.1.
1. For example, Wright (1988).
2. In a letter to *The Times* in 1960.
3. Data on tone-unit length from Crystal (1969), p. 257.
4. Miller (1967), chapter 1.

Chapter 6
Title quotation: *Ham*. 3.2.2.
1. The first quotation is from Spedding (1870), p. 77; the second from Bamford (1936), p. 197.
2. Rodenburg (2002), p. 64.
3. Kökeritz (1953), pp. 86–157.

Chapter 7

Title quotation: *Cym.* 1.6.75.

1. Kermode (2000), p. 45.

Chapter 8

Title quotation: *2H6.* 4.7.36.

1. For other examples of *thou/you* interaction, see Crystal and Crystal (2002), p. 451 and Ronberg (1992).

Chapter 9

Title quotation: *TGV.* 1.3.31.

1. See Sokol and Sokol (2000).
2. See further, Tanselle and Dunbar (1962).

Epilogue

Title quotation: *R2.* 4.1.8.

References and further reading

Alexander, Catherine M. S. (ed.) 2004. *Shakespeare and Language*. Cambridge: Cambridge University Press.

Bamford, Francis. 1936. *A Royalist's Notebook: the Commonplace Book of Sir John Oglander*. London: Constable.

Bate, Jonathan. 1997. *The Genius of Shakespeare*. London: Picador.

Bateson, F. W. 1975. Could Chaucer spell? *Essays in Criticism* 25, p. 3

Blake, N. F. 2002. *A Grammar of Shakespeare's Language*. Basingstoke: Palgrave.

Brook, G. L. 1976. *The Language of Shakespeare*. London: Deutsch.

Crystal, David. 1969. *Prosodic Systems and Intonation in English*. Cambridge: Cambridge University Press.

2004. *The Stories of English*. London: Penguin.

2005. *Pronouncing Shakespeare*. Cambridge: Cambridge University Press.

Crystal, David and Crystal, Ben. 2002. *Shakespeare's Words*. London: Penguin.

Goodwin, John (ed.) 1983. *Peter Hall's Diaries: the Story of a Dramatic Battle*. London: Hamish Hamilton.

Hulme, Hilda M. 1962. *Explorations in Shakespeare's Language*. London: Longman.

Kathman, David. 1996. The spelling and pronunciation of Shakespeare's name. http://shakespeareauthorship.com/name1.html.

Kermode, Frank. 2000. *Shakespeare's Language*. London: Penguin.

Kökeritz, Helge. 1953. *Shakespeare's Pronunciation*. New Haven: Yale University Press.

Maguire, Laurie. 2003. Shakespeare published. In Wells and Cowen, 582–94.

Miller, George A. 1967. *The Psychology of Communication*. Baltimore: Penguin.

Partridge, A. C. 1964. *Orthography in Shakespeare and Elizabethan Drama*. London: Edward Arnold.

Petti, Anthony G. 1977. *English Literary Hands from Chaucer to Dryden*. London: Edward Arnold.

Rodenburg, Patsy. 2002. *Speaking Shakespeare*. London: Methuen.

Ronberg, Gert. 1992. *A Way with Words: the Language of English Renaissance Literature*. London: Edward Arnold.

Salmon, V. and Burness, E. (eds.) 1987. *Reader in the Language of Shakespearean Drama*. Amsterdam: Benjamins.

Smallwood, Robert (ed.). 2003. *Players of Shakespeare*, Vol. 5. Cambridge: Cambridge University Press.

Sokol, B. J. and Sokol, M. 2000. *Shakespeare's Legal Language*. London: Athlone.

Spedding, James. 1870. *The Letters and Life of Sir Francis Bacon*, Vol. 3. London: Longman.

Spevack, Marvin. 1968–80. *A Complete and Systematic Concordance to the Works of Shakespeare*, 9 vols. Hildesheim: Olms.

  1993. *A Shakespeare Thesaurus*. Hildesheim: Olms.

Tanselle, G. Thomas and Dunbar, Florence W. 1962. Legal language in Coriolanus. *Shakespeare Quarterly* 13, 231–8; reprinted in Salmon and Burness.

Wells, Stanley and Orlin, Lena Cowen. 2003. *Shakespeare: an Oxford Guide*. Oxford: Oxford University Press.

Wright, George T. 1988. *Shakespeare's Metrical Art*. Berkeley: University of California Press.

Index